PRAISE FOR *INFANT BAPTISM:*

Well-known Lutheran theologian David Scaer shows that when Rationalism is welded to Lutheranism, faith doesn't become more credible but instead is lost. Unable to affirm "infant faith" with Luther, nineteenth- and twentieth-century German theologians no longer had a strong basis to baptize infants. If this practice were to be kept, they needed to skirt around the fact that infants were also sinful humans in need of a savior—and that Christ promises himself to all who are brought to him in the sacrament of baptism. Their attempt to compromise confessional loyalty with modern psychology whittled away the foundation of sacramental theology. This book will be of interest not only to systematic theologians, but also liturgists, pastoral theologians, ecumenists, and pastors seeking fidelity to scripture and the confessions.

—Mark Mattes, Ph.D.
Professor of Religion and Philosophy
Grand View University
Des Moines, IA

"They supported infant baptism but denied infant faith"—but how can one baptize children/infants, if one doesn't believe that they, too, believe? Even among Lutherans, not only among the Erlangen Theologians of the 19th century, this is a controversy that is erupting again and again. Its significance is by no means only historical, but also fundamental, dogmatic, and practical-theological. For without faith, according to Mark 16:16, there is no salvation.

Because the Church grows through Baptism and exists through it as a community in the body of Christ, this fascinating study by Professor Scaer has a fundamental and exemplary significance, not least for our understanding of faith: is faith an intellectual act of knowledge *(cognitio)* and assent *(assensus)*, or is it, like Luther and all orthodox theologians teach, a gift of God and work of the Holy Spirit (*fiducia)*, by which "*Christ dwells in us through faith*" (Eph. 3:17)?

For a theology and preaching that is one-sidedly fixed on the question of understanding, this study can be a point of teaching on how to consider anew Luther's interpretation of the third article in the Small Catechism.

—Reinhard Slenczka, D.D.
Professor emeritus
Erlangen Faculty of Theology

David Scaer proves his thesis well: something significant was lost in Luther's baptismal theology when nineteenth century Lutherans began to deny that infants are able to have faith. This lively and clear tour of key German theologians demonstrates from yet another angle the corrosive effects of Rationalism and Romanticism on Lutheran sacramental theology. A recovery of Luther's robust understanding of baptism is sorely needed in our churches. Dr. Scaer's careful study points to what must be said when we talk about God's powerful action in water and word.

—Mark D. Tranvik, Th.D.
Professor of Religion and Department Chair
Augsburg College
Minneapolis, MN

Luther wanted Christians to have no doubt that in their baptisms, God had made them his own, and this faith, received at baptism, was to be exercised each day in repentance and trust. Dr. Scaer shows how that confident confession was eroded by a fragmented modern understanding of the individual and a resulting defective theology. This book uncovers the errors, faulty logic and inconsistencies among 19th century theologians and serves to restore the confidence in baptismal faith as the Lutheran Confessions attest.

—Martin E. Conkling, Ph.D.
Associate Professor of Theology
Concordia College-New York

Real advances in the history of doctrine (*Dogmengeschichte*) come not through the publication of general treatises like Jaroslav Pelikan's five volume *opus*, but through research on specific theological topics (*loci*) in specific historical periods. David Scaer's book on the doctrine of infant baptism in the 19th century is a sterling example of such a real advance, containing both detailed descriptions and orthodox Lutheran critiques. Besides a brilliant defense of Luther's doctrine of the "faith-of-infants," this book also reveals the non-Lutheran anthropology of German Idealism that was the basis for most of the "Erlangen theology" in the 19th and 20th centuries.

—Rev. Martin R. Noland, Ph.D.
Pastor of Trinity Lutheran Church, Evansville, IN
Former Director of the Concordia Historical Institute

In this volume Dr. Scaer traces the theological challenges that confronted nineteenth-century Lutherans who had abandoned Martin Luther's teaching regarding infant faith. Lutherans two centuries down the line from the subjects of this book are still impacted by their thought and practice. This book is an indispensable resource for tracing the differing understandings about the nature of faith and its relationship to God's work in and through baptism that still affect the Lutheran tradition today.

—Rev. Lawrence R. Rast, Jr., Ph.D.
President and Professor of Historical Theology
Concordia Theological Seminary
Fort Wayne, IN

In this fascinating study Dr Scaer examines the way infant baptism was handled by nineteenth century Lutheran thinkers. With typical forthrightness he exposes their discomfort—and the theological gymnastics required of them as they sought to retain the practice whilst having discarded much of the theology which justified it, especially Luther's assertion of infant faith. This book deserves a wide readership not only amongst confessional Lutherans seeking a better understanding of their tradition, but amongst all who seek clarity and honesty in their theology and practice of baptism.

—Rev. Preb. Jonathan Trigg, Ph.D.
Anglican clergyman, Diocese of London
Author, *Baptism in the Theology of Martin Luther*

In this carefully researched and copiously documented volume, David Scaer examines the nineteenth-century crisis engendered by the Lutheran appropriation of rationalist thought. Focusing on the traditional practice of infant baptism—justified by Lutherans with the confession that infants were capable of saving faith, and questioned by rationalists who denied this—Scaer is to be commended not only for his deft analysis of this important episode, but also for persuasively demonstrating how the denial of infant faith not only undermines Lutheran baptismal theology, but the heart of Lutheran theology itself: justification by faith alone.

—Korey D. Maas, D.Phil.
Associate Professor of Theology & Church History
Concordia University
Irvine, CA

INFANT BAPTISM

Books by David P. Scaer

Author:

Discourses in Matthew: Jesus Teaches the Church

The Sermon on the Mount: The Church's First Statement of the Gospel

Mateo Enseña a la Iglesia

Contributor:

The Law in Holy Scripture: Essays from the Concordia Theological Seminary Symposium on Exegetical Theology

Women Pastors? The Ordination of Women in Biblical Lutheran Perspective

INFANT BAPTISM

IN NINETEENTH CENTURY LUTHERAN THEOLOGY

DAVID P. SCAER

Peer Reviewed

CONCORDIA PUBLISHING HOUSE • SAINT LOUIS

Peer Reviewed

Published 2011 by Concordia Publishing House
3558 S. Jefferson Ave., St. Louis, MO 63118-3968
1-800-325-3040 • cph.org

Manufactured in the United States of America

Library of Congress Cataloging-in-Publication Data

Scaer, David P., 1936-
Infant baptism in nineteenth century Lutheran theology / David P. Scaer.
p. cm.
Includes bibliographical references(p.) and indexes.
ISBN: 978-0-7586-2833-6
1. Infant baptism--Lutheran Church--History of doctrines--19th century. 2. Baptism--Lutheran Church--History of doctrines--19th century. 3. Lutheran Church--Doctrines--History--19th century. 4. Theology, Doctrinal--Germany--History--19th century. I. Title.

BX8073.5.S23 2011
234'.1612--dc23 2011024279

---

4 5 6 7 8 9 10 11 30 29 28 27 26 25 24 23 22

Contents

PREFACE

Sixteenth and seventeenth century Lutheran theologians followed Martin Luther in understanding that infants were included in Christ's command to baptize and could have faith. Eighteenth century Rationalists raised doubts about the legitimacy of infant Baptism and defined faith as a cognitive, reflexive act of the reason of which inarticulate children were incapable. Both the Reformed and Catholics had already explained how children without faith could be baptized, but this question was a new and more crucial one for Lutherans who held that justification was by faith alone. Friedrich Schleiermacher took over the Rationalist view in questioning the legitimacy of baptizing infants and denying them faith, but his concept of a religion based upon the God-consciousness of the Christian community awakened among German theologians an interest in Luther, the Lutheran Confessions and the seventeenth century orthodox Lutheran theologians. They supported infant Baptism but denied infant faith.

This book presents how these Lutheran theologians wrestled with their commitment to infant Baptism but without agreeing to Luther's doctrine of infant faith. How this dilemma is resolved is a factor in whether children baptized as infants are to be regarded any differently than those who were never baptized. Research for this book began with a dissertation then reworked to respond to more recent discussions on Baptism. Since this work surveys how Lutheran theologians from the end of the Enlightenment to the rise of Neo-orthodoxy thought about Baptism, it belongs to the history of doctrine. Systematic presentations are found in my *Baptism* (1999) and *The Law and the Gospel and the Means of Grace* (2008).

A major step towards publication was made by Trudy Behning's transcribing the dissertation into electronic form that made expansion possible. Graduate assistant Dr. John Sias worked through the expanded manuscript. Dr. Mark C. Mattes provided a detailed critique with suggestions that Adriane Dorr incorporated into the manuscript. Graduate assistant James Lee prepared it to meet the publisher's specifications. Andrew Gericke assisted in proofreading. Julia Hipkins patiently incorporated the corrections into the manuscript.

Permission to use copyrighted quotations was obtained by the Rev. Robert E. Smith, Electronic Resources Librarian at Concordia Theological Seminary. Assisting with the indices was graduate assistant Christopher Neuendorf. Dr. Martin Conkling carefully read through the manuscript in its final stages and provided recommendations for improvement. Graduate assistant Robert Paul was of immense help in preparing the second printing. Edward Engelbrecht and Sarah Steiner took care of matters at Concordia Publishing House. Remaining inadequacies can be laid at the feet of the undersigned. Karl Brinkel's *Die Lehre Luthers von der fides infantium bei der Kindertaufe* (1958) opened my eyes to Luther's understanding of infant faith. Church of England minister Jonathan D. Trigg's *Baptism in the Theology of Martin Luther* (1994) captured the reformer's thought on this issue as no one else had and proves himself to be a Lutheran in heart and soul. The years between the initial research and its appearance in print run parallel to my marriage to Dorothy who images the divine in making what seems at first impossible possible. Apologies to the thousands of students who put up with a lecturer who remains incorrigible in staying on topic.

DAVID P. SCAER
Epiphany 2011
Concordia Theological Seminary
Fort Wayne, Indiana

INTRODUCTION

In their dogmatical discussions of Baptism, Protestant and Catholic theologians are caught between two poles, recognizing on the one hand that, according to the New Testament, faith has a role for receiving Baptism and its gifts, and then, on the other hand, having to find a basis for baptizing children, especially infants, who are assumed by nearly all to be incapable of faith, at least the mature faith of an adult. Exceptions were Martin Luther, the Lutheran Confessions, the seventeenth-century Lutheran Orthodox dogmaticians, and the theologians of the nineteenth-century confessional Lutheran revival.[1] They held to baptismal regeneration and infant faith, *fides infantium*, and so they did not have to face the question of how children without faith could be baptized. Baptism was a means of grace through which the Word of God worked faith in children and forgave their sins.[2]

This study has to do with nineteenth-century Lutheran theologians who no longer accepted Luther's doctrine of infant faith, *fides infantium*, and so had to offer other reasons for baptizing children. Also included in this study is the Reformed theologian Friedrich Daniel Ernst Schleiermacher (1768–1834), who used both

---

[1] For a presentation of Luther's views on infant faith, see Karl Brinkel, *Lehre Luthers von der fides infantium bei der Kindertaufe* (Berlin: Evangelische Verlagsanstalt, 1958). Edmund Schlink, *Theology of the Lutheran Confessions*, trans. Paul F. Koehneke and Herbert J. A. Bouman (Philadelphia: Muhlenberg Press, 1961),151–55; Johann Gerhard, *Loci Theologi*, ed. Ed. Preuss (Berolini: Gust. Schlawitz, 1866), 4:355–60. For other overviews of Luther's position see John W. Riggs, *Baptism in the Reformed Tradition* (Louisville: Westminster John Knox Press, 2002), 25–30 and Mark David Tranvik, "The other sacrament: the doctrine of baptism in the late Lutheran reformation" (Th. D. Dissertation, Luther Northwestern Theological Seminary, 1992), 6–35.

[2] Francis Pieper carried these views over into the twentieth century in his *Christliche Dogmatik,* 3 vols. (St. Louis: Concordia Publishing House, 1917–1920). His discussion of infant faith (2:537–38) appeared before and separate from that of infant Baptism (3:325–27). His dogmatics appeared in English as *Christian Dogmatics*, 3 vols. (St. Louis: Concordia Publishing House, 1950–1953). Here see 2:448–49; 3:277–79. For a recent defense of the Baptism of infants and their faith, see David P. Scaer, *Baptism*, Confessional Lutheran Dogmatics, (St. Louis: Luther Academy, 1999), 135–56.

Lutheran and Reformed confessions in his influential *Der Christliche Glaube, The Christian Faith.*[3] His concept of consciousness as essential to human existence found its way in how many Lutheran theologians understood faith as a consciously made decision. According to this definition, infants and young children could not believe, though adherents of this view did not specify the exact age when this could happen. Catholics had long resolved the absence of faith in infants by substituting the faith of the sponsors or the Church. The Reformed spoke of a child's future faith that was assured by its place in the covenant by its birth into a Christian family. Because of Luther's emphasis on justification by faith, Lutherans did not have the luxury of avoiding the question of how infants could be baptized without faith.

Luther and the post-Reformation-era Lutheran theologians held that Baptism's validity did not depend on the faith of the baptized, but reception of its benefits did. Unlike Catholics and Protestants in the Reformed and Arminian traditions, Lutherans attributed faith to infants in connection with their Baptism.[4] Faith could occur before Baptism, but it was widely held that the Baptism created it.[5] Unencumbered by reason, the enemy of faith, an infant's faith was seen as superior to the faith of an adult. While many nineteenth-

---

[3] In finding a place for Schleiermacher among Reformed theologians, John W. Riggs says, "One hundred years after orthodoxy ended the seventeenth century and the pietism of August Sebastian Francke, Philip Spener, and others had produced fruit within Lutheranism and Anglicanism, the forces of orthodoxy, pietism, and the Enlightenment coalesced in the life of the most influential Reformed theologian of the nineteenth century, Friedrich Daniel Schleiermacher" (*Baptism in the Reformed Tradition*, 90). Schleiermacher was prominent in joining Lutheran and Reformed churches into the one administrative unit of the Evangelical Lutheran Church of Prussia, commonly known as the Prussian Union (1817), and then requiring one liturgy (1830). More than anyone else, Schleiermacher set the theological tone in the nineteenth century.

[4] Differing from classical Reformed theology with its doctrine of double election is Arminianism, which makes the free will determinative in salvation. Jacob Arminius, for whom Arminianism is named, was a Calvinist theologian in the post-Reformation century. Though his views on the free will and his denial of double election were rejected by Council of Dort (1618–1619), he belongs to the Reformed tradition on Baptism. This has allowed Lutherans to refer to Arminians as Reformed, though this usage appears to both groups as a lack of awareness of fundamental differences between them. However, Riggs speaks of "Arminian Calvinists" (*Baptism in the Reformed Tradition*, 38).

[5] For an overview of the doctrine of infant faith in the Lutheran theology of Baptism, see Scaer, *Baptism*, 147–56.

century Lutheran theologians reconsidered the older views, they did not completely dispense with the Rationalist view that reason was a factor in acquiring faith and hence for them infants could not have faith. This was enforced by Schleiermacher's view that without developed consciousness children were incapable of faith.[6] Since these Lutheran theologians held that children could not have faith at the time of their Baptism, they had to explain why infant Baptism should continue. Infant Baptism was more than an occasional religious ritual, but it meant or symbolized salvation and bestowed citizenship in the German states as it did in most of Europe. Some Lutheran theologians explicitly distanced themselves from Luther's doctrine of infant faith. Others simply avoided the issue. Sixteenth-century Reformed theologians saw Baptism as a sign of inclusion in the covenant and were not plagued by the Lutheran dilemma of how Baptism could be administered to children who were said to be without their own faith.[7] Arguments offered for infant Baptism by nineteenth-century Lutherans began to resemble traditional Reformed ones. The dilemma for Lutheran theologians was that they held that Baptism was a real means of grace that was fully effective only in faith, but this was lacking in infants. Subsidiary issues were historical questions about whether infant Baptism was an apostolic practice.

Mainline Protestant and Catholic churches have recognized Baptisms administered by the other churches using the Trinitarian

[6] Since Rationalism saw Jesus chiefly as a teacher, children could not benefit from His teachings until they reached maturity. For an overview of this era, see Horst Stephan, *Geschichte der Deutschen Evangelischen Theologie seit dem Deutschen Idealismus*, ed. Martin Schmidt (Zweite neubearbeitete Auflage; Berlin: Alfred Töpelmann, 1960), 61–74. Also see Brinkel, *Die Lehre Luthers von der fides infantium*, 95. "Fragen wir danach, was sich eigentlich in diesen, sich auf das Bewußtsein des Menschen berufenden Einwänden gegen Luthers Lehre von der fides infantium für ein Denken kundtut, so ergibt sich, daß es letztlich nicht in biblischen und reformatorischen Aussagen, sondern in idealistisch-humanistischen Voraussetzungen gründet. Es ist der Humanismus und Idealismus, der dem 'bewußten' Geist des Menschen zuerkennt. Es ist Schleiermacher gewesen, bei dem in der Theologie ein solches Denken eine besondere Zuspitzung erfahren hat. Schleiermacher versteht den Glauben vornehmlich als eine Beziehung des Subjektes Mensch auf Gott, wird doch nach ihm der Mensch in seinem Selbstbewußtsein Gottes inne und eben 'bewußt.' Nach ihm fällt daher in einem Menschen, in dem das Bwußtsein (sic!) noch nicht bestimmt genug auseinander traten, auch ein 'Gottesbewußtsein' noch gänzlich aus."

[7] See Jan Rohls, *Reformed Confessions: Theology from Zurich to Barmen*, trans. John F. Hoffmeyer, introduction by Jack L. Stotts, Columbia Series in Theology (Louisville: Westminister John Knox Press, 1997), 211–16.

formula.[8] From the time of the Reformation, the exclusion of infants from Baptism divided paedobaptists, those practicing infant Baptism (Catholics, Lutherans, Reformed, and later the Arminians), from those who did not (the Reformation-era Anabaptists, today's Baptists, and other groups like the Disciples of Christ). With the legalization of Christianity by the Roman Empire in the fourth century and its later establishment as a state-supported religion, infant Baptism became the accepted practice in Europe until the end of the twentieth century, when Christianity gave way to cultural and religious secularism. Today in Scandinavian countries one can be a member of the state-related Lutheran Church without being baptized. With the exception of the Anabaptists, who, in addition to opposing infant Baptism, were anti-trinitarian, the major parties to the Reformation era struggles continued to practice infant Baptism. A strong Baptist tradition in parts of the United States was a factor in infant Baptism not achieving the prominence it had in Europe, but it was practiced in colonial America among Protestants by the Puritans, the Episcopalians, the Reformed, and Lutherans. Infant Baptism belonged to the religious life of European immigrants in the nineteenth and early-twentieth centuries. Baptism served as the entrance rite into the community, but beneath external similarities were differences on how faith, grace, and Baptism were understood and how each related to the other.[9]

At the beginning of his reformation, Huldrych Zwingli offered arguments that the Anabaptists then used for discontinuing infant Baptism. To avoid this Zwingli defined infant Baptism as an entrance rite into the Christian community.[10] To argue for its practice, eighteenth-century Rationalist Lutherans, Schleiermacher, and most nineteenth-century Lutheran theologians adopted the same argument. Recent Lutheran baptismal liturgies also include the idea that Baptism

---

[8] Baptists use the Trinitarian formula but typically recognize only Baptisms administered in response to an oracular confession, often called a "decision for Christ." This is called adult Baptism or believers' Baptism and, in some cases, can be administered more than once.

[9] Seventeenth-century Lutheran Orthodox theologians were aware that Roman Catholics, Lutherans, and Calvinists offered different reasons for the practice of infant Baptism. Johann Andreas Quenstedt, *Theologia Didactico-Polemica sive Systema Theologicum* (Leipzig: Thomas Fritsch, 1715), 1126.

[10] Riggs, *Baptism in the Reformed Tradition*, 21–25; Rohls, *Reformed Confessions*, 212. For differences between Zwingli and Luther on infant Baptism and faith, see Karen E. Spierling, *Infant Baptism in Reformation Geneva* (Louisville: Westminster John Knox Press, 2009), 33–34.

is a community entrance rite.[11] For Reformation-era Lutherans and Catholics, Baptism was not just an entrance rite but also a vehicle of God's grace, though they defined grace differently. Catholics saw grace as a substantive quantity given in Baptism that had to be supplemented by additional graces given in confirmation and penance. Lutherans held that the grace given in Baptism was God's gracious attitude toward the sinner and was sufficient for salvation throughout life and did not have to be supplemented by other rites or preaching, though some nineteenth-century Lutheran theologians moved towards this view.[12] Whether faith was present or not—and for the sake of argument Luther proposed this in response to those who held that infants could not believe—Baptism was God's act and was to be administered only once.[13] For the Reformed, the Spirit worked in parallel to the water in Baptism, but the act itself did not bestow grace. It also symbolized the Spirit's working and ratified the covenant relationship in which a child participated by virtue of birth from Christian parents. It was not necessary for salvation, and so emergency Baptism was not practiced.[14] God's promises in Baptism took the place of the child's faith, of which the child was not cognitively capable.[15] Thus, the Reformed had no reason to administer Baptism to children in danger of death. Catholics and Lutherans did.

Lutherans, Reformed, and Catholics saw faith as the response to Baptism, but only Lutherans ascribed faith to infants at the time of their Baptism. Into the baptismal equation Catholics and the

---

[11] *Lutheran Worship*, a hymnal of The Lutheran Church—Missouri Synod, places into the baptismal rite a greeting from the congregation welcoming the child into the church. "We welcome you into the Lord's family. We receive you as (a) fellow members of the body of Christ, (a) child(ren) of the same heavenly Father, to work with us in his kingdom." (St. Louis: Concordia, 1982), 204. This is less intrusive but still present in its successor hymnal. "We receive you in Jesus' name . . . "*Lutheran Service Book* (St. Louis: Concordia, 2006), 271. See also *Lutheran Book of Worship*, the hymnal of the Evangelical Lutheran Church in America (Minneapolis: Augsburg Publishing House, 1978), 121–25.

[12] Scaer, *Baptism*, 111–12.

[13] Trigg summarizes Luther's position: "Faith is essential to the reception of baptism; baptism remains baptism in the absence of faith. Baptism understood as water which is embraced in the divine word of promise demotes all questions about the presence or absence of faith to a secondary level." Jonathan Trigg, *Baptism in the Theology of Martin Luther* (Leiden: E. J. Brill, 1994), 153.

[14] Parents' concerns about a sickly child were dismissed because God's grace covered them. See Spierling, *Infant Baptism in Reformation Geneva*, 34.

[15] Rohls, *Reformed Confessions*, 213–14.

Reformed factored a child's future faith which the parents and the Church had the responsibility of nurturing. In addressing questions about faith in the baptismal rite directly to the child, Catholic and Lutheran baptismal liturgies gave the impression that the baptized child actually believed, though only the Lutherans really held this.[16] Zwingli saw Baptism as a pledge made by both the baptized and the community, an idea that resurfaced later among Rationalists, who saw it as a social contract not personally affecting the child.[17] As much as Lutherans, Anabaptists, and, later, Baptists opposed each other on the legitimacy of infant Baptism, both saw faith as contemporary to administration of the rite; however, their definitions of Baptism and faith were different. Baptism for Reformation-era Lutherans was God's act and could be administered only once. Faith was trust in God for Christ's sake and did not require cognitive reflection. For Baptists, Baptism was an act of faith, obedience, and confession of which children were not capable. It symbolized the believer's faith and confession and could be administered more than once. Luther argued that one could not know for certain that adults had faith, since we only had their word.[18] In the case of children, we have God's word that they can believe. For Luther, the Baptism of infants is the norm.

Luther's belief about baptismal regeneration and infant faith in Baptism held sway in Lutheran theology until the eighteenth century, when Rationalist Lutherans no longer saw Baptism as a working of God's grace and hence not a factor in creating faith. Children lacked the rational capacity to believe. Infant Baptism was seen as an entrance rite into the community that could safely be omitted, a

---

[16] Chemnitz objects that by the belief that children are saved without faith, the Catholics had created "a certain middle state between faith and unfaith, between believers and unbelievers." Martin Chemnitz, *Examination of the Council of Trent*, 4 vols. trans. Fred Kramer (St. Louis: Concordia, 1974–1981). 2:170.

[17] Baptism as an act of the Christian community would appear in the Catholic and in Lutheran orders of Baptism. Riggs provides an analysis of the rite in the *Lutheran Book of Worship* of the Evangelical Lutheran Church in America. *Baptism in the Reformed Tradition*, 11–15. To provide a basis for infant Baptism, Zwingli stressed the objectivity of the word in Baptism, an idea the Reformed theologies of Baptism retained (25).

[18] "To have his confession is not to know his faith . . . so, whoever bases baptism on the faith of the one to be baptized, can never baptize anyone. Even if you baptized a person a hundred times a day you would not know whether he or she believes." "Concerning Rebaptism," *Luther's Works: The American Edition,* ed. Jaroslav Pelikan and Helmut T. Lehmann, 54 vols. (St. Louis: Concordia and Philadelphia: Fortress Press, 1955–72), 40: 240.

position close to Zwingli's. They also espoused historical-critical views that Jesus intended Baptism only for His time and that there was no evidence that the apostles baptized infants. Baptism as a sacrament for children arose in the post-apostolic era. Historical skepticism was not part of the Reformation-era debate on Baptism. Rationalists saw reason as a source of divine knowledge first as a supplement to revelation and eventually replacing it. The supernatural world was submerged into the natural or rational world and reason was key to understanding both. Faith was seen as a function of the reason that was able to sift through the physical evidences to find God. Of this process a child was incapable and so was found to be incapable of faith, a position already put forth by the Reformed.[19] The Council of Trent had gone so far as to condemn the Lutheran doctrine of infant faith.[20] By the eighteenth and nineteenth centuries, Rationalist Lutheran theologians had come around to the Catholic and Reformed view that infants could not have faith. Enlightenment theologians went further in holding that children were born without original sin, had no need of forgiveness, and, in any event, Baptism did not offer it. Baptism only ushered the child into the Christian community where moral improvement took place, but the baptized child had no advantage over the unbaptized one, since by birth both belonged to the community.[21] Rationalist Lutherans put forth convincing reasons for discontinuing infant Baptism, but instead of acting on the merits of their own arguments in dropping it like the

[19] Riggs, *Baptism in the Reformed Tradition,* 67. Calvin held that children could neither understand nor repent, hence at the time of their Baptism they could not grasp its promises. However, they are baptized into future repentance and faith. Johann Georg Walch (1693–1775), known for editing the twenty-four-volume edition of Luther's works (1740–1752), published a monograph in 1733, *Gedanken vom Glauben der Kinder im Mutter-Leibe and dem Grunde der Seeligkeit der verstorbenen ungetaufften Christen-Kinder*. The German edition of 1733 includes annotations by Adam Lebrecht Mueller; Walch's piece may have appeared first in Latin. An English translation was made from the German and published as *The Faith of Unborn Children*, trans. Otto F. Stahlke; ed. David R. Liefeldt (Nevada, IA: Lutherans for Life, 1998, 2005). Walch's polemic is against the Reformed, who hold that without reason, children cannot believe. Catholics are said to hold the same position (43–44).

[20] Chemnitz, *Examination of the Council of Trent,* 2:175.

[21] Calvin had to address the same issue in connection with his doctrine of election. Baptism did not change the condition of a child or an adult in his being elected to salvation or reprobation. Riggs, *Baptism in the Reformed Tradition*, 66.

Anabaptists had, they argued for its continuance and defined it as a rite holding Church and society together.[22]

In the beginning of the nineteenth century, Rationalism's confidence in reason had been undermined by Immanuel Kant, who held that human beings possessed a moral sense to decipher right from wrong. From this he argued for God's existence. Influenced by Kant, Schleiermacher replaced reason as the source of religious knowledge with the "feeling of absolute dependence," the equivalent of faith. Appropriately, he called his dogmatics *The Christian Faith* (*Der Christliche Glaube*). Jesus possessed this God-consciousness, *Gottesbewußtsein*, to the highest degree and in sharing it with His followers, the community of believers—the Church—came into being. Within this community, one's consciousness developed from self-consciousness to God-consciousness. Like the Rationalists, Schleiermacher defined the Church sociologically as a society and was unconvinced by the biblical arguments for baptizing infants, who lacked the consciousness requisite for faith. Baptism could serve as an entrance rite into the community where God-consciousness could be awakened.

There is wide agreement among those who practice Baptism that it is administered in response to a confession of faith. For some, Baptism is part of that confession. Two arguments against baptizing infants are their inability to believe and to articulate their faith, if they had any. Catholics substitute the faith of the sponsors or the Church for the child's faith, a solution not possible for Protestants, who hold that one is justified by one's own faith. Baptists address the faith issue by baptizing only adults or more mature children who make their confession of faith. Children cannot believe, and their innocence exempts them from the consequences of original sin. This compromises the Reformation principle of justification by faith. The Reformed practice infant Baptism but agree with the Baptists that infants are incapable of faith.[23] Their Baptism serves to confirm the covenant relation they already possess by birth from Christian

---

[22] For how this was understood by the Reformed, see chapter one, "Introduction: Infant Baptism and the Definition of Community," in Spierling, *Infant Baptism in Reformation Geneva*, 1–31.

[23] Various Anabaptist leaders criticized Zwingli and Calvin for betraying the Reformation by baptizing children, who were incapable of faith. Spierling, *Infant Baptism in Reformation Geneva*, 33.

parents, and it anticipates future faith.[24] To allow for infant Baptism, nineteenth-century Rationalist Lutheran theologians offered views that were indistinguishable from Reformed ones. Children of non-Christian parents were ineligible for Baptism. Recent Catholic liturgical reforms laid down similar guidelines.

Seventeenth- and early eighteenth-century Lutheran Pietism, typified by Philip Spener and August Francke, did not formally set aside Luther's definition of faith as trust in Christ, but Pietism expanded its definition of faith to include self-examination and a conversion type experience to raise ordinary faith to a higher level. Infant Baptism remained in place, but a personal, articulate confession of faith was made at confirmation.[25] Pietism's concentration on spiritual self-improvement was replaced by Rationalism's goal of moral self-improvement. Both movements saw the rite of confirmation for adolescents as providing for the confession lacking in infant Baptism. Some nineteenth-century Lutheran theologians also saw confirmation as a supplement for what was missing in infant Baptism.[26] For Luther, Baptism, including that of infants, was complete in itself.

Schleiermacher's concept of faith as God-consciousness within the community awakened in nineteenth-century Lutherans an appreciation of Luther and classical Lutheran theology. Wilhelm Löhe, Carl Ferdinand Wilhelm Walther, Friedrich Adolf Philippi, and Francis Pieper returned to Luther's position of infant faith, but they were a minority. Others began to see Baptism as a sacrament that conveyed grace, but following the Rationalists and Schleiermacher, they saw faith as a cognitive or self-reflective act of which infants were incapable. Infant faith was not an option. They wrestled with keeping Baptism as a Sacrament for infants but without attributing faith to them.

In the twentieth century, a major challenge to infant Baptism was mounted by Karl Barth, who devoted one volume to it in his massive

---

[24] Riggs notes that faith precedes Baptism and its benefits, but with infant Baptism it is a fruit of the election that follows faith. To overcome what Riggs calls a problem, some attributed to children "inactive regeneration" or "sleeping regeneration" and the "potency of faith." *Baptism in the Reformed Tradition*, 96–97.

[25] Arthur C. Repp, "Reconstructing Confirmation for Our Day," The Lutheran Church—Missouri Synod, *Seventy-Sixth Convention Proceedings of the Western District, June 12–16, 1961* (St. Louis: Concordia, 1961), 35–36.

[26] For the checkered history of confirmation among Lutherans, see David P. Scaer, "Confirmation as Sacramental Rite," *Logia* 15:1 (Epiphany 2006): 49–58.

Church Dogmatics.[27] He was influenced by Luther and Calvin, but mostly by Zwingli. Under Barth's influence, some Lutheran pastors refrained from baptizing their own children, though they were required to baptize other children. Like Zwingli, Barth saw Baptism as an act of faith and had doubts about infant Baptism, but unlike the Zurich reformer he did not overcome them. Since he did not advocate rebaptizing those baptized as infants, Barth was not a Baptist in the strictest sense.[28] At times, he sounded sacramental in holding that Baptism was "the event in which God in Jesus Christ makes a man His child and a member of His covenant, awakening faith through His grace and calling a man to life in the Christ."[29] However, Barth moved in Zwingli's direction in holding that Baptism was no more than a picture, a witness, sign, or representation (*Abbild*).[30] He separated the inner Baptism of faith from the Baptism with water, the latter of which was of little consequence.[31] Like Luther, Barth stressed the objectivity of the divine action in Baptism and referenced Luther's Small Catechism to explain that the word and not the water accomplishes salvation. At the same time, he rejected Luther's and Catholic views as *ex opere operato*.[32] Baptism was not the water of salvation and did not regenerate.[33] It was the divine pledge of the certainty of salvation and required the assent of the baptized. Even without faith, Baptism was effective and not to be repeated.[34] Barth could not even agree with Calvin that in Baptism the Spirit worked in parallel with the water. Baptism for Barth was the believer's act of obedience, Zwingli's position, which later reemerged among

---

[27] Karl Barth, *Church Dogmatics*, trans. G. W. Bromiley, 4 vols. (Edinburgh: T. & T. Clark, 1969) was the major dogmatics work of the twentieth century. The fourth volume, *The Christian Life*, had four parts, with the last printed as a separate volume entitled *Baptism as the Foundation of the Christian Life* (trans. B. W. Bromly [Edinburgh: T & T. Clark, 1969]). This English translation was taken from Barth's *Die Kirchliche Dogmatik* (Zurich: EVZ Verlag, 1967), 4/4. Subsequent references are taken from that English translation.

[28] Barth, *Church Dogmatics*, 4/4:189.

[29] Karl Barth, *The Teaching of the Church Regarding Baptism,* trans. Ernest A. Payne (London: SCM Press, 1949), 14.

[30] Barth, *The Teaching of the Church,* 9

[31] Trigg, *Baptism in the Theology of Martin Luther*, 213.

[32] Barth, *Church Dogmatics*, 4/4:172.

[33] Barth, *The Teaching of the Church*, 19–27.

[34] Barth, *The Teaching of the Church*, 40.

Rationalist Lutherans.[35] Barth bluntly says, "Baptism is not a Sacrament,"[36] but reverses himself, or so it seems, with a book subtitled *Baptism as the Foundation of Christian Life*. However, Baptism represented only renewal by the Holy Spirit and association with Christ.[37] Luther's "I am baptized," *baptizatus sum*, was too magical.[38] Barth's dilemma with infant Baptism arose from his attempt to coordinate the classical Reformed theme of God's sovereignty with God's encounter (*Begegnung*) with the individual, the theme that characterized his theology. Divine sovereignty allowed for infant Baptism, but the encounter, which defined faith, did not.[39] In a lecture to Swiss theological students in 1943, he reluctantly declared he could no longer support infant Baptism. In his *Church Dogmatics*, he came out against it but without condemning it. While nineteenth-century theologians provided arguments for infant Baptism in spite of reasons for discontinuing the practice, Barth acted on his convictions and held that infants are better left unbaptized.[40] Unlike the Anabaptists and the Baptists, he upheld its validity and did not require another Baptism of those baptized as infants.[41] Kurt Aland, and Karl Barth's son, Markus, provided biblical arguments against infant Baptism.[42] At the turn of the twenty-first century,

---

[35] Barth, *Church Dogmatics,* 4/4:102. "[Baptism] is not, itself, a divine work and word. It is the work and word of men who are obedient to Jesus Christ and who have put their hope in Him."

[36] Barth, *Church Dogmatics*, 4/4:128.

[37] Barth, *The Teaching of the Church, 9, 54*

[38] Barth, *The Teaching of the Church*, 62.

[39] Barth, *Church Dogmatics*, 4/4:189. "The strongest argument—I myself used it for some decades—is that infant baptism is so remarkably vivid a depiction of the free and omnipotent grace of God which is independent of all human thought and will, faith and unbelief."

[40] Barth, *Church Dogmatics*, 4/4:182 and 168.

[41] Barth, *Church Dogmatics*, 4/4:150–51, 194. For example, Donald Bridge and David Phypers, *The Water That Divides* (Downers Grove: InterVarsity Press, 1977). Wayne Grudem likewise urges a mutual accommodation with "a common admission that baptism is not a major doctrine of the faith. . . . " (*Systematic Theology* [Grand Rapids: Zondervan Publishing House, 1997], 982–83). Cf. Richard Schluter, *Karl Barths Tauflehre* (Paderborn: Verlag Bonifacius, 1973).

[42] Kurt Aland, *Did the Early Church Baptize Infants?* trans. with an introduction by George R. Beasley-Murray (Philadelphia: Westminster Press, 1963). [*Die Säuglingstaufe im Neuen Testament und in der alten Kirche; eine Antwort an Joachim Jeremias* (München: C. Kaiser, 1961).] See also Johannes Schneider, *Die Taufe im Neuen Testament* (Stuttgart: W. Kohlhammer, 1952). Beasely-Murray was a leading Baptist authority on Baptism. Joachim Jeremias, *Infant Baptism in the First Four Centuries*, trans. David Cairns (Philadelphia: Westminster Press, 1958); *The*

Europe was secularized, ties between the state and Church were loosened, and so arguments about infant Baptism lost their importance.

Another challenge to infant Baptism has emerged from Catholics involved in liturgical reforms in connection with a decree of Second Vatican Council, *The Constitution on the Sacred Liturgy*, calling for new and separate rites for the Baptism of adults and infants.[43] Proponents of the Rite of Christian Initiation for Adults (RCIA) have followed the Reformed in seeing adult Baptism as the norm and the Baptism of infants as a tolerable aberration with the proviso that parents desiring Baptism for their children first take instruction, now called catechesis. In some cases, infant Baptism has been delayed or even omitted. Another group of liturgical scholars, called the Mature Adulthood School, favors abolishing Baptism for infants except in cases of imminent death. Another group gathered around the Rite of Baptism for Children (RBC) allowed the Baptism of infants whose parents exhibited a sincere commitment to Christian life, a view that

---

Origins of Infant Baptism: A Further Study in Reply to Kurt Aland, trans. Dorothea M. Barton (London: SCM Press; Naperville: Allensons, 1963). For summaries of Barth's views see Scaer, *Baptism* 167–80; on the Jeremias-Aland debate, 124–34. Markus Barth's *Die Taufe ein Sakrament?* (*Is Baptism a Sacrament?*) appeared in 1951. The lectures which Karl Barth developed into *Die Kirchliche Lehre von der Taufe* were given in 1943 (*The Teaching of the Church Regarding Baptism*, trans. Ernest A. Payne [London: SCM Press, 1948)]. His volume on Baptism in the Kirchliche Dogmatik appeared in 1967. Karl Barth died the following year. Both father and son answered the question of *Is Baptism a Sacrament?* with a clear 'no.' See Riggs, *Baptism in the Reformed Tradition*, 95. See *Scaer*, Baptism, 124–134.

[43] *The Constitution on the Sacred Liturgy* (December 4, 1963) called for commissions to prepare new liturgical rites. Provisions were made for an adult catechumenate, revised adult baptismal rites (*Constitution,* III, 65–66), and rites for infant Baptism with specified roles for parents and godparents (67). Local bishops were allowed to dictate the form and the age for administering confirmation (68, 69, 71). Commissions were commonly called by their initials: RCIA for Rite of Christian Initiation for Adults; RBC for Rite of Baptism for Children; RC for Rite of Confirmation; and RCIC for Rite of Christian Initiation for Children. See Kurt Stasiak, *Return to Grace: A Theology for Infant Baptism* (Collegeville, MN: The Liturgical Press, 1996), 11. Presuppositional for the Rite of Baptism for Children in the Roman Catholic Church is that children do not believe at the time of their Baptism and so the sponsers with the parents are pledged to give them a Christian upbringing. See Michael G. Witczak, *The Sacrament of Baptism*, (Collegeville: The Liturgical Press, 2011).

appeared among some nineteenth-century Lutheran theologians and reflected a view of faith found in Pietism.[44]

At issue in the various discussions surveyed above was the role of faith in baptizing infants. This study has to do with how nineteenth-century Lutherans dealt with it. An earlier draft of this study was entitled *The Doctrine of Infant Baptism in German Protestant Theology of the Nineteenth Century* to allow for the inclusion of Schleiermacher. Since it never engages any other Reformed theologian, it appears now as *Infant Baptism in Nineteenth Century Lutheran Theology*. Reformed theologians were not faced with the Lutheran dilemma of what to do with faith in infant Baptism. It is with this dilemma that this study deals.

[44] In support of the older practice of baptizing infants, the Sacred Congregation for the Doctrine of the Faith in 1983 issued *Pastoralis Actio* affirming the traditional teaching that John 3:5 required baptizing infants. For a detailed discussion of these positions, see Stasiak, *Return to Grace: A Theology for Infant Baptism,* 11–52.

CHAPTER I

RATIONALISM AND SUPRANATURALISM

In his 1807 monograph concerning Baptism, *Über die Taufe*, Adam Theodor Lehmus (1777–1840) described the Socinian attitude prevalent in his day that Sacraments were of little value. This indifference surfaced among the people who were negligent in having their children baptized. Baptism rolls then served as birth records, and the government had no other way to keep track of its citizens—a problem especially in regard to the boys who would be conscripted into the military. Thus, a royal decree was issued in Prussia on February 25, 1802, requiring every father to have his child baptized within six weeks of birth. Failure to comply resulted in the father being declared mentally incompetent and the child being taken away from him and given to a guardian.[1]

Rationalists and Supranaturalists were prominent at the dawn of the nineteenth century. They were so similar that they engendered a third school of thought bearing the name of both, Rationalistic Supranaturalism or Supranaturalistic Rationalism.[2] These schools of

[1] Adam Theodor Albert Lehmus, *Über die Taufe* (Heidelberg: Mohr und Zimmer, 1807), 7.

[2] H. Hohlwein, "Rationalismus II. Rationalismus und Supranaturalismus, kirchengeschichtlich," *Die Religion in Geschichte und Gegenwart*, ed. Kurt Galling (Dritte, völlig neu bearbeitete Auflage; Tübingen: J. C. B. Mohr, 1961), 5:799. Hereafter this is cited as *RGG*. For Rationalism reason was the sole arbiter of the truth and so the Bible was viewed like any other book. Supernaturalism took a positive view of the Bible but used reason to determine what in the Bible was useful for religion, *principium rationis sufficientis*. Rationalistic Supranaturalism, or as it was also called, Supranaturalistic Rationalism, incorporated Kant's critique of reason

thought were products of the age of Enlightenment and its philosophical Idealism.[3] Adherents of Rationalism and Supranaturalism adopted the Socinian basis. Original sin was denied, and Baptism was no longer a means of grace for creating faith. Finding the arguments of the Lutheran Confessions, Luther, and the Lutheran Orthodox theologians for infant Baptism no longer convincing, they had to offer other reasons for its continuation.[4] For them, the Baptism of a child was an initiation ceremony into the Christian society. As the child grew older, he would find inclusion in this society advantageous in making his own decisions about religion. It may be said that infant Baptism had become so secularized, that no specific religious benefits were given to the baptized child; in no way was he changed or given anything personally. All benefits were attached to his reaching maturity within the Christian fellowship. The rite or ceremony of infant Baptism itself actually had more significance for onlookers than for the one baptized; it stirred up certain religious feelings within them and caused them to remember their own initiation into this same society.

Since the Rationalists and Supranaturalists denied that infant Baptism had any sure scriptural foundation, they had to establish it on extra-biblical material. Their favorite argument was a negative one: just as Christ did not command it, so also He did not forbid it. Therefore, there can be nothing wrong in continuing the practice, although it is not mandatory. Another basis for infant Baptism was said to be the practice of the Ancient Church. Here there could be no historical doubt that it was practiced.

The Rationalists and Supranaturalists took a negative attitude, for reasons previously offered, toward the practice of infant Baptism. Their negative principles may be succinctly grouped into six points: (1) There is no reference to infant Baptism in the Scriptures by way of command, example, or deduction. (2) The Baptism of the New Testament is for adults only. (3) Faith is created by the spoken or preached Word only and not by Baptism. (4) Since children are not sufficiently conscious or rational, they are not able to come to faith

---

and constructed a Christianity on his moral principles. This did not prove successful and Rationalism reappeared.

[3] Horst Stephan, *Geschichte der Deutschen Evangelischen Theologie seit dem Deutschen Idealismus*, ed. Martin Schmidt (Zweite neubearbeitete Auflage; Berlin: Alfred Töpelmann, 1960), 61–74.

[4] Johann Andreas Quenstedt, *Theologia didactico-polemica sive systema theologicum* (Lipsiae: Thomas Fritsch, 1715), 1125.

through the preached Word. (5) Because children are baptized without having faith, their Baptism is to be considered incomplete. (6) This incompleteness is corrected when the child comes to faith through the spoken Word.

This last point concerning a so-called incomplete infant Baptism's need of later completion has two ramifications: First, since the Baptism itself is incomplete, it is necessary that a pledge be given at Baptism by either parents or sponsors that the child will come into contact with the preached Word. Thereby the child will be given an opportunity to come to faith and thus correct the incompleteness of his Baptism. Second, the correcting of this incompleteness is often associated with the rite of confirmation in which the child can make his own confession of faith.

These six negative principles are specifically noted here since they constantly reappear throughout the Lutheran theology of the nineteenth century. There were certainly many exceptions to the principles denying the scriptural foundations of infant Baptism. But concerning the principles dealing with the efficacy of Baptism for children in creating faith and infant Baptism's being incomplete, there were no exceptions save for the Repristination theologians. Already in the first years of the century the presuppositions common to the entire century were set forth. To present the situation of Lutheran theology in Germany at the beginning of the nineteenth century, Julius Wegscheider (1771–1849) has been chosen from among the Rationalists and Franz Reinhard (1753–1812) from among the Supranaturalists.

JULIUS AUGUST LUDWIG WEGSCHEIDER

Wegscheider's *Institutiones Theologiae Christianae Dogmaticae* was the leading dogmatics book during the last generation of Rationalism. Between 1815 and 1844, it appeared in eight editions.[5] The space Wegscheider devotes to infant Baptism is not extensive. Nevertheless, his views are important, since they reappear in part in most of the nineteenth-century theologies. These views include the lack of biblical command or example concerning infant Baptism, the denial of infant faith, and the importance of a guarantee given at the time of Baptism that the Word will subsequently be applied to the child, thus causing faith to arise.

[5] Stephan, *Geschichte der Deutschen Evangelischen Theologie,* 64.

Wegscheider introduces his discussion on Baptism by dissociating himself from what he calls the older theologians. Undoubtedly, he is referring to the Lutheran theologians of the sixteenth and seventeenth centuries. Their views are said to be superstitious and contrary to what the New Testament says about Baptism. What the New Testament says about Baptism's essence and effects refers to adults only. To say that Baptism has any magical or supernatural force is contrary to what we know from both reason and experience. When Wegscheider speaks of a magical or supernatural force in Baptism, he is referring to the regenerating power of Baptism in creating faith in infants. Newborn infants are not capable of having faith of any kind, since the capability of having faith is dependent upon a certain level of consciousness in the individual. Children are said not even to be conscious of themselves; thus they are excluded from having faith. Therefore, the reason for baptizing infants cannot be that Baptism gives them faith or that they are able to believe. Neither can infant Baptism be defended from the point of view that Baptism is absolutely necessary, since the Scriptures know of no absolute necessity concerning Baptism. The custom cannot be defended from the familial connection a child born of Christian parents has with them, since the New Testament references to Baptism apply only to those who have already joined themselves to the fellowship of Christian saints. There is nothing in the Scriptures that says that Jesus ordered Baptism for those who would be born within the fellowship of Christians in all succeeding generations.[6]

Despite his criticism of other theologians' attempts to establish Baptism, and more specifically infant Baptism, as a Church custom, Wegscheider does offer reasons for continuing Baptism. Chief among these is basically an argument from silence: just as Jesus did not say that Baptism was to be used for all time, neither did He set a certain limitation on the length of time it was to be used. Likewise, if Jesus did not command Baptism of children, neither did He forbid it. Further evidence in favor of continuing infant Baptism is found in the practice of the church, where Baptism has always been a sign of initiation and regeneration. Therefore, Baptism may now be applied to those joining the Christian society.[7]

---

[6] Jul. Aug. Lud. Wegscheider, *Institutiones Theologiae Christianae Dogmaticae* (Edito tertio emendata et aucta; Halae: Io. Iac. Gebauer et Filii, 1817), 364–65.
[7] Wegscheider, *Institutiones,* 365.

Wegscheider does speak of a certain moral efficacy that is attributed to Baptism in giving certain outward advantages and rights to the one who is receiving it. Baptism brings its object into Christendom, *civitas Christiana*. Here the individual is brought into contact with Christian fellowship. In this fellowship are those things that will stir up in the baptized person the feelings of religion and virtue. Whether religion and virtue will arise in the baptized person depends completely on the disposition of his mind.[8]

It should be noted that, for Wegscheider, Baptism is no longer, strictly speaking, a means of grace; rather, it is a means of entering a fellowship where religion can be acquired. Such a concept of Baptism might best be called a means to the means of grace. It can be seen how infant Baptism could rationally be tolerated as such. By being baptized, children do not directly participate in salvation but only in the outward fellowship. When they attain the use of their reason, they can obtain religion for themselves from the Christian fellowship.

What has been said so far regards Baptism in general. Wegscheider has a special paragraph dealing specifically with infant Baptism. For him, the practice of infant Baptism can be defended rationally, and his two reasons correspond to those already given for maintaining Baptism in general. First, the Scriptures say nothing against infant Baptism. Second, the practice of infant Baptism received almost universal support in the Ancient Church. When the church accepts infants into the Christian society through the rite of Baptism, it also takes upon itself the responsibility of giving such infants religious instruction at the proper time. Concerning the giving of this instruction, the Church is to admonish very seriously both parents and sponsors. All those who participate in the act of Baptism are to be reminded of their great responsibilities.[9]

For Wegscheider, confirmation is not only a useful but a necessary ceremony, which is to be given in addition to Baptism. Baptism as the ceremony of initiation does not have to be repeated. Confirmation gives the youth who has been baptized as an infant the opportunity of being instructed in the Christian religion. Thus, he himself can examine the Christian religion of which he was made a member by Baptism and can make a decision concerning it.[10]

---

[8] Wegscheider, *Institutiones*, 365.
[9] Wegscheider, *Institutiones*, 366.
[10] Wegscheider, *Institutiones*, 366.

In reality, the person of the child is not immediately effected by the act of Baptism. The outward effects of Baptism are of no use to the infant until the time of reasoning. In the Baptism of infants, the only ones immediately affected are the parents and others participating in the act. It is they who accept the obligations concerning the child's education in the Christian religion.

Also included in the discussion on infant Baptism is a section on the rite of Baptism itself. It is of prime importance to Wegscheider that infant Baptism should be performed only by a called teacher of religion, that is, a pastor. This was John Calvin's position. It excludes all lay Baptism, in a manner in keeping with Wegscheider's position that the absolute necessity of Baptism is a fiction of which the New Testament knows nothing. Since Baptism is not an absolute necessity and does not effect the personal salvation of the child being baptized, there is no necessity for an emergency lay Baptism. That Baptism should be performed by *religionis doctoribus publicis* might further indicate that the service is to be performed before the congregation or in the presence of parents and sponsors. This would further substantiate the idea that Baptism really has more significance for those observing and participating in the rite of Baptism than for the child being baptized.[11]

The act of Baptism itself is performed by the application of water with the accompanying recitation of the words of institution in Matthew 28:19. Other customs mentioned in connection with Baptism but not of equal importance with the act itself are the giving of the name, the signing of the cross, prayers, the imposition of the hands, and the benediction. These ceremonies can still have a use in the church. Exorcism, however, is to be omitted.[12]

Obviously missing from the enumeration of the ceremonies accompanying Baptism are the renunciation of Satan and the addressing of the questions to the child concerning his faith. Insofar as exorcism is rejected, one wonders why the renunciation and the questions concerning faith are not also rejected. What is the significance of these if infant faith is denied? Surely they were known to Wegscheider, since he mentions the signing of the cross and the laying on of hands, certainly less important ceremonies. It is unusual that Wegscheider explicitly rejects exorcism, which began to fall into disuse two centuries before, but fails to mention the questions and

---

[11] Wegscheider, *Institutiones,* 366–67.

[12] Wegscheider, *Institutiones,* 367.

answers that were still used in many places at that time. It is obvious that, had they been mentioned, they would have been rejected together with exorcism. What makes it even more unusual is that all others who treat the baptismal rites in the nineteenth century treat the problem of the questions. Perhaps the best explanation of their absence is that Wegscheider did not want to oppose a commonly used practice.

FRANZ VOLKMAR REINHARD

The Supranaturalist Franz Reinhard gives a more extensive treatment to infant Baptism in his *Vorlesungen über die Dogmatik* than does the Rationalist Wegscheider. Present in Reinhard's understanding of infant Baptism are the same fundamental concepts that are purposed by Wegscheider. Infant Baptism cannot be proved by scriptural command or example. There is no infant faith in connection with infant Baptism. As a rite, it was the acceptance of the child into the outward fellowship of the Christian Church. Reinhard's discussion is superior, since it spells out more clearly the negative attitude of the Rationalists and Supranaturalists toward the biblical evidence traditionally used in the defense of infant Baptism, and presents equally well the secular approach, which had partly usurped the place of the traditional biblical one.

Already in his definition of Baptism and the Holy Communion, Reinhard gives evidence of a moralistic approach. Baptism and Holy Communion are defined as religious ceremonies through which God works for the betterment of man.[13] Baptism does not really bring anything new to its object, but it only improves that which is already there.

In a more specific discussion on Baptism, this Sacrament is called that ceremony through which a person is received into the religious fellowship of Christians. It is a festive act symbolizing the entrance of the individual into the Christian religion. In the act of Baptism, the one who is to be baptized confesses the religion Christ and His apostles taught. To be baptized in the name of the Father, Son, and Holy Spirit means that the baptized confesses solemnly the religion of the Father, Son, and Holy Spirit. With this confession, the baptized

[13] Franz Volkmar Reinhard, *Vorlesungen über die Dogmatik*, ed. Johann Gottfried Immanuel Berger (Zweyte verbesserte Auflage; Nürnberg und Salzbach: J. E. Seidelschen Kunst-und Buchhandlung, 1806), 554–55.

person is given to understand that he accepts this religion out of conviction and that he wants to fulfill the demands of this religion. In accepting these demands, the baptized vows that he will tenderly love all who belong to the fellowship confessing this religion and that he will lead an upright and blameless life according to its precepts.[14] In this definition of Baptism, the promise or the giving of grace is absent. Those acting in Baptism are the congregation, which receives the baptized person into its fellowship, and the baptized person, who confesses Christ's religion and vows to live up to its demands. It is nowhere mentioned that God is performing anything on the baptized through this act. Also important in this definition of Baptism is that everything should be done with solemnity. This indicates that Baptism is not so much a matter of immediate personal salvation as it is of belonging to a society and coming into social association with those who profess the religion of Christ and the apostles.

In being baptized, the person is also entitled to the rights and benefits bound up with the Christian religion. These rights and benefits would include waiting for the grace of God and for the forgiveness of sins for the sake of Jesus' death with which the hope of eternal salvation is inseparably connected.[15] Baptism does not give the grace of God or the forgiveness of sins, but it puts the person into a relationship where these blessings are obtainable. Here the same critique used of Wegscheider applies. Baptism is no longer the means of grace. But since it takes the individual into the fellowship where grace is available, it is the means to the means of grace. The real means of grace is the church's fellowship and not Baptism.

Also mentioned among the effects of the act of Baptism is the stimulation of the memories of those watching. First, previously baptized observers remember their own acceptance into the Christian religion through Baptism and all the happiness they have received by belonging to this religion. Second, they receive new incitement to fulfill obediently those duties to which they were obligated in Baptism. Third, they are reminded that they should treat the newly baptized as a brother and love him with all affection.[16] Thus, the act of Baptism has at least as much significance for observers as for the one baptized who receives in it only one real benefit: the enjoyment of those rights and privileges connected with the Christian religion.

---

[14] Reinhard, *Vorlesungen*, 566.
[15] Reinhard, *Vorlesungen*, 566–67.
[16] Reinhard, *Vorlesungen*, 567.

Again, Baptism is understood not so much as a matter of immediate personal salvation as it is an initiatory act into the Christian community. The focus of attention might be the person being baptized, but the ones benefiting most immediately are those baptized persons watching the act.

Reinhard also looks upon Baptism as a covenant with God. Through the festivities of a covenant, God can make clearer to men the duties to which they have bound themselves and can make it seem that they are performing these duties to God. Such festivities as those which are connected with a covenant are necessary because so often men can neglect to do their very best.

Just as God established a covenant with the people of Israel, so now He establishes one with us. In the covenant of Baptism, baptized persons vow to live according to the regulations of the Christian religion. This is supported by 1 Peter 3:21, where the Greek word *eperotema* is interpreted as a solemn obligation. What makes the obligation of Baptism more solemn in character is the presence of witnesses; this is said by Reinhard to be the origin of sponsors or baptismal witnesses.[17] In defining Baptism as a covenant, two concepts central to Reinhard's understanding of Baptism are again emphasized. In the covenant, it is man who is obligating himself. This covenant is distinguished from other obligations by its solemnity; to say that something is solemn, however, means only that it is performed in the presence of others. Thus, Baptism is not so much a matter of personal salvation as it is a matter of personal obligation in association with the Christian fellowship.

Those who serve as sponsors at infant Baptism have a greater responsibility than those who serve in connection with adult Baptism. They promise in the name of the child being baptized that he will observe the duties of the Christian religion. It is evident that inarticulate children require more help in their Christian upbringing and development than do adults. The sponsors are to provide for the child's upbringing and development should his parents no longer do so.[18] Even in the case of the Baptism of infants, Reinhard defines the function of the sponsors in terms of the vow laid upon the child through the act of Baptism. In that the sponsors are to provide for the upbringing of the child, they are helping the child fulfill the vow of Baptism. Again, two principles predominate in Reinhard's

---

[17] Reinhard, *Vorlesungen*, 567–68.
[18] Reinhard, *Vorlesungen*, 568.

presentation: first, Baptism is an act we do toward God; second, the act is solemnized by the presence of others.

Baptism is never to be applied to anyone by force. It is to be applied only to those who desire it. Should parents desire Baptism for their children, they also assume the obligation to care for the maintenance and wellbeing of the child.[19] Here the idea of obligation is again very prominent.

From the beginning, Reinhard sets out to disqualify any evidence from the Scriptures that might be offered in defense of infant Baptism. The Scriptures can be of no use in determining whether or not infant Baptism is either permitted or commanded as a rite for the Church, since they know absolutely nothing about it.[20] Reinhard substantiates this assertion by examining and dismissing five passages that had been used in defense of infant Baptism: the baptismal command (Matthew 28:19), the Synoptic pericopes of Jesus' blessing of the children (Matthew 19:14; Mark 10:14; Luke 18:16), the necessity of rebirth in Jesus' discussion with Nicodemus (John 3:5), the analogy of circumcision and Baptism, and the examples found in Acts where entire households are baptized.

The universality of the command to baptize in Matthew 28:19 cannot be used to establish infant Baptism, since Christ's words in verse 20 and the parallel in Mark 16:15 might be taken as limiting the field to those capable of receiving religious instruction, which, of course, would be adults.[21] The pericopes of Jesus' blessing the children (Matthew 19:14; Mark 10:14; Luke 18:16) are also not legitimate evidence in the matter of infant Baptism; these passages do not actually deal with children, but with those who have minds like children, who are obedient and docile like children. To such as these, and not to children themselves, is the kingdom of heaven ascribed. On that account, it cannot be argued that if children are excluded from Baptism, they would be excluded from the kingdom of God.[22] John

[19] Reinhard, *Vorlesungen*, 570.

[20] Reinhard, *Vorlesungen*, 572.

[21] Reinhard, *Vorlesungen*, 572. The Rationalist Jakob Eckermann (1754–1812) also interpreted these passages as referring to adults only and found no command in the Scriptures to baptize children. Jakob Eckermann, *Handbuch für das systematische Studium der christlichen Glaubenslehre*, 4 vols. (Altona: Johann Friedrick Hammerich, 1803), 4:327.

[22] Reinhard, *Vorlesungen*. 572. The same thought is even more positively expressed by Adam Theodor Lehmus. He writes: "Auch kann nicht entschieden werden, ob der Erlöser die Kindertaufe ausdrücklich befohlen habe, denn die Stellen, welche die

3:5 likewise does not belong in the discussion concerning infant Baptism, since it deals with the change of attitude in adult human beings.[23]

The analogy between circumcision and Baptism cannot be used as evidence that Baptism should be applied to children. If it is to be deduced from the similarity between these two rites that Baptism should be given to children, it could also be deduced from the same similarity that Baptism, like circumcision, should not be applied to children of other nations or races. Reinhard claims that what can be proven from analogy in one case can also be proven in the other case.[24] Also of no importance in the question of infant Baptism are those passages in Acts where it is reported that entire households were baptized. While it is certain that entire households were baptized, it is uncertain that children were there. If they were there, it is uncertain whether they were baptized. To say that children were baptized on these occasions can be maintained as little as the circumcision of the women in Abraham's house in Genesis 17:27.[25] Reinhard's arguments are not foolproof. Passages in Acts make no distinctions as to sex or age. He might have paid closer attention to Genesis 17:27, which specifically lists men. Infant male children are included by saying "all men born into the household."

Since Reinhard claims that the correctness of infant Baptism cannot be demonstrated from scriptural evidence, he attempts to establish it on other bases. Three bases are posed as questions to which Reinhard then answers affirmatively. The three definitive questions are: Was it usual to baptize children in the Ancient Church? Is the custom of baptizing children tolerable to the nature and purpose

---

historischen Vertheidiger derselben anführen bewiesen theils die Innigkeit des menschfreundlichen Mannes, Matth. XIX, 14. Marc. X, 14 Luc. XVIII, 16, theils dringen sie auf neuen kindlichen Sinn, den der Mensch gegen die Gottheit nähren soll, auf ein Schuldloswerden mit Bewußtsein, gleichwie Unschuld ohne Bewußtsein der Charakter der Kindheit ist. Marc. X, 15. Luc. XVIII, 17." Lehmus, *Über die Taufe*, 9.

[23] Reinhard, *Vorlesungen,* 572–73. Eckermann understands this passage as excluding not only children, but also adults as a class. For him this refers to the Jews who thought they had a claim to the Messianic kingdom. "Joh. 3, 5. ist schon im dritten Band erklärt. Nicht in Beziehung auf Erbsünde, sondern in Beziehung auf die Meynung der Juden, daß sie als Juden schon ein Anrecht auf das Messiasreich hätten, sagte Jesus: Ihr Juden könntet nicht Bürger des Reiches Gottes werden, wenn ihr nicht erst eine neue wahre Religion annehmen werdet." Eckermann, *Handbuch,* 328.

[24] Reinhard, *Vorlesungen*, 573.

[25] Reinhard, *Vorlesungen*, 573.

of Baptism in general? Is it necessary and useful to continue the baptizing of children in the Church? While the second question remains within the scope of Scripture, the first and the third questions by their very wording must be answered from extra-biblical material, from reasons of antiquity and usefulness.[26]

To the first question, that of antiquity, Reinhard answers that infant Baptism was practiced in the Ancient Church, even though certain objections were raised against it. That infant Baptism was occasionally objected to in the Ancient Church indicates that it was introduced at a previous time. It should also be considered that in general it received common approval and only an occasional objection.[27]

More important for Reinhard than the practice of the Early Church in the matter of establishing the correctness of infant Baptism is determining whether or not the nature and purpose of Baptism can tolerate baptizing infants. According to Reinhard, the purpose for Christ's institution of Baptism was that it should be useful in a variety of ways and that the baptized should be made to participate in important benefits. If it can be shown that inarticulate children are susceptible to these benefits, then it may be concluded that they may be baptized. The chief benefit of Baptism is said to be acceptance into the religious fellowship of Christians. Along with and belonging to this acceptance, one is given outward privileges of membership as well as the right to await all the benefits of Christ's death. The ability of children to receive such blessings is self-apparent.[28] Infant Baptism is valued not as a means of regeneration for the child but for its

---

[26] Reinhard, *Vorlesungen*, 573.

[27] Reinhard, *Vorlesungen*, 573. Eckermann holds that it cannot be proved from the Scriptures that the apostles did not institute infant Baptism or that it had other than apostolic origins. In the post-apostolic period there were still those who had known the apostles and could have shown that it was of post-apostolic origin. He agrees with the older Lutheran theologians that Baptism was practiced by the apostles, but unlike them, he argues not from the biblical texts but only early church tradition. Eckermann, *Handbuch*, 334–35.

[28] Reinhard, *Vorlesungen*, 574–75. Here also Eckermann is in agreement. "Es ist ferner unleugbar, daß die christliche Religionslehre die einzigen wahren Grundsätze aller wahren Religion enthält, und den Menschen zur richtigen Erkenntniß und würdigen Verehrung Gottes führt. Wie wichtig ist es daher nicht für ein Kind, von seinen frühesten Jahren an, sobald es derselben fähig ist, der Segnungen und Wohlthaten der christlichen Religion theilhaftig zu werden. Und zum Antheil an allen diesen Wohlthaten weiht und führt die Taufe das Kind." Eckermann, *Handbuch*, 338–39.

placing the child into a community in which he can share in future benefits.

Last of all, Reinhard says that it is necessary and useful to maintain infant Baptism in the Church, because by it inarticulate children would be received into the Christian community with understanding and affection. Much help, brotherly affection, and love are required in giving guidance to young children. Since infant Baptism gives the congregation an opportunity to exercise these spiritual virtues, infant Baptism is useful for them.[29]

It is necessary because if infant Baptism should no longer be practiced, the mixture of baptized and unbaptized would be detrimental to the peace and unity of the family.[30] This is a novel argument and could easily be answered by Baptists who would respond that eventually no children would be baptized and so unity

---

[29] Reinhard, *Vorlesungen*, 574–75. In the first decade of the nineteenth century there appeared three monographs written on Baptism which contained the same thought as expressed here by Reinhard, namely that infant Baptism was a useful ceremony for the congregation. The writers of these monographs were Christian Eisenlohr, Adam Theodor Lehmus, and Karl Michahelles. Eisenlohr said, first, just as infant Baptism was the preliminary solemn rite for the benefit of the parents and sponsors, Baptism as a religious rite was said to awaken and revive various religious thoughts and emotions in those watching. Second, it obligated the parents and sponsors to give the child a Christian education. Third, Baptism gives all involved a chance to remember their Baptism. Of course, the child being baptized must wait until maturity to enjoy this benefit of Baptism. Christian Eisenlohr, *Historische Bemerkungen über die Taufe* (Tübingen: Jacob Friedrich Herbrandt, 1804), 132–34. Similarly Lehmus quite specifically says that infant Baptism is not for the child's benefit, but is for the fulfillment of the adults' needs. "Die Kindertaufe ist also nicht um des Nutzens der Kinder willen vorhanden, sondern nothwendiges Bedürfniß christlicher Frommen, und also nichts sagend den Einwurf, daß Kinder eine so heilige noch verstehen können." Lehmus, *Über die Taufe*, 93. Michahelles sees in the rite of infant Baptism an opportunity to impress upon parents their ethical obligations to their children. "O wie viele Eltern bedärfen noch immer einer feyerlichen Aufforderung, ihre Elternpflichten auch in Ansehung der christlich sittlichen Bildungen ihrer Kinder zu erfällen! Gewiß die Fahrläßigkeit mancher Eltern in Ansehung derselben würde noch weit großer seyn, wenn nicht noch die Verpflichtung, die sie bey der Taufe ihrer Kinder auf sich genommen haben, dieselben bey sich zu entwickelnen Verstandkräften in der Lehre Jesu unterrichten zu lassen, gerade noch so viel Einfluß auf ihr Gemüth behauptete, daß sie nicht ganz umhin können, dieser Verpflichtung wenigstens einigermassen nachzuleben, und ihren Kindern, sey es auch nur den nothdürftigsten Religionsunterricht angedeyhen zu lassen, der doch immer besser ist als gar keinen." Karl Friedrich Michahelles, *Über den christlichen Ritus der Taufe und besonders der Kindertaufe* (Nürnberg: Wiegel und Rießner, 1816), 23–24.

[30] Reinhard, *Vorlesungen*, 576.

would be restored. More apparently, faith and the lack of it and not Baptism or the lack of it cause dissensions in families.

In spite of the biblical reasons for not practicing infant Baptism, Reinhard defends the practice, since it does not involve any improprieties. Any improprieties attached to infant Baptism are fabricated.[31] He deals more extensively with the alleged impropriety of the sponsor's making a promise in the name of the child of which the child knows nothing. If this is to be considered an impropriety, then the making of no contract advantageous to the children should be permitted.[32] Baptism does not compel children to remain disciples of Christ. A baptized person has the freedom of choice to determine whether or not to remain in the Christian fellowship. The Church makes it the duty of the baptized youth to test the religion of Jesus with mature reason. Should it appear necessary to the youth after testing the religion of Jesus to leave that fellowship of which he is a member by virtue of his Baptism, he may do so.[33]

Reinhard concludes his section on infant Baptism with a discussion of infant faith, which he discredits. He opposes the doctrines that Baptism is necessary or that through it Christ works faith in the soul of the child. The doctrine of infant faith in connection with Baptism arose when those biblical passages designating Baptism as the bath of regeneration were applied to children. This, in turn, depended on interpreting Baptism as the working and imparting of faith. To most theologians, the doctrine of infant faith has great difficulties and is repulsive.[34] Baptism does work faith in children, if faith is defined as the soul's predisposition for moral perfection in the future and a tendency to do good. Such predisposition for future moral perfection and a tendency in the soul to do good would be a mere capability in the child, which would presuppose neither consciousness nor knowledge.[35]

---

[31] Reinhard, *Vorlesungen*, 576.

[32] Reinhard, *Vorlesungen*, 576. Michahelles compares infant Baptism to an ancient family rite entitling the family to certain privileges. Unless the children undergo this solemn act, they cannot participate in family privileges. He points out that the parents would be fools if they did not let their children participate in the rite simply because the children did not have the mentality to estimate the value of the privileges given along with this rite. Michahelles, *Über den christlichen Ritus der Taufe,* 23–24

[33] Reinhard, *Vorlesungen*, 576.

[34] Reinhard, *Vorlesungen*, 576–77.

[35] Reinhard, *Vorlesungen*, 577.

Reinhard acknowledges that the kind of faith he attributes to infants is not taught in the Scriptures. He offers five reasons why children cannot have the faith about which the Scriptures speak: (1) Passages in which Baptism is connected with regeneration deal with adults. Whether it has anything to do with children is another question. (2) Regeneration is an expression that cannot be used of children but only of adults, who alone have the faculties of introspection and consciousness to better their minds. (3) Luke 1:15, where the leaping of John the Baptist in the womb of his mother Elizabeth is recorded, is an exceptional instance and does not belong in the discussion of infant faith. (4) Since the Scriptures do not know of infant Baptism, it cannot be known with certainty whether faith is produced by such a Baptism. (5) There is no evidence from experience that Baptism works a good disposition in the soul of the child. Reinhard concludes that infant faith remains a hypothesis that, indeed, does not involve any contradiction, but the evidence offered for it is hardly sufficient.[36]

CONCLUSION

Early nineteenth-century Rationalists and Supranaturalists agreed that infant Baptism lacked a firm biblical basis. Baptism was without saving efficacy, and children were incapable of faith. In their Baptism, children had no personal immediate participation in salvation. Thus, other reasons for the practice were identified. Through this rite, the child would have the advantage of becoming a member of a society in which to learn religion. Just as infant Baptism was not taught in the Scriptures, it was not prohibited, and so there was no good reason to discontinue a practice that could be traced back to the Ancient Church. The Rationalists and Supranaturalists understood infant Baptism less as a religious rite with immediate benefits for the baptized child and more as an induction ceremony into a society with religious aims.

Their tenets are not unique to them. Before them, the Reformation-era Anabaptists and Socinians had held that infant Baptism was without biblical support and denied that children were capable of regeneration. The Rationalists and the Supranaturalists saw that the logical conclusion of their theologies meant the cessation of infant Baptism, but for their own reasons made its continuation a

[36] Reinhard, *Vorlesungen*, 577–78.

matter of indifference. This the Anabaptists did not do but completely abolished its practice in their fellowships. Schleiermacher, who would come to dominate the theological world of the nineteenth century, saw his theological program as a protest against the Rationalists but lived within the same inconsistency of finding no biblical support for infant Baptism but not calling for its abolishment.

Arguments offered for infant Baptism by the Rationalists and Supranaturalists were more convincing in eighteenth and nineteenth century Europe—where the Church and state were coextensive—than they would be today. Baptism not only initiated one into the Church but made one a citizen of the country in which it was administered. Even without bestowing salvation, the rite introduced the child into a society in which he could receive citizenship and enjoy future benefits. In a Europe that was already on the road to secularization in the Age of the Enlightenment, Baptism was seen as necessary to obtain certain legal rights.[37] In the world of the nineteenth century, the Church and the state were still seen as one kingdom of God and so within this dimension infant Baptism had a place. Today secularization in Europe is almost complete and benefits of citizenship can be granted without Baptism. Putting aside secular benefits attached to Baptism, the Reformed held that religious benefits can be conferred by birth to Christian parents quite apart from Baptism. So this element in Rationalist thought was not entirely new. However, parents in the Reformed Church who refused Baptism for their children would be seen as not living up to the commands of the covenant and, thus, less likely to provide the environment in which their children could come to faith.

If Baptism is merely an initiation into this Christian society, as the Rationalists and Supranaturalists held, it might be asked if another mode of initiation might be substituted for Baptism. Or would birth to parents belonging to this society be considered sufficient for membership? These questions were not addressed by the Rationalists and Supranaturalists. Earlier, the Socinians raised these questions, and unlike the Rationalists and the Supranaturalists, they let infant Baptism fall into disuse.

Another reason for infant Baptism is the emotional stimulation that it stirs up among the observers, but is this a good enough reason

[37] As Michahelles points out, apart from any spiritual benefit which Baptism might or might not give, children should be baptized so that they may enjoy the benefits of citizenship. Michahelles, *Über den christlichen Ritus der Taufe*, 23–24.

for continuing any practice? Another ceremony might do this more effectively. Then there is the reason that infant Baptism gives a child great advantages for later in life, since he is made a member of a particular society.[38] A society is not prevented from abolishing or at least changing its rules of initiation and letting the unbaptized enjoy the benefits previously allowed only by the baptized. Since Baptism may not have been commanded for all times, making Baptism optional is possible. Reasons offered for infant Baptism by the Rationalists and Supranaturalists were pragmatic in their connection with the social and religious circumstances of Germany in the early nineteenth century. A change in circumstances would allow for its discontinuation.

Biblical passages traditionally held to teach the universality of the baptismal command, the necessity of baptismal regeneration, and the place of children in the Kingdom were discounted. Underlying this reinterpretation was the denial of original sin, and so for theological and not just biblical reasons, Baptism was not seen as necessary for

---

[38] This argument for infant Baptism shows how secularized the understanding of infant Baptism and the Church had become at this time. Typical of this approach was Karl Michahelles who urged parents to have their children baptized. With some parents there was no difficulty, since they wanted their children to share in the benefits of the Christian religion. Those parents who have no regard for the Christian religion should realize that the state gives many privileges to its Christian citizens which it does not give to non-Christians. Hence, even if parents do not care about the spiritual values of Christianity, they should have their children baptized in order to enjoy certain civic benefits and privileges. Since this is a crass example of the secularization of infant Baptism, the pertinent section is herewith included. "Entweder sind die Eltern der zu taufenden Kinder selbst von dem Werthe und von der Vortrefflichkeit; haben bereits schon in Hinsicht des Geistes und des Herzens die herrlichsten Erfahrungen davon gemacht, sind durch sie aufgekläret am Verstande, gebessert am Herzen und beruhiget am Gemüthe geworden, was Wunder, daß sie nicht genug eilen zu können glauben, auch ihre Kinder frühzeitig durch die symbolische Handlung der Taufe zu einer Religion einzuweihen, von welcher sie hoffen, daß sie in der Folge bey ihren Kindern sich durch gleiche segensreiche Wirkungen verherrlichen werde. Oder es ist der andere Falle, daß zwar die Eltern nicht jene erste Überzeugung von jenem hohen inneren Werthe der christlichen Religion haben, sich aber dennoch selbst gestehen müssen, daß sie doch wenigstens als äußerliche Bekenner des Christenthums so manche nicht unbedeutende, sondern vielmehr höchst schätzbare äußere Vortheile christlicher Stadtsbürger genießen, auf die keiner, der Nichtchrist ist, Ansprüche zu machen hat; sollten sie nicht schon aus Sorgfalt für die äußerliche künftige Wohlfahrt ihrer Kinder dieselben bey Zeiten zu einer Religion feyerlich einweihen lassen, wodurch ihnen, abgesehen von ihren höheren innersen Segnungen alle jene äußeren Wohlthaten und Vortheile schon von Jugend auf zu Theil werden, die die christlichen Staaten zu genießen pflegen." Michahelles, *Über den christlichen Ritus der Taufe*, 23–24.

salvation, especially for children who were seen as morally innocent. Not only were they incapable of regeneration but they did not require it. Lutheran Rationalists and Supranaturalists offered a theology completely different from that of Luther, who saw that all, including children, stood in need of regeneration through Baptism.[39] One reason offered for the practice of infant Baptism by the Rationalists and Supranaturalists was the silence of the Scriptures. This argument has some validity, but it proves less convincing when it is coupled with the denial of original sin and the saving ability of Baptism and the capability of children to have the kind of faith required by the Bible. Rationalist and Supranaturalist arguments from the post-apostolic period cannot be discounted but lose their force when the evidence from the apostolic writings is found to be inconclusive. By making infant Baptism's usefulness a reason for its continuation, these theologians provided probably the best reason for its discontinuation. These reasons had been taken over from the eighteenth century.[40] They also were finding a place among Lutherans in America who had

---

[39] Luther's teaching is maintained in The Lutheran Church—Missouri Synod, whose rite for infant baptism begins by saying that children as all men are born in sin and under the wrath of God. These children would be lost unless they are delivered by our Lord Jesus Christ (*The Lutheran Agenda* [St. Louis: Concordia, 1941], 1).

[40] The concepts concerning infant Baptism found in the early nineteenth century Rationalism and Supranaturalism were already present in the previous century. The most prominent school of theological Rationalism in Germany in the last half of the eighteenth century was the *Neologen*. Johannes Christoph Döderlein (1745–1792), a member of the theological school of Neology, published a dogmatical work which appeared in six editions between 1780 and 1797. In this work Döderlein has the same basic arguments for and against infant baptism as do Wegscheider, Reinhard, Eckermann, Eisenlohr, Michahelles, and Lehmus. Döderlein dismisses the necessity of infant Baptism and sees its purpose in attaching the child to the outward association of the Church in stimulating the memories and inciting to moral virtues. Here appears his entire discussion of the matter, "De Paedobaptismo."
"Sequitur ut de baptismo infantum, doctorum gratia, aliquid addamus, qui, tametsi ne eius *necessitas* e mandato Christi Matth. 28, 19. Ioh. 3, 5. Marc. 10, 14. nec usus sat antiquus potest demonstrari, tamen tantum abest, ut prohibeatur, ut contra multa sint, quae eum *iuste* et *utiliter* conferri parvulis persuadent: *iuste* quidem, cum infantes haud incapaces sint nec societatis populi Dei (*fidei* externae, nam *internam* non capiunt) in quam hoc ritu, ut olim Iudaei infantes circumcisione, adoptantum nec iuris beneficiorum Christi, cuius non ultima pars etiam conferri in infantes potest: *utiliter* autem, sive propter pueros, quibus memoria beneficii per omnem vitam solatia virtutisque incitamenta adferet, sive propter parentes, quos valde interest, consecrare suos Christo atque ad officia sua obeunda religione arctio contingi." *Institutio Theologi Christiani* (Editio Quinta; Norimberg und Altorf: n.p., 1791), 719–20.

fallen under Rationalist influences.[41] The time would come when infant Baptism would no longer be seen as useful and so would be discontinued. For the most part, that time has come in Europe.

[41] The Rationalistic attitude in North American Lutheranism towards infant Baptism found its ablest proponent in Frederick Quitman (1760–1832), president of the Evangelical Lutheran Synod of New York and a student of Johannes Semler (1725–1791), the father of the historical critical method and a leading German Lutheran theologian in the Enlightenment. Quitman puts forth his views on baptism in his *Evangelical Catechism,* written for use in the New York Synod. Two Rationalistic traits are evident in his approach to infant Baptism. (1) Stress is on the moral and ethical advantages of the rite. (2) The evidence for infant Baptism is purely historical. Nothing is mentioned of theological reasons, i.e., original sin and the need for regeneration. His views were in line with the German Rationalists. Here follow the pertinent sections of his *Evangelical Catechism.*

"1 Q. What is a Sacrament? A. A Sacrament is a sacred rite, instituted by Christ Himself, with a view to improve His followers in faith and holiness, and to confirm the promises of the Gospel to those that make proper use of it.

"10 Q. What does sacred history declare concerning this subject? A. Sacred history makes frequent mention of whole families having been baptized by the apostles, and the history of the primitive Christian church exhibits some unquestionable traces that infant baptism prevailed in the church as early as the close of the second century.

"11 Q. What induces you to believe that the very apostles baptized infants? A. Because as converted Jews, they had the Mosaic institution concerning the circumcision of young children before them, and also the example of their Rabbis, who, according to their own accounts, baptized not only adult proselytes from paganism but also children.

"12 Q. Has infant baptism any moral tendency? A. Yes; parents that offer their children for baptism manifest a religious sense highly beneficial to their family and offspring, while children that are early made sensible of their allegiance to Christ will be induced to become acquainted with their Lord and benefactor." *Evangelical Catechism* (Hudson: William E. Norman, 1814), 109–11.

Even though Quitman says that infant Baptism is scriptural, he does so on historical grounds and not theological ones. That infant Baptism is scriptural is shown only to be highly probable because of the apostolic association with the Rabbinic traditions and because of evidence found in the late second century.

CHAPTER II

FRIEDRICH DANIEL ERNST SCHLEIERMACHER

INTRODUCTION

The early nineteenth century marked the end of the Enlightenment for German Protestant theology. With it, Rationalism significantly waned as a specific theological force, though some of its tenets remain in place up to the present. Opposing theological Rationalism was Friedrich Daniel Ernst Schleiermacher (1768–1834), who was contemporary with the last of the Rationalist theologians, with whom he studied. Brought up in the home of a Reformed military chaplain with contacts with Moravian communities, he came under these influences. Like the Pietists, Moravians were Lutheran in theology but stressed living the Christian life over doctrine. Meeting Rationalism in his university studies, Schleiermacher came to the edge of unbelief. After serving as a pastor and a university professor in Halle, he helped found the University of Berlin, where he taught for the last years of his life (1810–1834).

Where the Rationalists had made reason the criterion of theology, Schleiermacher made the Christian feeling, *das christliche Gefühl*, or the divine consciousness, *das Gottesbewußtsein,* the center of his. Attention to the inner self can be traced through his Moravian upbringing to Pietism. By the turn of the nineteenth century, Rationalism's deistic, non-participatory view of God had effectively removed religion from German cultural life and emptied the churches. Schleiermacher's theological system provided a foundation on which religion, which for him was Christianity in the Reformed but also Lutheran traditions, could be re-established in a society that might be described not as irreligious but unreligious. Atheism had not taken hold, but Deism had pushed God to the edge of the universe so that He was no longer a player on the human scene.

In his *On Religion: Speeches to Its Cultured Despisers* (1799), Schleiermacher proposed that religion defined what it meant to be human. Organized churches were seen as religious associations. His crowning work was *The Christian Faith* (*Der Christliche Glaube*), by which phrase he meant that Christian faith was derived from the beliefs of the community of Christians. All people have a "feeling of absolute dependency," that is, they are conscious that the self and the world are mutually related and absolutely dependent on each other. This awareness includes being aware of being immediately related to God. Self-awareness or consciousness was the original source of all religions. Christianity's distinctiveness from other religions lay in God's decisive revelation in Christ, around whom the community known as the Church gathered.[1] For Schleiermacher, the source of belief was the totality of the first Christian community's experiences as recorded in the Scriptures, but it was not the only one. The traditional doctrine of the Trinity was revised. The Holy Spirit no longer had a personal existence with the Father and the Son within God, but He was seen as the spirit of the Church. Schleiermacher no longer held to the classical doctrine that Christ had two natures, divine and human. The Spirit's activities were those of the Church, by which He was limited. Through what the Church did, the Spirit brought members into fellowship with Christ.[2]

Sections in Schleiermacher's *The Christian Faith* were prefaced with sentences from the classical Lutheran, Reformed, and Anglican confessions, in order to create a unified theology for the European churches with roots in the Reformation. He used classical dogmatic terms but infused them with new meanings. Such familiar terms as Redeemer, Holy Spirit, and God were understood differently from their traditional usage in the Reformation and post-Reformation eras. Like the Rationalists, Schleiermacher saw the source of theology in each person. Jesus surpassed others in possessing God-consciousness; by sharing it with others, he established the Christian community

[1] John W. Riggs, *Baptism in the Reformed Tradition* (Louisville: Westminster John Knox Press, 2002), 90–93.

[2] Friedrich Schleiermacher, *Der Christliche Glaube nach den Grundsätzen der evangelischen Kirche*, 2 vols. (Dritte unveränderte Ausgabe; Berlin: Druck und Verlag von Georg Reimer, 1836), 2:280–82.

known as the Church. Although Schleiermacher did not come to terms with the question of whether other religions could also be valid expressions of the feeling of absolute dependence, it is hard to see why his program was not universalistic. The Rationalists he replaced as the dominant force in theology were explicitly universalists. Since theology was done only within the Christian community, to which he belonged, Schleiermacher did not have to address this question. Whether he believed in a personal God is beyond the scope of this paper, but it remains an intriguing question.

Schleiermacher's concept of absolute dependence did not allow for infant Baptism, but his understanding of the Church as those who were joined together by the feeling of absolute dependence provided a reason for its continuance. Baptism provided infants with Church membership through which, upon reaching maturity, they could come to faith through the spoken Word. Schleiermacher agreed with the Rationalists that regeneration was accomplished not through a rite like Baptism but through the oral Word and that the Christian community provided the environment for creating faith though, for Schleiermacher, faith is the feeling of absolute dependence, not an exercise of reason, as the Rationalists held. Rather than forging a new path in his discussion of infant Baptism, he took over many of their arguments, arranging them in new ways. He agreed with them that the New Testament knew only adult Baptism and that infants lacked faith because they were incapable of the sense of absolute dependence on God. Only in maturity is faith possible. Rationalists and Schleiermacher had taken different roads to the same conclusion.

In attributing the creation of faith to the spoken Word, Schleiermacher aligned himself with Luther and not Calvin, who held that faith resulted from the inner working of the Spirit in a parallel operation with the preached Word. However, in denying that Baptism creates faith, Schleiermacher remained in the Reformed tradition. Done without faith, infant Baptism is an incomplete Baptism that can be rectified by confirmation, a view offered by some Rationalists. Without confirmation as a supplementary rite, infant Baptism is contrary to Christ's ordinances. Considering that Schleiermacher had studied with Rationalist theologians, it is not surprising that he absorbed some of their views into his own. Like them, he came under the spell of the philosophical Idealism that flourished in the German

Enlightenment.[3] Rather than finding reasons for infant Baptism in the Scriptures or the early post-apostolic Church, Schleiermacher looked for a place for the rite under ecclesiology, as had the Rationalists. For the latter, the Church was a place for moral improvement; for Schleiermacher, it was a place to nurture the feeling of absolute dependence on God.[4] In both cases, the Church was sociologically defined.

In some of his arguments for continuing infant Baptism, Schleiermacher parts ways with the Rationalists and Supranaturalists, who, in their approaches, constituted one group. He makes no use of their argument that since Christ did not prohibit it, it can be practiced. Unlike the Rationalists, he does not bring into his discussion the Ancient Church practice of baptizing infants. Schleiermacher knows that up to the Reformation infant Baptism was the universal Church practice, but this does not provide him with a reason for continuing it. Schleiermacher's understanding that faith originates within the Christian community obligates him to give historical belief a prime place in his system, as is evident in his referencing the historic Reformation-era confessions, but this particular history he ignores. This seems at odds with a theology that is historically oriented. Here Schleiermacher's concept of the feeling of absolute dependence on God determines which segments of the Church's history he will accept; in this sense he operates with a predetermined dogmatic concept as the standard of his theology.

Working with the Rationalist discovery that the New Testament knew of only adult Baptism and that it requires faith, Schleiermacher concludes that infant Baptism is a poorly administered Baptism that would better be omitted from Church life. He is not absolute in this, since the head of each household has the Christian freedom to have his children baptized. Baptisms administered in infancy are as valid as those administered to adults, but without faith, infant Baptisms are of a lower caliber. A little more than a century later, Karl Barth, who presented himself as Schleiermacher's opponent, offered a strikingly similar position. Like Schleiermacher, Barth suggested that those

---

[3] Horst Stephan, *Geschichte der Deutschen Evangelischen Theologie seit dem Deutschen Idealismus*, ed. Martin Schmidt (Zweite neubearbeitete Auflage; Berlin: Alfred Töpelmann, 1960), 180

[4] Heinz-Horst Schrey, "Walther, Christian: Typen des Reich Gottes Verständnisses. Studien zur Eschatologie und Ethik im 19. Jahrhundert," *Theologische Literaturzeitung*, 87/10 (October 1962): 774.

practicing believers' and infant Baptisms recognize the validity of the other's Baptism.

Adult Baptisms administered with the Trinitarian formula in Baptist churches have been recognized by churches baptizing infants and adults. Groups practicing believers' Baptism have not reciprocated, though there are exceptions.[5] Like the Socinians a century before him and Barth a century later, Schleiermacher's opposition to infant Baptism does not require another Baptism for those baptized as infants. Unlike Barth, however, he redefined the Trinitarian definition of God so that it was closer to Socinian modalism. The divine persons are hardly more than three manifestations of God.[6] Schleiermacher, like the Rationalists before him and Barth after him, could not act on his convictions that infants were not fit candidates for Baptism, which, as they all agreed, lacked power to regenerate.[7]

BAPTISM

Christ established Baptism as an act of reception into the Church, but it functions at the same time as an act of the individual will. In the Church's fellowship, God's promise becomes effective. Since Baptism serves as the rite of introduction, it can be considered a means, though Schleiermacher does not use the traditional phrase "means of grace." Since Christ commanded Baptism and He wills that people be brought into the Church by it, Christ performs it. During His lifetime, Christ brought people into His fellowship not through Baptism but through the word of forgiveness He spoke and by His call to enter to discipleship. Christ taking the person into fellowship with Him was itself the act of reception, so Baptism as an additional act of reception would have been superfluous. Now that Christ is not on earth, Baptism replaces His personal choosing of the individual.

---

[5] For example, the renowned Baptist biblical scholar George Beaseley-Murray: "When an applicant was baptized as a child and was later received in due form into membership of a church by confession of faith, no matter by what ritual, he should be received into a Baptist congregation as if he came from another Baptist congregation, that is, by transfer." Quoted from Edmund Schlinck, *The Doctrine of Baptism*, trans. Herbert J. A. Bouman (St. Louis: Concordia, 1972), 149.

[6] Schleiermacher, *Der Christliche Glaube,* 2:540–43.

[7] Schleiermacher has been the object of much scholarly study, but John W. Riggs notes that as far as he has been able to determine, a monograph on his theology of Baptism or the sacraments in general is lacking. John W. Riggs, *Baptism in the Reformed Tradition* (Louisville: Westminster John Knox Press, 2002), 158–59, n. 82.

What Christ once did, Baptism now does.[8] This belief that ministers act in the stead of Christ reflects the Lutheran view of the ministry.[9]

Baptism is a Trinitarian act since the Word belonging to Baptism is a Word about the Father, Son, and Holy Spirit. On it, the discipleship of Christ rests. This Word about the Father, Son, and Holy Spirit has a double use, expressing what the Church intends to do in Baptism and what the candidate for Baptism desires; that is, his assent to the Church's intention and his making the Word his own. This Word is that of both the Church and the baptized—a view proposed by Zwingli that Baptism was a human response to a divine covenant.[10] As much as Calvin stressed Baptism as a divine covenant, the concept of covenant required a receiving agent, so Schleiermacher's position had precedent in the two leading Reformed fathers.

Essential to Baptism is the fact that this Word must be known and confessed by the one who is to be baptized. This is apparent in the command to make disciples, which can only happen through the power of the Word, so the Word comes before Baptism is administered. According to apostolic practice, Baptism took place only after the Word was acknowledged and confessed; without this confession, Baptism would have been unthinkable. Since the baptized's confession of the Word belonging to Baptism necessarily belongs to the act, it follows that faith should be required of the one who is to receive Baptism. Schleiermacher cites Matthew 28:19–20 and Mark 16:16 to show that faith is required of the candidates for Baptism. With faith, Baptism becomes what it intends to be, and that necessary faith is worked by preaching, as taught both by Peter in his sermon on Pentecost and by Paul in Romans 10:17. Baptism, thus, does not disrupt the function of the preaching of the Word but serves to confirm it.[11]

A Baptism not received in faith is poorly administered and received, since it is not done according to what Christ requires. The Church can never be indifferent to baptizing unbelievers along with believers. Here Schleiermacher hedges his bets: he sees no need to repeat a Baptism not offered in faith, though until the person comes to

---

[8] Schleiermacher, *Der Christliche Glaube,* 2:362–64.

[9] Apology of the Augsburg Confession VII, 28, 47. Latin: "quia ministri funguntur vice Christi, non repraesentant suam personam." German: "denn sie reichens an Christus statt und nicht für ihre Person."

[10] Riggs, *Baptism in the Reformed Tradition*, 35.

[11] Schleiermacher, *Der Christliche Glaube*, 2:375–81.

faith by preaching such a Baptism has many imperfections.[12] Baptizing those without faith militates against the entire apostolic practice as well as the total experience of the Church. The Church is not to increase its membership by baptizing *en masse*. Where the Church baptizes an unbeliever, preaching of the Word, and not Baptism, produces the faith that completes Baptism. Schleiermacher claims that the truth of this statement is apparent even to the simple Christian.[13] One must ask, though, whether it is so obvious to the simple Christian that the Word and not Baptism creates faith, given that for over a thousand years before Schleiermacher, many simple Christians believed just the opposite.

For Schleiermacher, infant Baptism falls into this category of an erroneously applied Baptism, because the necessary conditions of faith and confession outlined in the New Testament are not present. After the child reaches the age where he can intellectually appropriate the preached Word, he can come to faith, but there is no guarantee. Baptism, properly administered in the case of adults and improperly with infants, does not cause faith. Only the Word can accomplish this. Schleiermacher maintains the Lutheran and Reformed belief that Baptism's benefits can only be received in faith but remains in the Reformed tradition in rejecting the Lutheran belief that Baptism itself works the faith that receives Baptism's benefits. Calvin in the 1539 edition of the *Institutes of the Christian Religion* (4:15.1) wrote this:

> *Baptism is the sign of initiation by which we are received into the society of the church, that we might be engrafted in Christ and reckoned among the children of God.* Again baptism was given us by God for this purpose (which I have taught to be common to all sacraments), first to serve our faith before him; and then to serve our confession before others.[14]

Schleiermacher's definition of Baptism as an entrance rite to the Christian community requiring the commitment of the one being baptized belonged to Zwingli's definition and that of the later Calvin, though the founding Reformed fathers did not see eye to eye on Baptism.[15] For Schleiermacher salvation was given in Baptism as an entrance rite into the community. Here salvation occurred. Baptism

---

[12] Schleiermacher, *Der Christliche Glaube*, 2:378.

[13] Schleiermacher, *Der Christliche Glaube*, 2:378.

[14] Quote from and italics by Riggs, *Baptism in the Reformed Tradition*, 48.

[15] Riggs, *Baptism in the Reformed Tradition*, 25.

did not give the baptized a particular benefit; membership in the community did.

Schleiermacher recognized the problem that, since faith is required before Baptism, the candidate for Baptism possesses salvation before joining the community. To this he replied that a certain enjoyment of salvation is only found within the congregation of believers. As faith develops in those outside the community, so a desire to enter into the fellowship of believers also develops. Since Baptism takes the believer into the fellowship of believers, it works salvation and is a sealing with divine grace, a classical Reformed view. Baptism is a justifying act of God, because by it He admits the believer into the common life of the congregation fellowship where he can take possession of the forgiveness of sins and of the right of being adopted by God.[16]

If the Baptism of infants is problematic for Schleiermacher because they lack the faith to receive its benefits, one has to ask why believing adults should be baptized, if they already possess some of the benefits of salvation. Believers possess salvation before Baptism, and the fate of unbelieving children is not changed by Baptism, a view that fits within Reformed thought. Schleiermacher does not make a sharp distinction between justification and sanctification. Both are seen as progressive with the unbeliever progressing to faith and the believer progressing to greater faith. This progression is assisted by participation in the community in which faith is created and confirmed, but it can occur before. For the believer, Christ's perfection and salvation begins with Baptism, but not until he comes to faith. By remaining outside the Christian community, the unbeliever deprives himself of an opportunity to attain salvation. A believer who refuses Baptism deprives himself of those benefits of salvation present in the community. When the Church is responsible for keeping a believer out of the community by refusing him Baptism, he is deprived of fewer benefits than is the one who willfully refuses Baptism.

Schleiermacher understands that his views on Baptism fail to do justice to those Protestant confessions, such as the Lutheran Confessions, that claim Baptism creates faith and gives salvation, but for him such a Baptism has a magical force.[17] Clearly he has in mind the Lutheran belief that Baptism regenerates by creating and

[16] Schleiermacher, *Der Christliche Glaube*, 2:378–79.
[17] Schleiermacher, *Der Christliche Glaube*, 2:379–80.

confirming faith and forgiving sins—all of which for him take place within the fellowship of believers. Baptism does belong to the process of regeneration as the first of a series of acts leading to the salvation of an unregenerate person. For believers, Baptism is necessary in bringing them to full participation in Christ's salvation.

To summarize, Baptism is both a voluntary act of the individual, whereby he enters the community of believers, and an act of the congregation, which receives the baptized into its fellowship.[18] The Word in Baptism, about the Father, Son, and Holy Spirit, has a double purpose in expressing the congregation's intentions to receive the baptized person and his assent to join it. This assent involves individual confession and faith; where these are absent, Baptism is poorly administered and remains incomplete until faith is worked by preaching. Under no circumstances can Baptism be said to work faith. Schleiermacher belongs to the Reformed tradition, but he accommodates the Lutheran view in speaking of Baptism working salvation, only in the sense that it is the first of the Church's many acts through which faith will arise. Where faith is present before Baptism, the believer who is then baptized experiences a greater enjoyment of salvation in the fellowship of the congregation. In these definitions, Schleiermacher has understood salvation in two different ways. For the unbeliever, Baptism creates salvation by his being brought into the community of believers wherein faith can be created. For the believer, Baptism creates salvation in bringing him to the fuller enjoyment of salvation found only in the Christian congregation. Perhaps it would be better to see salvation as a process that begins when unbelief is still in place and completed when the full benefits of membership in the Christian community are enjoyed. Infant Baptism fits the first understanding. As an unbeliever, the child in Baptism undergoes the first step towards a fuller faith. Within these dimensions, Schleiermacher, without fully endorsing infant Baptism, provided for himself reasons for recognizing its legitimacy.

---

[18] The Reformed belief that Baptism is both a confession of the baptized and a sign of God's promises found its way into the *Articles of Religion of the Church of England*, commonly known as The Thirty-Nine Articles. So Riggs: "Article 27 discusses baptism and gives a twofold Calvin-like definition that baptism is both a sign of human profession and sign to which God has appended divine promises of forgiveness of sin and adoption as children." *Baptism in the Reformed Tradition*, 83. Schleiermacher included the Thirty-Nine Articles in his system of Protestant theology.

INFANT BAPTISM

For Schleiermacher, infant Baptism is and remains incomplete until completed by an act of confession on the basis of instruction.[19] He cannot support infant Baptism from the New Testament, since he has adopted the Rationalist conclusion that it contains no traces of it. All supposed references to infant Baptism in the New Testament have been superimposed upon the texts. Baptizing infants is not in harmony with the apostolic practice, which required that the candidate for Baptism at least have a minimal faith and be penitent. Infant Baptism is a deviation from the original practice. Historical evidence is lacking about the circumstances in which infant Baptism arose, but Schleiermacher speculates that infant Baptism arose from the common Christian feeling, *das christliche Gefühl*. First, Christians desired to count their children among those who died in the Lord. They pondered the fact that their children might die before they were old enough to receive the Christian instruction required before being baptized. Second, as some parents may be negligent in providing Christian instruction for their children, infant Baptism was a way to obligate the members of the Christian congregation to give instruction to children born of Christian parents who did not. Finally, the act of Baptism separated the children of Christians from those of Jews and heathens. After infant Baptism had become an established church custom, it expressed the confidence of Christian parents that their children did not lack the working of the Holy Spirit.[20]

Schleiermacher is critical of certain approaches to baptizing infants. He faults those Protestant confessions that do not discuss the historical origins of infant Baptism and justify it with inadequate theological reasons, which he finds contradictory. For example, an unacceptable reason for infant Baptism is that children as God's possession should be baptized. Should they be God's possessions, he argues, they already have the grace Baptism offers and hence would not be in need of it. On the other hand, if they did need Baptism, they could hardly be God's possessions. It seems as if Schleiermacher is addressing the Reformed belief that as members of the covenant

---

[19] Schleiermacher, *Der Christliche Glaube*, 2:382. "Die Kindertaufe ist nur eine vollständige Taufe, wenn man das nach vollendetem Unterricht hinzukommende Glaubensbekenntniß als den letzten dazu noch gehörigen Act ansieht."

[20] Schleiermacher, *Der Christliche Glaube*, 2:383–84.

through their birth of Christian parents, children are to be baptized.[21] Schleiermacher's argument uncovers a problem in the Reformed position that leaves children unbaptized until the eighth day and does not allow for emergency Baptisms by lay people before then. Also of no value for Schleiermacher is the argument that God wanted to include the posterity of Christians in the Church and that Christ poured out His blood for them. This argument goes too far. Since Christ poured out His blood for all men, it would require us to baptize everyone we could get our hands on.[22] Schleiermacher might have in view the Geneva Confession (1536).[23] Also unacceptable is the Lutheran reason for infant Baptism, though it is not labeled as such: that it effects a change in the person of the child. The child is the same after his Baptism as he was before. Just as the child was not unholy before his Baptism, he was not holy afterwards. Before Baptism, the child was not consciously repentant and so after his Baptism he has no awareness of his adoption by God. There is no evidence that Baptism works faith in children.[24] Schleiermacher's position is well within the bounds of classical Reformed theology.[25]

Having dismissed unacceptable reasons for infant Baptism, Schleiermacher treats it as an insufficient and incomplete Baptism, because Baptism's benefits must be received in penitence and faith—which children lack. Simply put, they are not fit recipients for Baptism. Their Baptism is incomplete and this deficit needs to be rectified. Even if Baptism does not change the person of the child,[26] it benefits the child in bringing him into the outer circle of the Church, where, in contact with the Word, he may come to faith. So he is

---

[21] Jan Rohls, *Reformed Confessions: Theology from Zurich to Barmen*, trans. John F. Hoffmeyer, introduction by Jack L. Stotts, Columbia Series in Theology (Louisville: Westminister John Knox Press, 1997), 214–15.

[22] Schleiermacher, *Der Christliche Glaube*, 2:384.

[23] Rohls, *Baptism in the Reformed Tradition*, 77. "Here we see (1) that baptism testifies to God's grace toward humankind (adoption); (2) that baptism portrays the cleansing from sin and human regeneration that come through the blood of Jesus and the power of the Spirit; and that the covenant appears as the reason for baptism."

[24] Schleiermacher, *Der Christliche Glaube*, 2:385.

[25] Calvin wanted to maintain Baptism's sacred character but "wanted to avoid the error that would enclose the 'cause of justification and power of the Holy Spirit' within the elements." Riggs, *Baptism in the Reformed Tradition*, 57.

[26] Though Calvin saw God's action in Baptism, he wanted to avoid "the error of sacramental instrumentalism" by "reemphasiz[ing] that human faith was necessary in order to accept the promise of which the sacrament was the sure sign." Riggs, *Baptism in the Reformed Tradition*, 58.

baptized in regard to his future faith and confession. As with Calvin, a child's future faith is a reason for his Baptism.[27] Schleiermacher believes that he has avoided the pitfalls of the two reasons for infant Baptism he previously criticized, namely that children already are in the Church and that Baptism commends them to the grace of God. He follows Calvin in holding that through children's birth to Christian parents, they already have a natural connection with the Christian order in which God has placed them. So they are already commended to the grace of God. This natural order allows them to be brought into the Church through Baptism. Their Baptism is consummated in the child's making his own confession. The baptized child must make his own confession of faith and adhere to it.[28] As a poorly administered Baptism, infant Baptism is incomplete but nevertheless valid. It joins children to the kingdom of God, but it does not give them the possession and enjoyment of salvation. Here Schleiermacher can only understand the kingdom of God in sociological terms as a society and not as the fellowship of believers. By being made members of the outward fellowship of the Church, children become objects only of

---

[27] Calvin: "In short, this objection ['since children were capable of neither repentance nor faith']—they are baptized into future repentance and faith (qu'ls sont baptisez en foy et penitence pour l'advenir)—which although they are not yet formed in them, the seed of both lies concealed in them through the secret operation of the Spirit." As quoted by Riggs, *Baptism in the Reformed Tradition*, 67, 153, n. 84. Rohls points out that Calvin's metaphor of a seed could be understood that baptism acted as a sacrament in bestowing grace, a position which he, later, no longer held (68–69).

[28] Schleiermacher, *Der Christliche Glaube*, 2:385–86. Schleiermacher is speaking of the connection children have with the church. One of the more interesting attempts to explain this relationship was offered by Isaak August Dorner (1809–1888), who was greatly influenced by Schleiermacher. Dorner tried to explain how unbelieving children can belong to a church consisting of believers. Dorner argues that it is not given to the church to distinguish the believers from the unbelievers. The parable of the tares growing among the wheat is cited to support that unbelieving children should be retained in church membership. Here follows the pertinent section. "Wird für die Spättaufe der dogmatische Begriff der Kirche als der *Societas fidei et spiritus sancti* geltend gemacht und daraus gefolgert, die Kirche dürfe nur aus Wiedergeborenen bestehen, zu denen Unmündige nicht gehören, so ist dagegen zu erinnern, daß der Kirche die untrügliche Sicherheit versagt ist, zu wissen, wer wahrhaft gläubig und wiedergeboren ist. Daher kann auch nicht ihre Aufgabe sein, die Mitgliedschaft in der Kirche so zu bemessen, daß jeder von ihr ausgeschlossen sei, der noch nicht wiedergeboren ist. Vielmehr ist ihr ja sogar gesagt: 'Lasset beides mit einander wachsen bis zur Ernte.'" *System der Christlichen Glaubenslehre*, 2 vols. (Berlin: Verlag von Wilhelm Hertz, 1886), 1/1, 840–41. It seems as if this parable is concerned about retaining recognized unbelievers in church membership and not admitting those without faith, including, in Schleiermacher's case, children.

the preparatory work of the Holy Spirit. Their Baptism does not measure up to the Baptism of Christ's institution, which included confession. Still, the incompleteness of infant Baptism does not make it invalid, as if it were a perverted Baptism. When Lutherans speak of the invisible and visible Church, they refer respectively to believers and the outward assembly in which unbelievers are mixed with believers. Schleiermacher follows the Reformed belief that includes believers' children who do not believe but who share in the covenant of their parents.[29]

Zwingli provided the Anabaptists with their reasons for not baptizing infants but then had to reverse himself. Schleiermacher's arguments against infant Baptism led him to the Anabaptist position, and so it seems as if he had to ask himself why he did not wholeheartedly adopt it. The Anabaptists were right in baptizing only those who made a confession of faith but were wrong in requiring that Baptism be reapplied to those who may already have received it in infancy. Should infant Baptism be invalid on account of its incompleteness, then every Baptism would be invalid for being incomplete. Christians always lack complete holiness. In the midst of continued progress towards Christian holiness, they possess no certain sign that real regeneration has taken place. Justification is merged into sanctification, which is seen as a process. Schleiermacher condemns the Ancient Church practice in baptizing persons only shortly before they died, because they were still lacking in Christian holiness. Lack of holiness in an individual does not invalidate Baptism. This is also true in the case of infant Baptism, which, though it is administered without faith, is still valid. Its efficacy, however, remains suspended until the child acquires his own faith.[30] Schleiermacher sees life between unbelief and belief as a continuum, and so he finds no necessity to pinpoint the origin of faith or the application of grace in Baptism, which he denies.

To correct the incompleteness of infant Baptism, confirmation, which presumes instruction, must follow. Confirmation, in which the

[29] Jan Rohls, *Reformed Confessions*, 170.

[30] Schleiermacher, *Der Christliche Glaube*, 2:386. See Riggs, *Baptism in the Reformed Tradition*, 93. If confirmation is an application of the Word for Schleiermacher, it is difficult to explain that its character is compromised by seeing it as a separate rite. Luther did away with confirmation but allowed its practice by other reformers. Not surprisingly Lutherans had no common understanding of the rite. See David P. Scaer, "Confirmation as Sacramental Rite," *Logia* 15:1 (Epiphany 2006): 49–58.

child makes his own confession, brings the Baptism administered in infancy into line with Christ's original ordinance. To make sure that the child will be confirmed and thus by instruction bring his Baptism into conformity with Christ's intentions for this rite, the Church obligates itself to provide Christian instruction for them by baptizing infants. Schleiermacher does not allow that confirmation should be detached from infant Baptism as a separate sacrament, which is the Catholic view. When this is done, a Baptism applied in infancy remains incomplete and ineffective.[31]

Schleiermacher reconstructs the historical situation in which he believes that infant Baptism arose. Parents began having their infants baptized when they started to have their children educated in the Church, something the Church had not previously experienced. Baptism was chosen as the symbolical act to express that children belonged as much to the congregation as they did to their parents. Schleiermacher saw no reason that Baptism had to serve this purpose any more and proposed that infant Baptism cease with the proviso that the Baptisms of those baptized as infants would not be regarded as invalid. Its omission would not harm children. Only those who hold that Baptism possesses magical powers—by which he means Lutherans with their sacramental views—believe that Baptism gives children an advantage in the life of the world to come. A magical view of Baptism must be rejected because it takes the focus off Baptism's benefits in this life. Baptism does not give a child who dies before renewing his baptismal covenant any advantage over an unbaptized child. The decision of whether to baptize children may be left up to the individual household, as long as those who baptize children do not hold to the magical view that Baptism gives an advantage to children in the afterlife. Preferable for Schleiermacher is delaying Baptism until children can make their own confession.

Schleiermacher's position had ecumenical potential. Making adult Baptism the norm would have the added advantage of expressing the willingness to remove the Reformation-era confessional verdict of condemnation against the Anabaptists. This in turn would allow Lutherans and Reformed to enter into Church fellowship with them. For their part, the Anabaptists would recognize infant Baptism as a valid Baptism with the proviso that it was supplemented by a confession that might be given in confirmation.[32]

---

[31] Schleiermacher, *Der Christliche Glaube*, 2:387.

[32] Schleiermacher, *Der Christliche Glaube*, 2:387–88.

CONCLUSION

For Schleiermacher, infant Baptism deviates from biblical practice; Baptism is only improperly administered to infants who lack faith and repentance. Schleiermacher finds a reason for the practice in the corporate consciousness of Christians who wanted to include their children among the saved should they die, a reason he finds unacceptable. Another reason was that it obligated the congregation to educate children whose parents were not so inclined. Still another reason was distinguishing children of believers from those of unbelievers. Some had argued that children should be baptized because they belong to God. These reasons are also unacceptable to him.

It would be better that infant Baptism fall into disuse, but those who continue the practice should see to it that they connect children with the Word. Infant Baptism can also signify that through their birth within Christendom they are commended to the grace of God, a view remarkably similar to Calvin's. All said and done, Baptism is erroneously applied to children, but this is said with the understanding that this decision to baptize children belongs to the freedom of each household. Failure to baptize them would not affect their condition in the afterlife.

Ceasing infant Baptism would allow fellowship with the Anabaptists, who have a superior practice in baptizing adults and not infants. On their part, they would be required to recognize the Baptisms of those who received Baptism in infancy. Schleiermacher's view of a unified Protestant Church—including Lutherans, Reformed, and Anglicans—would then be expanded to include Anabaptists in the nineteenth century, not those of the Reformation era but Baptists. Though he worked to incorporate all these views into his theology, he belonged more to the Reformed tradition than to the Lutheran whose sacramental views he labeled as magical. Those would also include Catholic understandings, but his concept of the Christian community did not include them. He attempted to accommodate the Lutheran view of the means of grace in calling Baptism a ladder (*Leiter*), by which he means that by Baptism one can join the Christian fellowship within which salvation comes to its fullest expression on earth.[33] This

---

[33] Cf. F. Kattenbusch, "Taufe. II. Kirchenlehre," *Realencyklopädie für protestantische Theologie und Kirche*, ed. Albert Hauck (Dritte verbesserte und vermehrte Auflage; Leipzig: J. C. Hinrichs'sche Buchhandlung, 1907), 19: 422.

is hardly the Lutheran understanding. As with the Rationalist theologians of the Enlightenment, he saw the kingdom of God as a purely earthly phenomenon lacking heavenly dimensions. Christ and the Holy Spirit work through the Church, or Christian fellowship, by which they are limited. God's Trinitarian life is confined to the life of the Christian community, by and in which Christ and the Spirit are limited.[34] Salvation is understood in terms of participation in the Christian community in which the feeling of absolute dependency on God is found. Schleiermacher's definition of faith is not Luther's trust in the saving merits of Christ but a disposition of the mind to walk in the footsteps of Christ. The church is no longer the congregation of the faithful gathered around Word and Sacraments, as both Luther and Calvin saw it, but the association of those seeking ethical improvement. Baptism confers benefits, not because of the act itself, but because it ushers one into a community where these benefits are available.

While some Lutheran theologians incorporated some of Schleiermacher's principles into their theologies, they did not follow him in calling for the cessation of infant Baptism. Rather, they found themselves in the perpetual Reformed dilemma of allowing for Baptism's benefits to be given before faith was present. Schleiermacher's arguments against baptizing infants might be used for ceasing Baptism altogether, since Baptism is neither a benefit nor a detriment to the condition of the one receiving it. Benefits available in the fellowship of the Christian community can be enjoyed before joining it, even though in smaller measure.

Schleiermacher weighs the historical evidence from the apostolic era, which provides no evidence for infant Baptism, against his own theological arguments in favor of it and concludes the reasons for ending the practice are not convincing. Baptism does not play a prominent part in his concept of the Christian community, and so ultimately its practice is a matter of indifference, especially when he considers that it has no benefits in the next world. It is an entrance rite into a community to enjoy its benefits and no more. Even unbaptized children and adults can share in them. Membership in the community assists salvation in the sense of moral improvement but does not guarantee it.

Confirmation plays a prominent role in making infant Baptism an acceptable practice. Without it, infant Baptism remains an improperly

[34] Schleiermacher, *Der Christliche Glaube*, 293–303.

administered Baptism. Ironically, the historical origins of confirmation are less discoverable than those for infant Baptism.

Justification is swallowed up or subsumed into sanctification as a process. Schleiermacher presented his theology as an antidote to Rationalist theology, but agreed with them that Baptism did not convey grace directly to the recipients and that only the Baptism of adults was the New Testament practice. For both, Baptism was an entrance rite into a Church that was defined sociologically. Original sin was denied, redefined, or ignored, so even if Baptism had supernatural powers, which both the Rationalists and Schleiermacher denied, it was of no value to the child. Schleiermacher differed with the Rationalists in not speaking about the emotional impetus coming from watching an infant being baptized. He says nothing about advantages for the observers, but agreed with them that the Baptism obligates the Church. Rationalists did not call infant Baptism an erroneously applied Baptism, as he did, but like them, he had to find reasons for its continuation.

Schleiermacher set the tone for the remainder of the nineteenth century, even for Lutheran theologians who incorporated his fundamental principles but were a bit more positive towards infant Baptism. His idea of infant Baptism as a community rite obligating the Church has found its way into contemporary Lutheran baptismal liturgies. Making certain that faith is present is fundamental to the Catholic Rites of Christian Initiation for Adults (RCIA). For theologians associated with the movement surrounding these rites and the Rite of Baptism of Children (RBC), it is a reason for excluding some infants from Baptism. In regard to influence, Schleiermacher has a prominent place with Luther in contemporary baptismal thought and practice.

CHAPTER III

ERLANGEN THEOLOGIANS (PART 1)

INTRODUCTION

In a reaction to eighteenth-century Rationalism, the nineteenth century experienced a renewed interest in the classical Lutheran theology of the Reformation and post-Reformation eras. Theologians involved in the movement were not of one mind in how far this should go. Those calling for as complete a restoration as possible were known as Repristination theologians. In Germany, their prominent leaders included Friedrich Adolf Philippi (1809–1881), a professor at the University of Rostock, and Wilhelm Löhe, a Lutheran pastor in Neuendettelsau and the sponsor of Concordia Theological Seminary in Fort Wayne, Indiana (1846).[1] In America, the German university-trained Carl Ferdinand Wilhelm Walther (1811–1887), founder of Concordia Seminary (1839), now in St. Louis, Missouri, and later president of The Lutheran Church—Missouri Synod, took the lead.[2] American-born Charles Porterfield Krauth produced a Lutheran dogmatics in English. His roots went back to the German Lutherans who had come in America's colonial period. The

---

[1] Horst Stephan, *Geschichte der Deutschen Evangelischen Theologie seit dem deutschen Idealismus*, ed. Martin Schmidt (Zweite neubearbeitete Auflage; Berlin: Alfred Töpelmann, 1960), 167–88.

[2] See Stephan, *Geschichte der Deutschen Evangelischen Theologie*, 170. "Nur die Lutheraner, die sich durch Auswanderung nach Nordamerika dem deutschen Geistesleben entzogen (Missourisynode), machten vollen Ernst mit der Lutherischen Orthodoxie. Sie gingen sogar auf Luther zurück (Neudruck von J. G. Walchs Lutherausgabe St. Louis 1880–1904), scheuten sich auch nicht wie die deutschen Repristinatoren vor seinem Prädestinatianismus. Folgerecht verwarfen sie das ganze neue deutsche Luthertum als Abfall vom rechten Glauben. Leider nahmen sie auch die theologische rabies des 17. Jahrh. auf und entfalten eine neue Streittheologie."

confessional Lutheran heritage was carried into the twentieth century by Francis Pieper (1852–1831), who was born in Germany; his dogmatics translated into English is still widely read.[3] These theologians were committed to the doctrine of Luther and of the Lutheran Confessions, which taught that infant Baptism created faith in infants who were burdened with original sin.[4] Their baptismal liturgies addressed questions about faith directly to infants who were also asked to renounce Satan before being baptized. These liturgical elements had fallen into disuse in the Rationalist era.[5]

Those who came to be known as the Erlangen School were part of the Lutheran revival, but they wanted to incorporate the insights of the Rationalists and Schleiermacher into their theology. As the name suggests, their leading proponents were professors on the theological faculty of the University of Erlangen. They had a greater following than the Repristination theologians.[6] Into a basic Lutheran theology they combined elements taken from Roman Catholicism, Romanticism, and other philosophies.[7] Baptism planted the "seed of faith" into the body, and so this Sacrament was regarded as an act on the body or its nature and not the soul as the rational part of human existence. The child was given the Holy Spirit, as the cause of faith, and faith's effects, that is, forgiveness, salvation, and eternal life, but not faith itself. Baptism affected their nature but without faith. Like the Rationalists and Schleiermacher, these theologians insisted that

---

[3] Pieper's discussion of infant Baptism is surprisingly brief. Franz Pieper, *Christliche Dogmatik*, 3 vols. (St. Louis: Concordia, 1920), 3:325–27 and *Christian Dogmatics*, 3 vols. (St. Louis Missouri Publishing House, 1950–53); 3:277–78. His section on infant faith is included in his general discussion of faith (2:448–49) and not on Baptism.

[4] L[ewis] W. S[pitz], "Lutheran Theology after 1580," *Lutheran Cyclopedia*, ed. Erwin L. Lueker (St. Louis: Concordia, 1954), 639–40. For a study of Luther's theology of Baptism, see Jonathan D. Trigg, *Baptism in the Theology of Martin Luther* (Leiden: E. J. Brill, 1994). Also see Karl Brinkel, *Luthers Lehre von der fides infantium bei der Kindertaufe* (Berlin: Evangelische Verlagsanstalt, 1958). The Repristination view held at the turn of the twenty-first century is put forth by David P. Scaer, *Baptism*, Confessional Lutheran Dogmatics (St. Louis: The Luther Academy, 1999).

[5] Friedr[ich] Ad[olf] Philippi, *Die kirchliche Glaubenslehre*, 5 vols. (Gütersloh: C. Bertelsmann, 1864–1875), 5/2: 90–91.

[6] H. Graß, "Erlanger Schule," *Die Religion in Geschichte und Gegenwart*, ed. Kurt Galling (Dritte, völlig neu bearbeitete Auflage; Tübingen: J. C. B. Mohr, 1958), 2:566–68. Hereafter this edition is cited as *RGG*.

[7] Stephan, *Geschichte der Deutschen Evangelischen Theologie*, 179.

faith could be produced only by the audible Word in rationally conscious persons.

Prominent in their understanding of Baptism was the word order of Matthew 28:19, in which Baptism preceded teaching. Both were necessary to effect a complete salvation. Baptism brought the gifts of salvation and teaching in the Word worked faith. The working of one could not be ascribed to the other. Therefore, salvation in the fullest sense could only be ascribed to a person who had been both baptized and taught the Word by which he could come to faith. Only an incomplete salvation was possessed by baptized children who had not been taught the Word and by adults who had faith through the Word but were unbaptized. Both Baptism and faith worked through the Word were considered necessary.

Included in the Erlangen School were Johannes Höfling (1802–1853), Hans Lassen Martensen (1808–1884) of Denmark, Gottfried Thomasius (1802–1872), Carl von Zezschwitz (1825–1886), Ernst Hory (1870–1914), Rudolph Rocholl (1827–1905), and Franz Delitzsch (1813–1890). Though their doctrine of Baptism was distinguished by a direct or immediate effect on the physical side of a person—his nature—they attempted a synthesis between older Lutheran theology and Enlightenment principles.[8] On account of this, they were opposed by the Repristination theologians. At the base of the Erlangen theology was a particular anthropology that held that the real essence of a person was his physical, unconscious nature, out of which, in maturity, his consciousness with reason developed. Reason or consciousness was the seat of the thinking process. In this anthropological definition, the unconscious, physical nature, the part possessed at conception, took priority in defining what a person was.[9]

---

[8] Spitz, "Lutheran Theology after 1580," 639–40, and Stephan, *Geschichte der Deutschen Evangelischen Theologie*, 181. Cf. also H. Graß, "Erlanger Schule," *RGG* 2:566–68.

[9] Francis Pieper offers this critique. "But there are also later Lutherans who speak in Roman fashion of a communion with Christ, even of a regeneration through Baptism, without the simultaneous presence of faith in the forgiveness of sins. They imagine the effect of Baptism to be some sort of physical action (*Naturwirkung*), or the infusion of a substance, for the experience or reception of which, they say, no faith is necessary. Proponents of this theory assert that apostates among the baptized remain members of Christ, or that unbelievers among the baptized nonetheless carry within them the Spirit of Christ, 'deposited in them as a dowry for their whole life.' " Pieper has in mind Franz Delitzsch and Gottfried Thomasius. *Christian Dogmatics*, 3:266–67.

A child possessed only the unconscious nature and was devoid of reason, which would develop as he matured.

Corresponding to this dichotomous definition of a person as unconscious nature and reason were Baptism and the spoken Word. Baptism was the means of grace directed to man's physical, unconscious nature and the spoken Word was directed to the reason. Baptism had the superior role in applying grace to one's nature. The preached Word informed the developed reason of God's gracious action in Baptism. Lack of reason or a thinking mind did not disadvantage the child, in which Baptism found an excellent receptor in the unconscious nature. Baptism applied grace to a child's nature without the participation of the mind. Without the Word but through Baptism, Christ and the Spirit come directly into the child's nature and dwell there. Baptism is sacramentally efficacious on the body and has no effect on the reason. Only after the child acquires the use of reason is it possible for him to handle the spoken Word and thus come to faith. In the case of a child, Baptism's benefits are received without faith.

This approach to the application of baptismal grace apart from the Word and faith might be termed *theosophical* because at the heart of this belief is the idea that a direct relationship is established between God and one's unconscious nature. Without participation of the reason, this view can be described as mystical or magical without ascribing to it the classical Lutheran view that Baptism regenerates. Application of grace in Baptism without the disposition of the child could also be described as *opus operatum*. These are fair descriptions of the particular concept that in Baptism God directly addresses a child's unconscious nature. Since these terms are used in other contexts, the Erlangen concept will here be termed "naturalistic." Naturalism refers to a philosophical worldview and corresponding movements in art and literature that deny the supernatural.[10] In its use as descriptive of the Erlangen theology, naturalistic refers to God's operating sacramentally in Baptism on a person's unconscious nature apart from the Word and faith.

Here the Erlangen theologians combined elements of classical Lutheran theology, Rationalism, and Schleiermacher's theology with nineteenth-century German Romanticism. In line with the older Lutheran theology, the Erlangen theologians regarded Baptism as a means of salvation for children. Since, however, it worked apart from

---

[10] Stephan, *Geschichte der Deutschen Evangelischen Theologie*, 174–75.

and before the presence of faith, their position also resembled the Roman Catholic view. Regarding Baptism as a means of salvation was a deviation from both the Rationalists and Schleiermacher, who did not ascribe any saving activity directly to the act of Baptism itself. Another influence was the naturalistic philosophy of Romanticism, which elevated man's nature over his reason or mind. Johann Fichte had placed the ego—or the self—in the center and subordinated the physical world to it. Friedrich Schelling reversed this scheme in designating nature as a form of the absolute ego. Nature was the visible mind, the mind was the invisible nature, and man was nature's highest form. In man, nature becomes objective to itself. This philosophy was taken into the anthropology of the Erlangen theologians, who prized a person's nature over his reason.[11] As the human being develops, his nature can reflect on itself, and this reflection is mind or reason.

Common to mainline Christianity is the belief that God comes to man in Word and Sacrament. In the Erlangen theology, this is reversed to fit the dichotomous view of a human being as unconscious nature and rational mind, with Baptism conferring grace on one's nature and the Word addressed to the mind or the reason to create faith. Though the Erlangen theology was in part a reaction to Rationalism in reviving traditional Lutheran belief, it held to the Rationalist belief that only a mature reason was capable of a faith based on the preached Word, a view also held by Schleiermacher.

As much as the Erlangen theologians wanted to return to classical Lutheran beliefs, their view resembled those of the Rationalists and Schleiermacher in six points:[12] (1) Faith could only be worked on reason through the spoken Word and not through Baptism. (2) Mature reason or consciousness is a necessary prerequisite for faith. (3) Without reason, a child cannot comprehend the Word and hence cannot believe. (4) Though the Erlangen theologians, in holding that Baptism gave the Holy Spirit and conferred faith's benefits, differed from the Rationalists and Schleiermacher, they agreed with them that Baptism did not work faith. (5) A child's lack of faith at Baptism

---

[11] Stephan, *Geschichte der Deutschen Evangelischen Theologie*, 174–75, and Karl Ludwig Wilhelm Heyder, "Schelling, Friedrich Wilhelm Joseph von," *A Religious Encyclopaedia*, ed. Philip Schaff (New York: Funk & Wagnalls, Publishers, 1883), 3:2118–20.

[12] The Erlangen theologians consciously adopted Rationalistic principles into their theology. See Spitz, "Lutheran Theology after 1580," 639–40, and H. Graß, "Erlanger Schule," 556–58.

renders the Baptism incomplete until the child is rationally mature enough to obtain faith through the preached Word. (6) Like the Rationalists and Schleiermacher, the Erlangen theologians held that Baptism could only be dispensed to children under the condition that the child would later hear the Word. Unique to the Erlangen theologians was their teaching that Baptism had a mystical effect on a child's unconscious nature.

The naturalistic concept attached to the doctrine of infant Baptism had several proponents in the last half of the nineteenth century. Johannes Höfling, a professor at the University of Erlangen, referenced the word order of Matthew 28:19—first baptizing and then teaching—to argue for the priority of Baptism over the spoken Word. Hans Lassen Martensen, a Danish theologian who nonetheless wrote his dogmatics in German, is generally classified with the Mediating theologians, but his views on the Sacraments allow him to be grouped with the Erlangen theologians.[13] A professor at the University of Copenhagen and later bishop of Seeland, Martensen provided a clear and an adequate presentation of naturalistic anthropology, which was fundamental to the Erlangen view of infant Baptism. Gottfreid Thomasius, professor at Erlangen, was the well-known proponent of the kenosis theory that Christ's divine nature was inoperative in works towards the world (*opera ad extra*).[14] Within the Trinity (*opera ad intra*), Christ maintained His relationship with the Father and the Spirit. Thomasius's teaching that Christ suspended His divine nature during His state of humiliation corresponded to the view that children could be devoid of rational faith while sharing in the benefits of Baptism. His comprehensive systematic presentation of the naturalistic working of Baptism provided for him a basis for infant Baptism. Naturalistic concepts of Baptism appeared in the theologies of others, among whom were Carl Gerhard von Zezschwitz of Erlangen; Ernst Hory, a Lutheran pastor, who also showed the connection between the kenosis theory of the incarnation and the naturalistic concept of infant Baptism; Franz Delitzsch of Erlangen,

---

[13] Stephan includes Martensen under the section entitled "Die Vermittlungstheologie," *Geschichte der Deutschen Evangelischen Theologie*, 195. The following reservation is made: "Freilich übernahm der Martensen dabei auch die Schwächen der deutschen Restaurationstheologie, z. b. die Kenotik und die neulutherische Sakramentslehre."

[14] Pieper, *Christliche Dogmatik*, 2:117.

who in his early years was associated with the founders of the Missouri Synod; and Rudolph Rocholl, a Lutheran pastor.[15]

JOHANN WILHELM FRIEDRICH HÖFLING

Höfling published his *Das Sakrament der Taufe* (*The Sacrament of Baptism*) in two volumes in 1846 and 1848, respectively. He had an interest in tracing the historical references to the practice of Baptism in the writings of the Ancient Church. These two volumes contain a wealth of material on the early history of Baptism and are often referenced as authoritative in this matter. Höfling's work also addressed dogmatic and exegetical questions that show how he argued for infant Baptism. Prominent in his understanding of Baptism is the clear and sharp division between it and the preached Word. Each possessed an independent efficacy; one was, nevertheless, dependent on the other in bringing complete salvation to man. This understanding of Baptism and the preached Word is established primarily on his exegesis of Matthew 28:19–20, which he interpreted to mean that both Baptism and preaching are necessary to convey a complete salvation.

Infant Baptism fits into the scheme of this passage, since children receive Baptism first and then the preached Word. Only after receiving both do they possess salvation by faith. For Höfling, both Baptism and the preached Word are means through which God bestows entire salvation on the individual. The efficacy of the one is dependent upon the efficacy of the other, but in such a way that the efficacy of each is peculiar to its own nature. The efficacy of each is distinct yet complementary to that of the other.[16] Baptism and the preached Word are qualitatively and not quantitatively different; neither can be omitted if complete salvation is to be effected. Gifts given by one are not given by the other. Intensified or repeated use of one cannot compensate for the omission of the other. Thus, if one has received the gifts of the Word, one will not receive the gifts of Baptism no matter how often one hears the Word.

---

[15] F. Hübner, "Rocholl, Rudolf," *RGG*, 5:1131. He left the Evangelical Church of Prussia, a government-mandated union between Lutherans and Reformed, for the Hannover Lutheran territorial Church. He later joined the *Altlutheraner*, "the old Lutherans," in Prussia who formed an independent Church outside of the Prussian Union.

[16] Joh[ann] Wilhelm Friedrich Höfling, *Das Sacrament der Taufe,* 2 vols. (Erlangen: Palm, (1844–46), 1:16.

Even though Baptism and the preached Word have qualitatively different effects, both impart the Holy Spirit. What Scripture attributes in the one place to the former, it attributes to the latter in another place. Since both Baptism and the preached Word work toward the one and the same goal of imparting the Holy Spirit, the Church can begin with either in its task of bringing complete salvation to the individual. Circumstances determine for the Church whether it shall first dispense the preached Word or Baptism. Here the Church does not act arbitrarily or indiscriminately, but according to the personal disposition and receptivity of the individual. In each the Holy Spirit is effective in distinctive ways in the hope that the one will follow the other and complete the application of the other. Höfling objects to the traditional distinction of *verbum audibile* and *verbum visibile,* if this means that Baptism is only a declaration and symbol God commanded, in which the promise of the Word of grace is applied to the individual. Baptism does more than merely symbolize, declare, and offer salvation to the individual. Rather, inherent in God's institution is the promise that from the moment of its being applied, Baptism has a continuous effect on the baptized. Baptism is the New Testament means of grace for effecting the saving fellowship with God through Christ. God does not merely speak about salvation but delivers it. Through the preached Word, God speaks to man, but in Baptism, God actively works on the very person of the man and his action and conveys what the preached Word describes and offers to man.[17] Grace and salvation given in Baptism constitute the power that can effect fellowship with God in Jesus Christ.[18]

Another difference between the two means of grace is that the Word has spiritual efficacy only, or is directed only to one's spirit, while Baptism is directed to the entire individual. Because preaching focuses now more on one point in human existence and less another and not the entire person, it does not effect a complete regeneration. No single word from God can do it. Baptism ranks higher than the preached Word in bringing about regeneration because it addresses a human being in his totality. Since the institution of Baptism requires the use of an earthly material in its application, it is a very concentrated working of God directly on the basic spiritual and corporeal nature of the individual (*geistige und leibliche Natur*) and not only on his spirit and spiritual personality, as in the case of the

[17] Höfling, *Das Sacrament der Taufe*, 1:16–17.
[18] Höfling, *Das Sacrament der Taufe*, 1:18–19.

Word.[19] Even though Höfling does not offer an explicit anthropology, it emerges in his division of the preached Word and Baptism and how they and their effects are each addressed to a person. The preached Word addresses the mental personality (*geistige Persönlichkeit*), a person's capacity to think. This effects one's knowledge of salvation but not salvation itself. The other part of man is the mental-corporeal nature (*geistige und leibliche Natur*) on which Baptism works directly. Höfling's view of Baptism can be termed naturalistic, as it has been defined above, in that it has an effect on the baptized apart from the Word and faith. Within this understanding of Baptism and the preached Word, Höfling develops his teaching on the Baptism of infants.

Baptism's unique work is placing the individual into what he calls the grace-filled fellowship of the Lord's death and resurrection. The power, fruits, and blessings of these redeeming acts are appropriated in Baptism.[20] Baptism's symbolical character points to how it works. It cannot be considered merely a religious washing that only symbolizes that the baptized person has received the necessary inward purification and cleansing. If it were only this, then Baptism would not be a distinctively Christian institution.[21] Baptism works what it symbolizes and demands; rather than Baptism's symbolical nature being lost, it is raised to a higher level. No tension exists between what Baptism should be and what it really obtains, but as a symbol it effects what is contained in the symbol.[22] This thinking is well within the bounds of traditional Lutheran doctrine, though the doctrine that Baptism works apart from faith is not.

INFANT BAPTISM

Unlike Wegscheider, Reinhard, and Schleiermacher, Höfling holds that infant Baptism has a biblical basis even if he does not locate specific examples. New Testament accounts of baptizing entire families are inconclusive, since it can never be proved with certainty whether inarticulate children were present on these occasions. On the other hand, it cannot be proven from the Scriptures and the Early Church fathers that they were not present and baptized.[23] Rather than

[19] Höfling, *Das Sacrament der Taufe*, 1:19.
[20] Höfling, *Das Sacrament der Taufe*, 1:20–21.
[21] Höfling, *Das Sacrament der Taufe*, 1:23.
[22] Höfling, *Das Sacrament der Taufe*, 1:21.
[23] Höfling, *Das Sacrament der Taufe*, 1:99–101.

citing biblical examples, Höfling derives the basis for infant Baptism from accumulating certain passages: the command of Christ in Matthew 28:19–20; Peter's sermon on Pentecost in Acts 2:39; the pericopes of the blessings of the children as found in the Synoptic Gospels; the comparison of Baptism to circumcision in Colossians 2:11–12; and the special status of children born to Christians in 1 Corinthians 7:14.

In Matthew 28:19–20, children are included in all nations and so are to be made disciples. They are objects of the Lord's command. Since teaching is inaccessible to children's level of development, Baptism is the only means by which they can be made disciples. They are capable of receiving Baptism. The Holy Spirit speaking through the mouth of Peter in Acts 2:39 includes children in the promise. In the pericopes of the blessings of the children, the Lord scolded those who wanted to prevent the parents from bringing their children to Him, so that He might lay His hands on them and bless them. If children are prevented from being baptized, the only door is closed through which they can enter into communion with Christ. According to Colossians 2:11–12, the Sacrament of Baptism has taken the place of the Old Testament institution of circumcision. If in the Old Testament the circumcision of the flesh was not only permitted but even commanded for those in infancy, then Baptism as the "circumcision of Christ" should not be denied to them.[24] The last passage, 1 Corinthians 7:14, states that the children of Christian parents are holy. The children of Jews and heathen stand outside of the area of the calling grace of God, because their connections are with families of unbelievers. Children of Christian parents have the advantage of already standing within the sphere of the calling grace of God. It is on this account that Paul calls the children of unbelievers unclean and the children of the believers clean. The natural connection that children of Christians have with Christian fellowship and with the calling grace of God not only makes them holy in antithesis to the children of unbelievers, but also imparts to them a special capacity for grasping, developing, and maintaining the grace of Baptism. It can be said that through their birth they have a special right to receive this grace.[25]

Along with his biblical arguments for infant Baptism, Höfling offers theological reasons for it. Children need baptismal grace and

[24] Höfling, *Das Sacrament der Taufe*, 1:102–03.
[25] Höfling, *Das Sacrament der Taufe*, 1:104.

have the capacity for it; thus, they should receive it. Höfling does not use the term original sin, but since he cites the passages typically cited in the presentation of this doctrine, he is probably referring to it. He cites Genesis 8:21, which says that the imagination of a man's heart is evil from the time of his youth. In Psalm 51:7, David says that he was conceived by his mother in sin. Paul designated all men as children of wrath by nature, Ephesians 2:3. The Lord expressly says in John 3:3, 5–6 that a man must be born again and must be born of water and of the Spirit if he is to see the kingdom of God. What is born of the flesh is flesh, and what is born of the Spirit is spirit.[26] It seems unlikely that he is not referring to original sin.

The other reason for baptizing children is their capacity to receive the grace of Baptism. Even though Höfling does not precisely define what their capability is, it is evident from what he says elsewhere that this capability exists in the child's mental and physical nature (*geistige und leibliche Natur*) as opposed to their spiritual, that is, psychological part (*geistige Persönlichkeit*), which is not actively present in infants. The children's capability for receiving the grace of Baptism is taught by the pericopes of Jesus' blessing the children. To the children belongs the kingdom of heaven. All those who want to enter the kingdom of God, that is adults, must become like them. Children receive the grace of Baptism without resisting it. That children are nonresistant in receiving the grace of Baptism follows quite naturally from Höfling's concept that children possess only a mental and physical nature, *geistige und leibliche Natur*, and not a psychological part capable of reason. Children do not respond with faith to the grace of Baptism as do adults, who have adequate reason to respond to the preaching of the Word. Höfling, however, hedges his arguments in carefully pointing out that children are not completely devoid of every aspect of faith; they just do not possess the faith of adults.[27] He points out that faith is a product not of our own human knowledge, emotions, and desires, but of the Spirit and of grace. Faith is defined as the reception of the Spirit, of grace, and of the power of the Lord. In the sense that the children receive these through Baptism, they have faith, but this hardly fits what is commonly understood as faith, that is, one's putting one's trust in

[26] Höfling, *Das Sacrament der Taufe*, 1:100.

[27] "Freilich haben die Kinder den Glauben nicht, und können ihn nicht haben im Sinne der Erwachsenen." Höfling, *Das Sacrament der Taufe*, 1:100.

Christ for salvation.[28] In not including self-awareness as a component in faith, Luther and classical Lutheranism may have differed from the definitions of the Reformed, Rationalists, and Schleiermacher, but all parties agreed that faith was something the believer, not God, did. For Höfling, children's so-called faith is nothing more than regarding them as objects of the Spirit who creates faith, and they possess grace and power as the fruits of faith. Only at maturity do they have the ability to trust in Christ. They are objects of Him who causes faith and have its effects, but their faith does not include knowledge or trust. Children possess the Spirit and His blessings immediately or directly without coming to belief themselves. So when Höfling says that they have faith in a certain sense, he means that they do not believe and trust in Christ at all. Their lack of faith as an act of the will that trusts in Christ is made more explicit in his discussion on infant Baptism and faith, where Höfling describes the manner in which children receive the grace of Baptism.

In receiving the grace of Baptism, children offer no resistance. Unlike adults who have a developed consciousness and will, they do not resist. Mature persons must first take their consciousness and will under control so that they do not shut out the divine grace as it is found in Baptism. They must make an effort not to resist obstinately the grace in Baptism. It is required of them that they come into agreement with this grace. Before they can appropriate the grace of Baptism to themselves, they must employ their minds and their wills in hearing the preached Word. Quite different is the situation where the will does not exist and the mind is not conscious of itself. Such persons do not have to use their minds and wills in hearing the preached Word. Without mind or will, it is impossible for them to resist the grace of Baptism. Children are such persons who have neither mind nor will. Baptizing adults against their will or without their knowledge would be foolish, but with children it is different. Since they are incapable of reasoning and willing, they cannot hinder the grace of Baptism.[29] With children, thinking, knowing, and willing

---

[28] Höfling, *Das Sacrament der Taufe*, 1:101.

[29] Höfling, *Das Sacrament der Taufe*, 1:101. Franz Reinhold von Frank (1827–1894), known as the dogmatician of the Erlangen Theology, similarly taught that Baptism demanded no responsive action from its object. "Wir kennen die Taufe als Sacrament der Wiedergeburt, welche ihrem Begriff nach keine entgegenkommende oder mitwirkende Action fordert; wir kennen das neutestamentliche Heil als solches, welches nur die *aptitudo passiva* um dem Menschen sich zu vermitteln voraussetzt."

are developed later. God's grace works in the child's fundamental nature, *geistige und leibliche Natur*, which lacks consciousness, and not in the mind, where thinking takes place (*geistige Persönlichkeit*). Only with adults is grace worked through the mind. Baptism works grace apart from a person's consciousness and therefore children who have no consciousness can receive it. In support of his position that the Holy Spirit can be given to children without the mind, Höfling cites the example of John the Baptist, who was filled with the Holy Spirit when still in his mother's womb.[30] Höfling's arguments for infant Baptism are consistent. The condition of infants requires it and their nature, which has not yet reached the level of consciousness and remains without reason, is capable of receiving its benefits.[31]

Höfling finds his position supported by Matthew 28:19–20, from which he understands that making disciples consists of the application of Baptism and preaching of the Word as two separate but complementary acts. Baptism and preaching the Word are indissolubly connected, and, within this connection, Höfling finds the circumstances under which infant Baptism may be dispensed.[32] Since Baptism and preaching are both necessary in delivering a complete salvation to the individual, it follows that those baptized as children should be instructed upon reaching maturity. Since neither Baptism nor preaching of the Word is complete in and of itself, one may not be isolated or separated from the other. Each performs its unique function in connection with the other. One cannot be taken out of its relationship with the other. Though both work toward the same goal of imparting the entire salvation to the individual, they work in

---

System der Christlichen Wahrheit, 2 vols. (Dritte verbesserte Auflage; Erlangen und Leipzig: A. Deichert, 1894), 2:285.

[30] Höfling, *Das Sacrament der Taufe*, 1:101–02.

[31] Höfling, *Das Sacrament der Taufe*, 1:102.

[32] That baptizing and teaching were both necessary for becoming a disciple was explicitly taught by many who held to the naturalistic working of baptism. Frank approvingly cites Johann Christian von Hofmann in his interpretation of Matthew 28:19–20. "Gewiß ist die Meinung der genannten Stelle diese, daß das μαθητεύειν in der zwiefachen Form genannten Stelle diese, des βαπτίζειν und διδάσκειν mit wohlbemessener dieser Actionen, sich vollziehen solle, keineswegs diese, das μαθητεύειν solle nur nicht ohne ein βαπτίζειν und ein διδάσκειν bleiben (v. Hofmann)." *System der Christlichen Wahrheit*, 2:283. Cf. also Ernst Hory, *Die Taufe als Kindertaufe auf Grund heiliger Schrift* (Stuttgart: n.p., 1872), 26–27, and Hans L[assen] Martensen, *Die christliche Taufe und die baptische Frage* (Gotha und Hamburg: Andreas Pepthes, 1843), 23–24.

qualitatively different but complementary ways. For salvation, both are necessary. Neither is sufficient by itself.

For children, this means that Baptism must be followed by the preaching of the Word or instruction in it. In the case of children, it is not necessary for the Word to be applied before Baptism, since without reason or consciousness they are not capable of reacting to it. Their nature, *geistige und leibliche Natur,* is capable of receiving Baptism with its accompanying grace. However, after his Baptism, a child must come in contact with the preached Word without which the grace given in Baptism never belongs to the will. Where the preached Word is not applied to baptized children, they lose the grace of Baptism. Unless they come under the influence of the Word, they are without faith and no longer possess what Baptism gave them. Where grace exists only in the *geistige und leibliche Natur*, which is the case of a baptized child who does not come to faith through the preached Word applied to his mind, the *geistige Persönlichkeit*, grace is completely taken away. An exception is made for children who do not mature normally into adulthood.[33]

Since Baptism and the preached Word belong inseparably together as the two means for making disciples or for imparting the full salvation to the individual, infant Baptism should take place only within the scope of the Christian family and congregation. Both family and congregation can give the assurance that baptismal grace will be complemented by the application of the preached Word. Thus, a child's need for Baptism and his capability of receiving the grace given him are not sufficient reasons for baptizing infants.

In holding that faith can only arise in a Christian environment and not from the act of Baptism itself, Höfling has followed the arguments of Rationalists and Schleiermacher that only children with the probability of being raised as Christians are to be baptized. Already in the Reformation era, the Reformed proposed that faith was first possible for infants when their reason matured. Höfling also held this view but, unlike the Reformed, the Rationalists, or Schleiermacher, he held that Baptism worked on the child's nature, giving the Spirit and His gifts to the child. He agreed with them that faith arose only from the spoken or, as he called it, the preached Word and not from Baptism. Since no assurance can be given that the preached Word will be given to children of Jews and heathen, such children are not to be baptized. Höfling in no way denied that such

[33] Höfling, *Das Sacrament der Taufe*, 1:103.

children have a need for the grace of Baptism and are capable of receiving it.[34] They are excluded because Baptism exists in an inseparable relationship with the preached Word, which could not be expected to be applied to such children.

In his discussion of the Baptism of children of known unbelievers, Höfling further develops what he considers the necessary connection between Baptism and the preached Word. First he speaks to the issue of children who are snatched away from their parents and then baptized without their consent. This practice cannot be condoned, because God's grace cannot take the path of sin and injustice. Birth in a non-Christian family indicates that they are not to be considered objects of God's call of grace in Baptism. Baptizing children of Jews and heathens without the knowledge and will of the parents is a crime against the parental right. Administering Baptism in such a situation is also a crime against the Sacrament itself. Any administration of Baptism that does not contemplate the future preaching of the Word is a sacrilege, because the necessary connection between the two is broken. The danger of sacrilege against Baptism is greater in baptizing the children of unbelievers, because there is little hope that the preached Word will be applied.[35] Höfling's stress on the necessity of the preached Word following the Baptism of children is underscored in his discussion of cases in which unbelieving parents request Baptism for their children. Their consent is not sufficient reason to baptize them. As long as children remain under the care and authority of unbelieving parents, the danger of sacrilege is present, since Baptism is separated from the preached Word. Baptism in this case is not a violation of the parental rights but is a sacrilege against Baptism.[36]

By itself, Baptism can never bring salvation to those children who remain in this life and whose consciousnesses and wills develop according to the laws of nature.[37] For Baptism to be effective in

---

[34] Höfling, *Das Sacrament der Taufe*, 1:103–04.

[35] Höfling, *Das Sacrament der Taufe*, 1:125.

[36] Höfling, *Das Sacrament der Taufe*, 1:126–27.

[37] Frank, working with the principle that both Baptism and the spoken Word were necessary for bringing salvation to the individual, said that Baptism administered without parental consent was no Baptism. "Das keine Taufe ist, wo man Kinder ohne Wissen und wider Willen ihrer Eltern, in offenbarem Widerspruch eben gegen die Einsetzung welche das διδάσκειν mit dem βαπτίζειν zusammenbindet, 'tauft' und sie dann dem Heidenthum überlässet." Frank, *System der Christlichen Wahrheit*, 2:288. With such a concept of Baptism, Frank makes the validity of infant Baptism depend

accomplishing a full salvation in these cases, the preached Word must follow. Unless the Holy Spirit continues His work in the preached Word, that which was actually and objectively appropriated to the child through Baptism cannot become his possession of which he is really aware and which he desires. What was objectively given to the child in his Baptism without the preached Word can never become subjectively possessed with the mind and the will. For Höfling, what is objectively given in Baptism are the Spirit, the power of the Lord, and His grace. These gifts are given to the child's nature (*geistige und leibliche Natur*), not to his mind or spirit (*geistige Persönlichkeit*).

The situation of children who have received Baptism but not the preached Word is similar to that of those adults who have only received the preached Word but not Baptism. It is required of baptized children that the Word be preached to them. Adults who through the preached Word come to faith must be baptized. Neither children who have been baptized but lack the Word nor adults who believe the Word but lack Baptism enjoy salvation in its completeness. Baptized children can enjoy complete salvation when, through the working of the preached Word, the will and consciousness appropriate what was given in Baptism.[38] Baptism and the preached Word are necessary for complete regeneration. This is as true for adults as it is for children. Without being baptized, adults do not possess the blessings offered in this Sacrament. They exist in a state between being regenerate and unregenerate. Unbaptized but believing adults cannot be considered unregenerate because they have already taken to themselves the saving Word of God through preaching. In them, grace and the Spirit of God are already present and active. They have started on the way to the new life, but they are still not regenerate, because neither Baptism nor the preached Word alone can work regeneration. Baptism can give the blessings of

---

in part upon the parental consent. The exact opposite position is taken by Carl Ferdinand Wilhelm Walther. "Endlich wenn die Taufe einem Kinde wider den Willen der Eltern schon ertheilt ist, dann ist dieselbe nichts desto weniger gültig und kräftig, wenn alle wesentliche Stücke der Taufe vorhanden gewesen sind, wozu der Wille der Eltern nicht so schlechterdings erforderlich ist; indem hier die Regel der Rechtsgelehrten statt hat. Es gibt vieles, was eine erst einzugehende Ehe hindert, die eingegangene aber nicht auflöst; ebenso gehört nämlich mehreres zur Ertheilung der Taufe, was die ertheilte nicht ungültig macht." *Americanisch-Lutherische Pastoraltheologie* (St. Louis: Druckerei der Synode von Missouri, Ohio u.a. Staaten, 1872), 126.

[38] Höfling, *Das Sacrament der Taufe*, 1:137.

salvation and the preached Word can create trust within the person, but the functions and effects of each are not interchangeable. Full salvation or regeneration requires having both Baptism's blessings of salvation and the trust created by the preached Word. Without one or the other, full regeneration does not take place.

Either Baptism or the preached Word can initiate the Spirit's work of regeneration, but neither alone can complete it. In the case of baptized children, regeneration is complete when preaching follows Baptism. For believing adults, this happens first when they are baptized.[39] Appropriately, the Church does not consider adults as members before their Baptism. Baptized children are considered members only at the conclusion of their instruction, which is often their confirmation. Then they are really part of the faithful and recognized as self-sufficient members of the body of Christ with full rights. Believing adults without Baptism lack the objective part of regeneration. Baptized children without instruction in the Word lack the subjective part. Through the preached Word, unbaptized adults believe in Christ; nevertheless, they do not have the blessings of salvation given only in Baptism. Baptized children, on the other hand, have the blessings of salvation, such as the Holy Spirit, but are still without faith and so possess regeneration objectively. Believing adults possess regeneration subjectively. Instruction provides the subjective element to baptized children and Baptism provides the objective element to believing adults.[40]

Apart from the Repristination theologians, nineteenth-century Lutheran theologians had a commitment to the Baptism of infants but did not advance beyond the Reformed and Rationalist belief that they did not have faith at the time Baptism was administered. Such a Baptism for Schleiermacher was erroneously applied. Even though it was an erroneously administered Baptism, as infant Baptism was considered, it could be justified in view of the child's future faith, a view put forth by Calvin. Höfling follows Schleiermacher in maintaining that infant Baptism is given in view of the child's future faith. However, Höfling speaks of three types of faith in which infant Baptism is administered: (1) the ability to receive the Holy Spirit; (2) the belief of the Church; (3) the rational and conscious acceptance of Christianity. All three factored into Höfling's doctrine of infant Baptism. The first type of faith is the child's own receptivity to the

---

[39] Höfling, *Das Sacrament der Taufe*, 1:137.
[40] Höfling, *Das Sacrament der Taufe*, 1:139.

Holy Spirit and divine grace, which he receives without resisting. For children, this faith is sufficient for salvation. They do not need to be vicariously saved by the faith of others as if this kind of faith was insufficient to save them.[41] This faith is the reception of the Spirit's gifts in the child's nature (*geistige und leibliche Natur*). It does not involve the child's reason or the consciousness that comes later in life. The second type of faith on which children are baptized is the faith of the Church. If children of Christians were baptized in view of their own faith understood as a use of the will, then all children should be baptized without discrimination in the hope that they would be saved. If the faith, in the usual sense of actual belief, was created by Baptism, then by itself it would be adequate for obtaining complete salvation. Application of the preached Word would become superfluous. Since the preached Word can never be superfluous for those persons who have attained the use of their reason, it is necessary that a guarantee be given when the infant is baptized that the preached Word will be applied in maturity. Without this condition, Baptism should not be given to infants.

It is the faith of the Church that supplies the guarantee that the preached Word will be applied to the child and provides the environment in which the preached Word is applied to the child. A child's relationship to the Church created by Baptism entitles and qualifies the child to hear the preached Word and to have that faith that arises only from the preached Word. The faith of the Church and not the faith of the child is the cause for bringing the child to Baptism, which, in turn, puts the child in a position to hear the preached Word. In baptizing infants, the Church assumes a responsibility for them.[42]

Only from the preached Word comes that kind of faith, the third type, which trusts Christ. The third type of faith Höfling calls the *fides explicita*. It first arises when the child has attained the use of reason. *Fides explicita* is not present at the time Baptism is administered to infants but can come only through the preaching of the Word. Before the use of reason, a baptized child has *fides implicita*, that is, it possesses the Holy Spirit and grace, which exist in his nature until the rise of reason is sufficient for his salvation. At the age of reason, *fides explicita* is necessary. Since Baptism is administered to infants not only on the basis of their *fides implicita* but also their *fides explicita*, the *fides ecclesiae* is important in

---

41 Höfling, *Das Sacrament der Taufe*, 2:231.

42 Höfling, *Das Sacrament der Taufe*, 2:231–32.

guaranteeing that the preached Word will be given to the child and then can become *fides explicita.*[43]

In the sense that the child possesses the Spirit, he has faith, but in the sense in which it is required as he reaches rational maturity, he does not have faith, a view held first by the Reformed and then perpetuated by Schleiermacher. Only the faith created by preaching is active.[44] Höfling's anthropology, which divided the person into two parts, the *geistige und leibliche Natur* and the *geistige Persönlichkeit,* provides him the basis for his understanding of faith as *fides implicita* and *fides explicita.* His use of *fides ecclesiae* is not that the faith of the Church is substituted for the child's faith, the Catholic view, but refers to the view put forth by the Rationalists and Schleiermacher that a child comes to his own faith in a Christian environment. Höfling approaches the Catholic view in that the child possesses the Spirit and his blessing prior to and without his own faith.

Höfling's understanding of the relationship between Baptism and preaching and of faith is reflected in his attitude toward the Baptismal liturgy. The liturgy with which Höfling was familiar addressed the questions concerning faith to the child who was to be baptized. These questions are addressed to the child's future faith and not his present faith. Höfling does not advocate a change in the baptismal questions, as long as the questions are understood as referring to future faith. The questions have nothing to do with what is actually present in the child, including faith, before Baptism. Essential to Höfling is that faith comes through the preaching of the Word at the time of the child's rational maturity and not at Baptism. Since the questions are addressed to a child's future faith, they take on the character not only of a confession but of a vow to which Baptism obligates the child.[45]

In his discussion of baptismal questions addressed to the child, Höfling understands faith according to the traditional Reformation teaching as actual belief and trust, and so the questions address not what the child possesses in nature by the Spirit but his future rational and conscious comprehension of Christianity. Unless one knew Höfling's varied definitions of faith, an observer could only conclude from the liturgy that the child actually had faith at the time of his Baptism. This he does not allow, since it can only happen from the preached Word at the time of maturity. In baptizing a child, the

[43] Höfling, *Das Sacrament der Taufe*, 2:232.
[44] Höfling, *Das Sacrament der Taufe*, 2:233.
[45] Höfling, *Das Sacrament der Taufe*, 2:233.

baptismal liturgy used by Höfling would be at odds with this stated position. By removing the questions from the rite of Baptism, the Rationalists demonstrated theological integrity. Unknown is whether Höfling had to wrestle with a liturgy that said something entirely different than what he held.

The institution of sponsors also reflects Höfling's understanding of Baptism and the preached Word as well as his concept of faith. The sponsors represent the child, the congregation, and the parents. Since Baptism obligates the child towards God and the Church, as in Zwingli's view, the child needs guarantors and representatives in accepting these obligations.[46] The sponsors acceptance of the Apostles' Creed in the child's stead does not reflect a faith the child has before or through Baptism but a faith that will come later during rational maturity through the preached Word. So the confession made by the sponsors obligates the child in an anticipatory way.[47] The child fulfills these obligations with the application of the preached Word.[48]

The sponsors also represent the congregation's obligation to the child who has been born within it, making sure that the Baptism is properly performed and giving a special guarantee that the preaching of the Word and Christian education shall follow. Finally, the sponsors represent the parents, who are the first members of the congregation to concern themselves with the child.[49] This view fits within Höfling's understanding of the *fides ecclesiae* in providing the Christian environment in which the Word will be preached. Thus the unity of Baptism and Word is assured, so that no sacrilege is committed against Baptism.

CONCLUSION

At the base of Höfling's discussion of infant Baptism is the necessary relationship between Baptism and the preached Word for a complete regeneration to be accomplished. This concept he derives from his interpretation of Matthew 28:19–20, that making disciples is accomplished by baptizing and preaching. Should one of these be

---

[46] Höfling, *Das Sacrament der Taufe*, 2:240.

[47] Theodor Kliefoth (1810–1895) also recognizes the sponsors' duties as making a confession for the child which he will later make himself. *Theorie des Kultus der evangelischen Kirche*, (Parcim und Ludwigslust: Hinstor'schen Hofbuchhandlng, 1844), 186.

[48] Höfling, *Das Sacrament der Taufe*, 2:242.

[49] Höfling, *Das Sacrament der Taufe*, 2:243.

lacking, complete regeneration is not effected. Such a person is still not a full-fledged member of the body of Christ. Apart from his interpretation of the Matthean citation, Höfling does not cite additional biblical evidence for his view. While he offers multiple understandings of the word faith, he assumes but does not define regeneration. He is definite in saying that it must be brought about by both Baptism and the preached Word. Thus, between regeneration and unregeneration exists the condition of partial regeneration, though he does not use this term and, accordingly, does not say whether those caught between regeneration and unregeneration are saved or not. Without asking what he intends by regeneration, one is baffled by his belief that Baptism can give the Spirit, the power of the Lord, and grace, but it cannot give or work faith. Then, on the other hand, the preached Word can work faith, but it cannot give the blessings of salvation.

Although some Lutheran theologians, by lumping Baptism and the Word under the means of grace, may have failed to recognize their distinctive functions, Höfling's division of labor between Baptism and the preached Word leaves too many issues unanswered. He moves back to Luther's belief that Baptism accomplishes salvation and gives the Holy Spirit, but in place of Luther's concept of faith, he puts a concept of faith that fits the definitions of the Rationalists and Schleiermacher. His understanding of a human being as *geistige und leibliche Natur,* out of which a *geistige Persönlichkeit* develops, is as creative and speculative as his view that Baptism is intended for the former and the Word for the latter. Should this understanding of man prove wrong, his defense for infant Baptism would collapse. Questions concerning this anthropology shall be discussed more extensively in presentations of the views of Thomasius and Zezschwitz, which follow. Distinctive in Höfling's presentation is his understanding of regeneration as dependent on Baptism and the preached Word. This allows a middle ground between regeneration and unregeneration. Whether or not Höfling's views are compelling, he does reflect a not uncommon belief that infants can receive God's working in Baptism but not in the preached Word.

HANS LASSEN MARTENSEN

In 1843, when Martensen was professor of theology at Copenhagen, he published his monograph on Baptism, *Die christliche Taufe und die baptische Frage*. It was published again in 1860 after he had become the bishop of Seeland. Though Martensen was Danish, he participated in the main streams of German theology of his day, and many of his books were published in German, most noteworthy being his *Christliche Dogmatik*. Martensen held that Baptism and the Word each had its distinct efficacy directed to man's physical nature and reason. Like Höfling, he held that only the preached Word could effect faith, and that only in mature persons. Martensen describes how Baptism works on the child's nature and then how Baptism's effects develop into a real and active faith.

Martensen regards Baptism as that act through which the Lord chooses His disciples. During his earthly lifetime, Jesus personally chose His disciples, who did not need to be baptized. Paul had to be baptized because he was chosen after the Lord had left the earth.[50] In *Der Christliche Glaube*, Schleiermacher had already put forth the concept that Baptism was necessary only for those who did not know Jesus personally, but with Höfling, Martensen set forth his understanding of Baptism in relationship to the preached Word. Baptism and not the preached Word is the basis of faith, but the Word creates faith. Christ is actually given in Baptism, from which faith is built. Christ is not given in the preached Word. Without faith created by the preached Word, Baptism is unproductive. When Baptism is applied, faith created by the preached Word becomes active and productive. Faith created by the preached Word, whether it be before or after Baptism, has a temporal dimension since it comes into existence under the circumstances of time and experience. Baptism gives an eternal dimension to faith, since faith finds its everlasting foundation in Christ. The preached Word creates a faith that is limited by time and place, but Baptism gives a foundation to faith—Christ—who is not subject to either time or place. The great mystery of Christian faith is that Christ enters into an organic relationship with the baptized person. Christ is faith's foundation, from which faith and the desire to do good works develop. Baptism and not preaching creates that organic union between God and man out of which come all other blessings, including faith and good works.[51] Preaching has no separate functions, but it is understood in its relationship to Baptism. For those who have already been baptized, preaching

[50] Hans L[assen] Martensen, *Die christliche Taufe und die baptische Frage* (Gotha und Hamburg: Andreas Pepthes, 1843), 11.

[51] Martensen, *Die christliche Taufe und die baptische Frage,* 12–13.

develops the mystery of faith previously imparted through Baptism.[52] The preached Word develops the mystery of faith given in Baptism so that faith knows and trusts in Christ, who already dwells in the baptized. Infants possess the mystery of faith through Baptism and so still need the preached Word to develop this mystery into a living, active faith.

Martensen regards Baptism as more than just making grace visible along with a declaration and pledge of grace, which is the classical Reformed position. It is a real impartation of grace without which Christian life cannot be developed.[53] In holding that Baptism brings Christ directly to one's nature and the preached Word creates cognitive faith during maturity, Martensen's views are the same as Höfling's. Baptism bestows grace to the physical nature, and preaching declares it to the mind.

Lack of an explicit command in the Scriptures to baptize infants can be explained by the Scriptures being written from a missionary point of view. First, the apostles were commissioned to establish congregations where Christian education could take place. Since Baptism is inseparable from instruction in the Word, baptizing of children where instruction in the Word did not follow would be without any purpose. The requirement that the preached Word follow Baptism administered in infancy is dependent on Martensen's understanding that Baptism and the preached Word are necessarily related. Without the preached Word the mystery of faith given in Baptism cannot develop into a living and active faith. Lack of an explicit biblical mandate for infant Baptism does not concern Martensen; the Spirit and not merely the letter leads to a right understanding of the institutions God created and a correct use of them. Since doctrines do not have to be proved from a literal (*buchstäbliche*) reading of the Scriptures, Martensen follows Rationalist exegesis in dismissing passages such as Mark 10:14–15, 1 Corinthians 7:14, and 1:16, which have been traditionally used for infant Baptism.[54] Even though the Scriptures do not have an explicit command to baptize infants, Martensen finds a basis for it from his understanding of the relationship between Baptism and faith derived from his interpretation of Matthew 28:19–20 and of the apostolic practice. Greek words that are usually translated as "teaching" he

---

[52] Martensen, *Die christliche Taufe und die baptische Frage*, 13.
[53] Martensen, *Die christliche Taufe und die baptische Frage*, 16.
[54] Martensen, *Die christliche Taufe und die baptische Frage*, 23.

understands as "making disciples," which consists of both baptizing and teaching. A church desiring to remain true to the Lord's command must begin by first baptizing and then following with teaching or preaching, which effects the active, living aspect of faith that is conscious and alive.[55] For his view that first Baptism gives Christ as the mystery of faith and then the preached Word or Christian education develops it into a living and active faith, Martensen finds support in the word order of Matthew 28:19–20, where Baptism precedes teaching. Since in this passage Baptism comes before teaching, Martensen concludes that infant Baptism is a proper response to Christ's command. The Lord's command to make disciples of all nations through Baptism and Christian instruction is carried out as infant Baptism is practiced throughout the world.[56] Martensen substantiates his claim that the correct order is that Baptism has a priority over preaching by pointing out that the New Testament refers to the baptized as regenerate. The only requirement for Baptism is that the person has the receptivity for the kingdom of God that is common to all. This common receptivity of all men is the ability of a human being's natural part to possess Christ. Complete faith is not demanded of the candidate for Baptism. An unbaptized person does not have faith in the fullest sense but only the desire for faith. Since faith is initiated first through Baptism, neither faith nor regeneration were required of the candidates for apostolic Baptism.[57] That common receptivity for the kingdom of God that the apostles required of adults before they were baptized is the same receptivity that children already possess by nature.[58]

Martensen divides the person into the natural part and the mental or spiritual part. Receptivity for Baptism belongs to the first and more basic part of human existence, the natural part. This children possess long before the mental part develops, in which rational thought takes place. Their inborn receptivity for Baptism qualifies them to receive it. Though the need for Baptism suggests that the child is born with original sin, which needs to be remedied by Baptism, the real reason for his being eligible for Baptism is his receptivity, to which Höfling devotes his most extensive discussion.

---

[55] Martensen, *Die christliche Taufe und die baptische Frage*, 24.
[56] Martensen, *Die christliche Taufe und die baptische Frage*, 24.
[57] Martensen, *Die christliche Taufe und die baptische Frage*, 26.
[58] Martensen, *Die christliche Taufe und die baptische Frage*, 28.

Receptivity required of candidates for Baptism is not receptivity for a particular gift of grace, nor is it found in some and not in others. It is the common receptivity of human nature for the new creation and Christ. It can be understood as the possibility that human nature possesses because of its redemption and potential of reaching the point of perfection. This receptivity of Baptism is the human nature's slumbering, an indecisive shadowy condition within the nature of man that offers no resistance to grace. This non-resistance is expressed well by the Roman Catholic formula, *obicem non ponere*, which is not only the lack of resistance, but the inability to do so. The receptivity required of all who desire Baptism is present in children.[59] Along with a child's receptivity for Baptism, which is the inability to resist the grace of Baptism, the child's nature possesses an internal drive towards the kingdom of God and a deep longing for Christ. Within the child exist two impulses: one towards the kingdom of God and the other towards the world.[60] On the one hand, the child is drawn to God, and on the other hand, he is drawn to the world. Both are factors in infant Baptism because the part directed to the world needs what Baptism offers, and the part drawn to God makes the child a fit candidate for Baptism.

The receptivity required of candidates for Baptism exists naturally in children and does not have to be awakened in them as is necessary with adults. Children possess by nature the condition that can only exist in adults who in the preached Word hear about the universality of sin and salvation. The drive for the kingdom of God comes to the surface in adults only when they hear the Word. No longer are the "old I" and the world able to hinder the working of salvation. Preaching of the Word removes the sin that covers up the original nature that is able to receive Baptism. Then Baptism is no longer hindered by sin and can do its work. When the adult believes the preached Word, he is put in the same condition a child is in by nature. At this time, the adult is able to receive Baptism.[61] Thus, Martensen can say that after the preached Word has done its task, the Baptism administered to an adult is infant Baptism.

Martensen's argument for children's receptivity to Baptism is further developed by comparing it to his doctrine of the incarnation, by which he understands that Christ's deity slept during the

[59] Martensen, *Die christliche Taufe und die baptische Frage*, 29–31.
[60] Martensen, *Die christliche Taufe und die baptische Frage*, 31.
[61] Martensen, *Die christliche Taufe und die baptische Frage*, 31–32.

developing years of his childhood. Christ's lack of consciousness in the incarnation demonstrates that the divine nature can be united with the human nature at any level of conscious development. This can take place even before there is any consciousness at all.[62] Just as Christ possesses the Godhead without consciousness, so the child possesses Christ in a similar way. In denying that Christ is aware of His deity, Martensen moves away from the characteristic Lutheran christology that all the divine attributes are given to the human nature through which they work, the *genus maiestaticum.* The relationship of infant Baptism to the incarnation is reserved for the section on Ernst Hory, who discussed this more extensively.

In addition to children's receptivity as a reason for their Baptism, there is the fact that they need it. For Martensen, it is Pelagianism to say that children do not need a Savior because they are without guilt. To maintain the innocence of children and to deny their need of Baptism and the Savior is to deny the sinfulness of the human nature and to regard the Lord's childhood as superfluous and insignificant for the work of redemption.[63] Martensen speaks of the sinfulness of the human nature without speaking of original sin. Behind his argument that the childhood of Jesus would be superfluous if it did not contribute to redemption is the doctrine of Christ's active obedience. This means that during His entire life, including His childhood, Christ was fulfilling the Law perfectly for those who transgressed it. His holy and sinless infancy redeems the sinful infancy of human beings. If children were innocent, not guilty of sin, then, as Martensen maintains, Jesus' life as a child would not have had a part in the work of redemption and would have been superfluous and insignificant.

In Baptism, the sinfulness of the perverted human race is broken, but individual acts of sin are not redeemed.[64] After Baptism has been

---

[62] Martensen, *Die christliche Taufe und die baptische Frage,* 34–35.

[63] Martensen, *Die christliche Taufe und die baptische Frage*, 35.

[64] Johann Ernst Georg Stosch (b. 1851), who follows Martensen very closely in his understanding of Baptism, claimed that Baptism destroys original guilt and all sin as it develops later in life. "Die Taufe hat ein in die Zukunft gewandtes Antlitz. Sie tilgt die Erbschuld ebenso, wie sie die ganze kommende Entwickelung unter die Macht der Vergebung der Sünden." *Zeitgedanken über die Taufe* (Gütersloh: C. Bertelsmann, 1902), 85. Ernst Hory calls Baptism the antidote to original sin. "So sehen wir in der Kindertaufe das Antidon gegen die Erbschaft der natürlichen Geburt, die Erbsünde." *Die Taufe als Kindertaufe auf Grund heiliger Schrift* (Stuttgart: n.p., 1872), 120.

applied, one's sinful human nature no longer has to be a hindrance to salvation and the baptized person is able to desist from further engaging in sinful deeds. Baptism does not give sanctification and ethical perfection in any particular degree, but it offers the possibility of sanctification and perfection. Through Baptism, the newly created human race is planted into the body.[65]

Martensen details Baptism's specific effects. Baptism not only promises God's grace to infants but actually gives it to them. As the object of God's grace, he also becomes the subject who should predestinate himself in freedom to Christ, for salvation. The child is thus both the object and the subject of the action of Baptism. Predestination given to the child in Baptism is not a finished predestination, but an election to grace, calling the child to freedom. Those who have been elected in Baptism are to develop the gift given in Baptism by spiritual devotions and works, through the use of the Word, prayer, the congregational life, and the Lord's Supper.[66] Thus the predestination given to children in their Baptism is the election to a position or condition from which they can decide for themselves whether or not they will give heed to God's call of grace. That Baptism gives to children the possibility of sanctification, and not the sanctification itself, conforms with Martensen's concept that they are given a chance to predestinate themselves, and not a fixed predestination.

Through Baptism, the child becomes the unconscious carrier of Christ's objective righteousness. He is a *christophorus*, a bearer of Christ, without knowing it. The child is placed into an organic relationship with Christ, and in this relationship, the seed of faith is given.[67] When Martensen refers to the seed of faith, he is referring to what he has previously designated the mystery of faith, which is Christ. From this mystery of faith, which is really the indwelling of Christ in the child's nature, active faith arises. Martensen seems to use the term seed to refer to something which will be produced in the future.[68] The seed of faith is not faith, but it is the potential for having

---

[65] Martensen, *Die christliche Taufe und die baptische Frage*, 29.

[66] Martensen, *Die christliche Taufe und die baptische Frage*, 44–46.

[67] Martensen, *Die christliche Taufe und die baptische Frage*, 54–55.

[68] In his 1559 edition of the *Institutes of the Christian Religion*, Calvin said the seed of "future faith and repentance lies concealed in [children] through the secret operation of the Spirit." Quoted from John W. Riggs, *Baptism in the Reformed Tradition* (Louisville: Westminster John Knox Press, 2002), 67. Latin and French original, 153 n. 84.) Calvin held that the seed was given not *in* but *at* Baptism and

faith.[69] Objective salvation is given to the child as a gift and from this gift faith then develops. Faith is the product of the gift of Baptism. The grace given in Baptism is described as the mother of faith and not its result.[70] When the child is planted into Christ through Baptism, he is also given the Holy Spirit. The Spirit is the ultimate cause of any development that might occur in the child and its receptivity of Christ. The Spirit mediates the correct use of Christ's gifts.

The Spirit that Christ gives to the child in Baptism is the same Spirit active in the Christian congregation, and so He makes the child in whom He is dwelling a member of the congregation. In the congregation, the Spirit leads souls to Christ and confirms them in their Baptism.[71] In referring to the Spirit who is active in the congregation, Martensen is referring to the Spirit's action in the

---

referred not to what the baptized child then possessed but what he would possess in the future. Riggs discusses how the seed metaphor is problematic for Calvin in that it implies a nonpersonal activity of the Spirit, which did not fit his theology that faith was necessary (68–69). Like Calvin, Martensen uses the seed of future development, but unlike Calvin he holds to the Spirit's nonpersonal working.

[69] The phrase *Keim des Glaubens* is sometimes used by those holding to a naturalistic working of infant Baptism. Martensen uses this phrase interchangeably with *Princip des Glaubens* and *Wesen des Glaubens*. These phrases do not refer to faith itself, but to Holy Spirit as the cause of faith and Christ as its object. Rather than possessing faith, the child has the potential for it. A certain Pastor Dienemann wrote that little children "können noch nicht glauben." Then he went on to say: "Mit der Taufe, mit der Gabe des heiligen Geistes, mit der Wiedergeburt wird aber nun auch ganz selbstverständig in den Kindern der Keim des Glaubens hineingelegt." *Die heilige Taufe im Licht des göttlichen Worts und der Gegenwart* (Leipzig: Deichert, 1894), 53–56. Frank, who also denied infant faith, still could say that in Baptism the child receives "die Intiative zur Weckung und Herstellung des Glaubens." "Initiative" is for Frank what "Keim" is for Martensen. Frank, *System der Christlichen Wahrheitt*, 2:288. Even Alexander von Oettingen, who was closer to the Repristination theologians, denied the possibility of faith to infants because of insufficient consciousness. Still he asserted that through Baptism the child received the "Keim des neuen Lebens in Christo." *Lutherische Dogmatik*, 3 vols. (München: Beck'sche Verlagsbuchhandlung, 1897–1902), 2:417. Gotthardt Romberg said that in Baptism God worked on the child through the form of a "Trieb oder Keim." "Kindertaufe und Wiedergeburt," *Mecklenburgisches Kirchen-und Zeitblatt*, 31 (1903): 405. Ernst Sartorius (1797–1859) spoke similarily of Baptism's benefits. "Die Taufhandlung gleicht der Einsenkung eines Samens, oder Legung eines Keims, wobei die Handlung selbst nur einem bestimmten Zeitpunkt angehört und einen Angang bildet, aus welchem dann in continuirlicher Folge eine neue Lebensentwickelung hervorgeht, die in Zeit und Raum sich immer weiter ausbreitet." *Die Lehre von der heiligen Liebe*, 2 vols. (Zweite Auflage; Stuttgart: Liesching, 1855), 2:104.

[70] Martensen, *Die christliche Taufe und die baptische Frage*, 55.

[71] Martensen, *Die christliche Taufe und die baptische Frage,* 57.

preached Word, which creates faith in the mental or spiritual part of the person. The arising of faith in the mind confirms the presence of Christ, who through Baptism already lives in the child's nature. Schleiermacher saw the child's inclusion in the congregation where faith could arise as the one valid reason for infant Baptism.

In Baptism a child receives Christ and the Spirit of faith, both of which are the essence of faith, but he cannot comprehend this unfathomable mystery. The Holy Spirit is called the Spirit of faith, since by virtue of His dwelling in the child through Baptism, He becomes the cause of all future faith. A child's reception of Christ and the Spirit of faith, which are the essence of faith, occurs not by infusion but organically, so that the Holy Spirit becomes the "spirit" of the child's soul. God does not directly dwell in the child, but He begins to live alongside the child in what Martensen calls an immanent relationship.[72] From this relationship brought about by Baptism, faith develops.

At the time of his Baptism, the child is devoid of faith, understood as knowledge of and trust in God. Through Baptism, the child possesses Christ and the Holy Spirit without the benefit of faith, but Christ is the essence of faith and the Holy Spirit, the cause of the new life in Christ. Though the child possesses the essence of faith and the Spirit, he still does not have faith. A child has Christ, who has the essence and object of faith, but without a developed mind, he does not engage in trusting Christ. The Spirit lives in the nature of the child without creating faith, and Christ lives in the nature of the child without being believed.

Martensen uses Jesus as an analogy to explain this. A baptized child's lack of faith is similar to Christ not being conscious of either Himself or His deity. As an infant, Christ had no knowledge, although within Himself He carried all the treasures of knowledge in the form of a seed that would later be productive. Similarly, the child unconsciously carries within himself Christ and the Holy Spirit. He possesses the object and cause of faith but not faith. Martensen argues

---

[72] Martensen, *Die christliche Taufe und die baptische Frage*, 62. Georg Stosch, who follows Martensen, describes what actually happens to the baptized child. "Die Taufgnade ist nicht eine ruhende, die erst später bei Einzelnen durch den Glauben in Bewegung gesetzt wird und in Tausenden einen Todesschlaf schläft, weil der Glaube sie nicht erweckt. Vielmehr redet die Taufgnade schon zu der schlummernden Seele des Kindes, wie nur Gottes Geist zu einer Menschenseele in allen Stadien ihrer Entwickelung zu reden vermag." (*Zeitgedanken über die Taufe*, 85). In the naturalistic concept of Baptism, its benefits are given without the Word and faith.

that if a child had faith in the sense of knowledge and trust and of itself enters into a covenant with God, then he would also have to assert that Christ during His infancy made use of His knowledge as the incarnate God in a hidden way. This would mean that Christ's childhood was an act of deception. He pretended to be a child, but actually He was not. Not admitting children to Holy Communion shows that the Church holds that children do not actually have faith through their Baptism. Communing children was not universally practiced and is expressly condemned by the Protestant (*evangelisch*) Church.[73]

Even though the child does not have faith through his Baptism, he is given the Holy Spirit, who is responsible for the development of faith. Actual faith develops from that which was given in Baptism. The Church is given the task of assisting in developing (*entfalten*) faith from what was given in Baptism.[74] Historical faith is the first step toward developing real faith. Faith as historical experience or knowledge is based on what Martensen calls phenomenology, that is,

---

[73] Martensen, *Die christliche Taufe und die baptische Frage*, 60–62. Of course Martensen is right, but he might have been on safer ground had he said that the majority of Christendom does not administer Communion to children. Eastern Orthodoxy, constituting about one quarter of all Christians, does.

[74] The Word *entfalten* is related to the Word *Keim.* As a seed develops into a flower, so the gift of Baptism develops into faith. In this analogy the spoken Word is compared to rain, which causes the seed given in Baptism to develop and bring forth the fruit of faith. Stosch writes: "Das Wort hat schlummernde Keime und schlummernde Errinerungen geweckt. Wie licht ist oft das Sterben von Kindern, die in ihrer Taufgnade heimgehen. Gesetz und Evangelium ist als Geistessaat in das Herz und Gewissen der Getauften gesät. Die Saat keimt und bringt Frucht durch das Wort Gottes." *Zeitgedanken über die Taufe*, 76. Similarly Hory: "Dem Wort fällt die Aufgabe zu, dem aus den Hüllen der geistigen Natur die geistige Persönlichkeit zu entwickeln, diese Aufgabe, die ihm auf andern Gebieten des Lebens zukommt." *Die Taufe als Kindertaufe auf Grund heiliger Schrift*, 122. This process of the seed unfolding or developing given in Baptism was not only accomplished by the spoken Word but by the Lord's Supper as well. See A[ugust] F[riedrich] C[hristian] Vilmar (1800–1868), *Dogmatik*, ed. K. W. Piderit (Gütersloh: C. Bertelsmann, 1874), 257. Albrecht Peters describes the relationship of Baptism to the Lord's Supper as it was taught by the naturalistic theologians. "Ganz analog wird auch bei uns unterschieden zwischen dem äußeren sichtbaren Leib, der das Brot und den Wein empfängt; er ist dem 'natürlichen' Lebensproceß unterworfen, er ist der fortwährenden Selbstsauflösung, dem Tode preisgegeben, und dem 'inneren Leibeskeim,' der durch die Taufe in uns hineingepflanzt, durch Christi Leib und Blut zur Auferstehung und zum neuen Leben ernährt wird." *Realpräsenz: Luthers Zeugnis von Christi Gegenwart im Abendmahl* (Berlin: Lutherisches Verlagshaus, 1960), 13. Peters gives here a brief description of the naturalistic working of the Lord's Supper taught by the nineteenth century Lutheran theologians (12–14).

from one's experience of things. At each step of its development, historical faith must have the possibility of becoming real faith. Historical faith is a normal step in eventually obtaining real faith. As long as historical faith is in the process of developing, it does not damn because it is on the way to perfection. Only when historical faith is allowed to remain incomplete can it be detrimental. It is necessary that actual saving faith be potentially present in historical faith as it develops.

Faith in its final form, the faith which develops from what was given in Baptism and through the process of historical faith, is defined as comforting trust, the heart's laying hold of redemption and a spiritual hungering and thirsting after the righteousness that finds satisfaction in Christ alone.[75] This faith infants cannot have, since it is based on one's ability to experience phenomena. Of this, children are incapable. Martensen's position is characteristic of nineteenth-century Lutheran theology in general, in that true faith requires reason and consciousness upon which the preached Word works—a view carried over from the Rationalists and Schleiermacher.

Martensen's concept of infant Baptism is reflected in his attitude to the baptismal liturgy. He cannot account for the presence of questions in the baptismal rite, since they indicate that the child has a freedom of choice in answering "yes" or "no" to them, a position he does not allow. According to both reason and the Scriptures, the child has no such freedom of choice. If retention of the questions and answers becomes an issue, it would be better to delay the Baptism until such a time as when a child really has freedom of choice. Should there be any impression that the questions in the baptismal rite indicate that the child does have a freedom of choice in answering them, then infants must no longer be baptized. To avoid the impression that children really have faith, Martensen suggests that the questions should be addressed to the sponsors or that they should be put in a declarative form. In a liturgy in which questions are addressed to the sponsors or replaced with declarative sentences, the child does not thereby become a disinterested object, because he is a receiving individual and has the possibility of developing his own personality.[76] By removing the questions from the rite of Baptism, Martensen reflects his belief that infants do not really have faith but are passive recipients of Christ as the essence of faith and the Spirit

[75] Martensen, *Die christliche Taufe und die baptische Frage*, 67–69.

[76] Martensen, *Die christliche Taufe und die baptische Frage*, 73.

who creates faith. The concept that the child is active in making a choice in Baptism is condemned as Docetic. In the Ancient Church, the term refers to the christological heresy that Christ appeared to be human but was not. Martensen uses it of those who claim that children believe in Baptism, when in fact they do not. That the children do believe was Luther's view, but Martensen makes no mention of him.

Baptismal sponsors function in desiring for the child what a child desires for himself, of which he is at the time unaware. This desire resides in the natural relationship every human has to Christ. A child is born into the world in order to give witness to Christ and so from his inmost nature desires to develop that faith that the Church confesses. Since the child is born already with the desire to confess the Christian faith, the sponsors express that which the child himself desires.[77] A child's desire to confess the Christian faith was introduced by Martensen in his discussion of a child's nature that is an innate, inward drive towards the kingdom of God. This drive is the child's desire to confess the Christian faith. Sponsors express for the child this drive towards the kingdom of God and to confess the Christian faith.

When the faith whose foundations were established in infant Baptism reaches the point of being conscious of itself, then confirmation can serve as a personal ratification of the confession of faith. It also entitles the baptized to participate in the Lord's Supper.[78] With or without confirmation, infant Baptism's validity is unaffected. Baptism of an infant is proper and complete in itself.[79] While apart from confirmation such a Baptism is complete in itself, the act of salvation without the development of faith is incomplete. Salvation consists of both Baptism and the preaching of the Word.

CONCLUSION

With Martensen, as with Höfling, both Baptism and the preached Word are necessary for complete salvation, but with Martensen, the preached Word had a subsidiary function in its relationship to Baptism. It develops what is given in Baptism, which has the more significant role in giving Christ and the Holy Spirit and placing the

---

[77] Martensen, *Die christliche Taufe und die baptische Frage*, 73–74.
[78] Martensen, *Die christliche Taufe und die baptische Frage*, 74.
[79] Martensen, *Die christliche Taufe und die baptische Frage*, 75.

baptized into direct organic connection with God. This the preached Word does not do for either the baptized or unbaptized child or adult. For the baptized person, the Word creates faith, which includes making him aware of the possessions he already has. Baptism gives Christ and the Spirit as the essence of faith, and the Word creates faith whereby the baptized becomes aware of what he already possesses. Within this scheme, Martensen finds a place for infant Baptism, which he supports from Matthew 28:19–20 where baptizing comes before teaching.

Martensen's anthropology, like Höfling's, divides the person into the natural and the rational parts, which parallel Baptism and the preached Word. Just as nature is more fundamental to personhood than is reason, so Baptism is more fundamental to salvation than is cognitive faith. Even if the lack of reason makes faith impossible for the child, his nature is capable of receiving the grace of Baptism. In adults, reason becomes dominant over their nature and the preached Word functions in breaking through the reason or the rational part to allow the natural part to come to the surface. Released from reason, the natural part of a person no longer resists grace and now desires and longs for the kingdom of God and for Christ. This Baptism works on the person's nature.

Neo-Platonism sees the life of the soul as superior to that of the body. Martensen's anthropology, which he adopts from Romanticism, a matter discussed below, reverses this so that the body possesses a value superior to that of the soul or the reason. Preaching gives information about salvation to reason, which remains lost until delivered through Baptism. Baptized children possess Christ as the object of faith and the Holy Spirit, who works apart from faith, which can only be worked by the Word. Direct union between God and the baptized without the Word and faith can be seen as a type of mysticism.[80] Martensen makes a unique contribution among the

[80] Those who taught a naturalistic working of Baptism seemed to be aware that their views were considered by some to be magical. In the second edition of his *Die christliche Taufe und die baptische Frage*, Martensen goes to great lengths to refute this by arguing that this would entail a child receiving something of which his nature would be incapable. A magical concept would also affirm that Baptism without the other means of grace could work salvation (Zweite Auflage; Gotha: Andreas Perthes, 1860), vi-vii. Georg Stosch also claims that the naturalistic working of Baptism is not magical. *Zeitgedanken über die Taufe*, 91–92. Determining whether anything can be judged as magical depends on how this word is understood. An atheist might brand everything religious as magical. Protestants might see Catholic rites as magical, as

Erlangen theologians in describing how faith develops from what the Spirit gives in Baptism. Between the Spirit as the cause of faith given in Baptism and real faith worked by the Word is historical faith, which is created by an individual experiencing the evidences, the phenomena. Even though a faith based on the phenomena, that is, historical faith, does not know and trust Christ, it does not merit condemnation as long as it is in the process of growing towards the real faith worked by the preached Word.

As mentioned, Martensen remains under the influence of the Rationalists and Schleiermacher in seeing faith as developed reason or consciousness encountering the preached Word. He advances beyond them in returning to the Lutheran distinction between Word and Sacrament and avoids the Reformed view, also popular among Lutherans, that both have the same working. Martensen deviates from the Lutheran view by attributing the bestowal of Christ and the Spirit to Baptism and not to the Word, which only informs about what Baptism gives but does not deliver it. Preaching brings the gifts of Baptism to completion.

In faith, knowledge precedes trust, but this is a logical sequence and not a chronological one that allows a prolonged period for faith to remain as historical knowledge before trust in Christ arises. Martensen's scheme finds that faith as historical knowledge is acceptable as long as there is progress to a complete faith. (It seems as if historical faith, that is, knowledge about Christ without trusting in Him, was that kind of faith for which Jesus condemned His opponents.) A major item in Martensen's theology is that children who are incapable of real faith can nevertheless possess Christ and the Spirit. They do not possess reason, which is necessary to hear the preached Word and come to real faith. From this, it would seem that at the moment they attain reason they would be capable of complete faith and responsible for not having it. This is certainly the case with unbaptized adults who have historical faith but do not trust in Christ. Children given Christ and the Spirit in Baptism would have the greater responsibility of coming to faith as soon as reason begins to function, or so it would seem. Historical faith is cognitive acceptance of Christian truths but without seeing them as significant for one's

---

the Reformed do Lutheran rites. One definition of magical might be the bestowal of Christ, the Holy Spirit, and salvation's benefits without faith worked by the Word. Under the terms of this definition the naturalistic view of Baptism might be called magical, though the term might better be left unused.

salvation. Many people might be brought to true faith and salvation after a period of having only historical faith, but can this concept be introduced into the process of baptized infants coming to faith later in life?

Martensen develops his theology of Baptism with traditional Lutheran terms and concepts, but he incorporates other streams of thought into his beliefs. He remains indebted to the Idealism of Rationalism in seeing faith as an act of the mature reason. Martensen also embodies Schleiermacher's view of faith as the experience of individual consciousness without external phenomena within the Christian community. His concept of Baptism working on a person's inner being, his natural part, can be described as the theosophic or mystical concept, but faith can only arise when certain outward phenomena are brought into contact with the conscious or rational part of the person.

GOTTFRIED THOMASIUS

Gottfried Thomasius (1802–1872) was a professor of the University of Erlangen from 1842 until his death. He had been a student of Schleiermacher whose views on the Christian consciousness shaped his views on Baptism, but like other members of the Erlangen school, he was part of the Lutheran revival. His views on infant Baptism can be found in his dogmatical work, *Christi Person und Werk*, and resembled those of other members of the Erlangen school in that Baptism and the preached Word both worked in acquiring salvation, but each worked differently. Baptism was directed to the individual apart from that person's level of development and competence. Its mere application places the baptized into the fellowship of salvation. On the other hand, the efficacy of the preached Word depends on the level of one's psychological maturity. For conversion one must be conscious of oneself, a view corresponding to Schleiermacher's *Selbstbewußtsein*, self-consciousness. Baptism works on that part of a person that is able to receive material, physical (*natürlichen*) means of grace. The natural side of man makes one a member of the human race, and to this physical part, Baptism is directed. This natural or physical side of person's being is a mysterious realm lying beneath the consciousness. In this mysterious realm, the psychical and physical (*geistleiblichen*) forces of life originate. This part of human existence God has reserved for His own work. Here lies the conscience, the mysterious life that becomes the life with which God deals. The will resides in that conscious part of a human being and rests upon the foundation of this mysterious realm that exists within the natural part of man. Into one's hidden and mysterious realm, the Spirit of Christ sinks Himself through Baptism as the effective cause of the new spiritual life. This spiritual life planted by Baptism in man's hidden being has within itself the potential gradually to overcome the old self and cause the new one to come forth.[81] Baptism as the planting into Christ gives the baptized a new incarnate, *gottmenschliche*, life. The Spirit of the incarnate God dwells and works in the baptized person. Since Baptism is the means through which the Spirit lives in the baptized, it is the Sacrament of regeneration, but it neither creates a new consciousness nor changes the direction of the will.[82] Regeneration of a person's conscious and willing self is accomplished through the Word, which is directed to the person who is already conscious of himself. Baptism works regeneration in the natural or material side of a person whose consciousness and will remain unaffected by Baptism.[83] By Baptism, the Spirit lives in the physical part of a person and not in the will or consciousness. As with Höfling, Thomasius offers a bifurcated concept of regeneration that is initiated by Baptism in one's natural part and then completed in the will and consciousness through the Word.

Baptism creates a new life in the individual, but until faith is created by preaching there is no personal appropriation of salvation.[84] A new man is created and a new life begins in Baptism, but without faith created by the preached Word, the gifts found in Baptism are not appropriated. Only the preached Word can create faith and make what is offered in Baptism a personal and lasting possession for salvation. Baptism makes the offer of the forgiveness of sins and implants the seed of divine life, but only in faith do these effect justification in the individual's consciousness. The individual is placed by Baptism into the saving relationship with Christ, but he only appropriates Baptism's gifts through faith created by the Word. Faith makes the

---

[81] Thomasius, *Christi Person und Werk*, 3/2:5–6.

[82] Thomasius has given a definition of regeneration that does not include faith and thus he can ascribe regeneration to children, even though they are still incapable of believing. Alexander von Oettingen also claimed that children were really and effectively regenerated in baptism. However, he quite explicitly states that they are neither repentant nor converted. *Lutherische Dogmatik*, 2:417–8.

[83] Thomasius, *Christi Person und Werk*, 3/2:5–6.

[84] Thomasius, *Christi Person und Werk*, 3/2:5–6.

gifts of Baptism personal and fulfills the obligations of the covenant imposed by Baptism. Thus, faith becomes the condition for the efficacy of Baptism.[85]

INFANT BAPTISM

For infant Baptism, Thomasius does not offer extensive biblical arguments, but he nevertheless finds it in keeping with the intentions of Scripture. He acknowledges that God gave no express command for infant Baptism, and he finds no indisputable biblical example of the apostles baptizing children. Passages in Acts mentioning the baptizing of entire families say as much for infant Baptism as they do against it. It might be that only the head of the household believed and made his home a place where Christian fellowship could be cultivated, but within these passages lays the unmistakable intention that as soon as the Church attained a firm foothold in this world Baptism should become infant Baptism. Thomasius finds support for infant Baptism in Mark 10:13–16 and Matthew 19:13–15, where Jesus promises the kingdom of heaven to children. Not only does the Lord promise the kingdom to children, but He instructs the Church to receive them. Since Baptism is the means ordained by Christ for entering into the Kingdom, children should be baptized.[86] Thomasius finds a reason for infant Baptism in the children's need of this Sacrament and their ability to receive it, an argument put forth by Höfling and Martensen. The child's need of Baptism and his capability to receive it give the Church both the right and the duty to baptize infants. Their need for Baptism comes from their natural sinfulness, which has placed them under the common guilt of humanity and the wrath of God. This need approximates original sin, but Thomasius does not use the term here. The children's capability to receive Baptism is based on the objective power of Baptism and on the way in which Baptism works. This objective working of Baptism is the giving of the Spirit to the natural part of man apart from his will or consciousness. Since the child is part of the human race, he also can become an object of the Spirit's action and so in his nature he can be regenerated. Baptism as the Sacrament of initiation requires no other condition for its being received than the common ability of all men to be saved, and so a child can be baptized. This common ability is inherent in one's natural side. As part of the human race, the child

[85] Thomasius, *Christi Person und Werk*, 3/2:8–9.
[86] Thomasius, *Christi Person und Werk*, 3/2:149.

also has this ability. Since in the child the personal will has not awakened, this ability has a purely passive character (*capacitas passiva*).[87]

Through Baptism, the Spirit works in the child even though faith is not created by this activity. Baptism neither works nor is able to work a conscious attitude in the child. Faith is not worked by Baptism, but through it the Spirit of Christ mysteriously sways in those depths of the child where his natural life and personal life are connected in a direct unity. In Baptism, God grips the core of life that is characteristic of His creatures and changes the direction of this life. A child's inner self is unlocked by the Spirit but not in the sense that the child really believes. Baptism opens the inner condition of the child's human spirit for the work of divine grace. This condition is analogous to the child's life being opened to his mother's love. A child's receptivity for his mother's love exists long before he becomes aware of it.[88] In Baptism, the Spirit actually gives the child a divine substance that is God Himself, but this is not faith.

Part of Thomasius's doctrine of infant Baptism is how he understands faith and the reasons why children cannot have it. The Scriptures define faith as a conscious attitude of the mind, and at its heart, faith is personal trust that presupposes contrition. Since children are neither conscious nor capable of trust or contrition, they cannot have faith, which is always caused by the preached Word. Only through hearing is the Word transmitted to the mind. Thomasius finds support for this in Romans 10:17: "Faith comes by hearing and hearing by the Word of God." Such hearing is understood as a conscious reception of the Word of God. Hence children who are said to be incapable of consciously hearing the Word of God in their Baptism do not receive faith. What the Holy Spirit works in the nature of the child may not be called faith.[89]

---

[87] Thomasius, *Christi Person und Werk,* 3/2:143. What Thomasius calls the *capacitas passiva* corresponds to Frank's *aptitudo passiva* and to what Martensen called *obicem non ponere*. This passive quality exists in man's natural side, which in children exists to the exclusion of the rational part, which first develops with the process of reason.

[88] Thomasius, *Christi Person und Werk,* 3/2:144–45.

[89] Thomasius, *Christi Person und Werk,* 3/2:155. Vilmar, who like Thomasius teaches that Baptism works in the mysterious parts of the hidden life of the child, asserts that children can have faith. He makes the bold statement "so müssen wir eine *fides infantium* behaupten," even though his views on infant Baptism resemble those of Thomasius that infants do not have faith as adults do. Such a situation is indicative of the confusion that can arise in this matter. Even though both men agreed on the

CONVERSION AND THE BAPTIZED PERSON

Before a person can have faith, he must know his total sinfulness and have a sincere desire to be saved. Both the knowledge of sinfulness and the desire to be saved rest upon the recognition of the essence of sin. Without this, faith cannot come into existence. Only in bitter experience can a person separate himself from sin and turn to the grace of God. This personal putting away of the old natural direction of the mind is known as repentance. The positive side of repentance is personally laying hold of salvation. Together repentance and faith comprise conversion. To receive Baptism, one must first undergo this conversion, but for the baptized child, this process of coming to faith lies in the future. Through conversion, the person who has previously received Baptism as a child separates himself from sin and makes the gifts given in Baptism a personal possession. Even though Baptism has placed the person into the grace-filled covenant of reconciliation and has put him under the working of the Holy Spirit, the baptized person is still afflicted with the sinfulness of his nature. This sinfulness infects his entire being and makes him damnable before God.[90] The baptized person must through repentance separate himself from his sinful nature and through faith personally lay hold of Christ.

When a person with the grace given in Baptism does not come to faith, a contradiction is created between what he received in Baptism and what he should become in faith, between what God has given him in Baptism and his lack of faith. If this contradiction is not removed, the blessing of Baptism is taken away. Grace received in Baptism becomes the permanent possession of salvation only when the baptized person affirms this grace, keeps it, and lets it become effective in himself. This can only happen at the age when he is able to make his own decision.[91] Thomasius can speak of contradiction because the Spirit's work in a person's nature does not correspond to the lack of faith in his conscious, rational personality. An unbelieving person baptized as a child is regenerate according to his nature but unregenerate according to his personality. At least for a time, he is simultaneously regenerate and unregenerate. A Baptism administered during infancy affects the child as he approaches maturity in making

---

efficacy of Baptism on children, the one denied infant faith and the other affirmed it. Thomasius considers faith to be a trust in Christ. Vilmar does not. Vilmar, *Dogmatik*, 243–44.

[90] Thomasius, *Christi Person und Werk*, 3/2:145–46.

[91] Thomasius, *Christi Person und Werk*, 3/2:146.

him a better object for the working of the preached Word. When the Word encounters an individual baptized person as an infant, it finds a person who is not completely dead to spiritual things. Rather, the Word meets an individual who is already regenerate and in whose most inward parts the Spirit of Christ is dwelling. This point of contact exists in baptized persons but not in unbaptized ones.[92] The baptized person has already encountered salvation. Thus, to a baptized person the preached Word does not bring salvation for the first time, but rather the preached Word confirms an already present salvation. It takes the power that was given by God through Baptism from the nature of the child into his will. Characteristic of the Erlangen theology is that the preached Word has a function subsidiary to Baptism. What the Word is to the child's will, Baptism is to his

---

[92] Thomasius, *Christi Person und Werk*, 3/2:146. Stosch describes how the baptized child responds to the spoken Word of God. "Ein getauftes Kind beginnt, dem Worte Glauben zu schenken, durch ein inwendiges Licht erleuchtet. Der Anfang und die zweifelfreie Art seines Glaubens weist zurück auf einen früheren, durch Gottes verborgene Wirkung geschaffenen Anfang des Glaubens. Der Herr, an den sie glauben, ist ihnen nicht erst durch das Wort bekannt geworden. Das Wort hat schlummernde Keime und schlummernde Erinnerungen geweckt." *Zeitgedanken über der Taufe*, 76.

A relationship between God and the child exists through Baptism apart from faith and the Word. The Word comes first in its spoken form. Stosch also maintains that conversions are deeper in the baptized than in the unbaptized. "Erweckungen und Bekehrungen werden tiefer und wahrer, sie werden dem Evangelium gemäßer sein, wenn sie auf dem Grunde der Taufe geschehen, als wenn sie nur den luftigeren Grund bloßer Eindrücke unter sich haben." Thomasius, *Christi Person und Werk* 3/2:80.

It might be true that the reinstatement into Church membership of those who were baptized as children is easier than converting those who have never been baptized. However, Stosch's opinion falters, because for him children are not really converted in Baptism. If children are converted in their Baptism, then they can be returned to this faith.

Ernst Hory speaks of Christianizing the people through Baptism. "Die Taufe, und zwar als Kindertaufe, ist es in erster Linie, die das Völkerleben zu einem Boden der göttlichen Gnade weiht; die diesen Boden noch ganz unabhängig von der Entscheidung des Einzelnen das an sich wendende Wort mit den Säften und Kräften dieser Gnade tränkt; sie in erster Linie schafft sozusagen eine christliche Atmosphäre, die auch der persönlich noch nicht für das Christentum Entschiedene noch mitgenießen darf. So gewinnt das μαθητεύσατε πάντα τὰ ἔθνη eine ungemein weitreichende Bedeutung. Das Völkerleben wird hiesdurch zunächst christianisirt und mit Thau der in Christo erschienenen göttlichen Gnade befruchtet." *Die Taufe als Kindertaufe,* 130. Baptism might create a Christian atmosphere, but never apart from faith.

nature. The Word activates the salvation delivered by Baptism but in itself does not bring salvation.[93]

CONCLUSION

As Höfling spoke of two aspects of regeneration, Thomasius speaks of two regenerations, one effected by Baptism on man's natural part and the other by the preached Word on the consciousness. This bifurcation provides Thomasius a basis for infant Baptism. Following the logic of his own argument, one person can be both regenerate and unregenerate at the same time.[94] If it is agreed that only those who are regenerate in their life are saved, then the question arises at what time in a child's life the regeneration given in Baptism is inadequate for assuring salvation in the next life. Though their positions that the Spirit works mysteriously in the inner parts of a child are virtually indistinguishable from each other, Thomasius does not call this process faith as do Höfling and Vilmar. Martensen comes close to saying that a child has faith in saying that in Baptism a child receives the essence of faith, but the essence of faith is not faith. Thomasius makes it quite clear that what the Spirit does in Baptism is not faith, which is always man's action and not God's.

In comparison with the other Erlangen theologians Thomasius provides a descriptive theology of the naturalistic operation of Baptism on the child's nature. Like them he gives faith a subsidiary role, since the real gifts of salvation are given not through it but through the theosophic action of Baptism directly on the person apart from faith. The Word informs faith of what Baptism gives. Thomasius remains within the Reformation Lutheran understanding of faith as personally laying hold of Christ, but faith is an action subsequent to the reception of salvation for baptized infants and antecedent to the reception of salvation for baptized adults. Faith is

---

[93] Thomasius, *Christi Person und Werk*, 3/2:147.

[94] Chemnitz's critique of the Roman Catholic position is applicable here: "Some simply argue that all these and similar statements of Scripture pertain only to adults, not, however, to infants, whom they hold to be saved by the grace of God but without faith; nevertheless they do not want baptized infants to be numbered among the unbelievers. Therefore they are obliged to invent, without the authority of Scripture, a certain middle state between faith and unbelief, between believers and unbelievers. I cannot agree with this opinion, for the statements of Scripture are general. However, faith and unebelief, believers and unbelievers, are contradictory terms." *Examination of the Council of Trent*, trans. Fred Kramer, 4 vols. (St. Louis: Concordia, 1974–1981), 2:170.

the conscious response of the mind to the Word about salvation which already exists in the nature of the child through Baptism. Salvation is given directly to the nature of the child through Baptism quite apart from faith. Thomasius, like Höfling and Martensen, maintains the Idealism of the Rationalists in seeing faith as a response of the mature reason to the Word. Also incorporated into their views is Schleiermacher's understanding of a mature human being whose self-consciousness is a prerequisite for faith.

CHAPTER IV

ERLANGEN THEOLOGIANS (PART 2)

Belonging to the Erlangen School with Höfling, Martensen, and Thomasius were four others who also held to the naturalistic view that Baptism had a direct effect on man's physical life. Each developed a particular aspect of this view. Carl Adolf Gerhard von Zezschwitz gave a fuller explanation of the anthropology involved in the naturalist view. Ernst Hory related Baptism's naturalistic effect with the kenosis Christology that Thomasius had developed. Rudolph Rocholl referenced the philosophers whose views influenced the Erlangen School's anthropology that divided the human being into natural and rational parts. Franz Delitzsch's concept of Baptism was close to the Roman Catholic view.

CARL ADOLF GERHARD VON ZEZSCHWITZ

Zezschwitz held that a complete salvation depended on Baptism and the preached Word. Baptism was directed to a man's unconscious self and the preached Word to the conscious self. Each human being consisted of two parts, the spiritual natural part or self, *geistiger Naturgrund*, and the conscious part or self, the "I," *ich*. Together they comprise the individual, and one cannot be identified with the other, but the "I or conscious part is dependent on and governed by the natural or unconscious part. The "I" is positioned as a satellite over against the natural part of man. Tension between the two parts is most clearly seen in the area of religion. A man's mind, his "I," works arbitrarily and is independent from his natural self. Conscience belongs to the natural part of man, his *geistiger Naturgrund*, a permanent vestige of its original relationship to God within a person. The natural side of the spiritual life, the *kardia*, receives psychological impressions.[1] To each part of a person the Word comes in different forms. To the conscious or rational part, the "I," the Word comes as a Word of revelation whose effectiveness depends on its being received by a rational individual as an object. One's reason, the "I forms an "I-You" relationship with the Word of revelation. At work in Baptism is the Word of action, the creating Word, the Word of the Creator, through which the Holy Spirit addresses the unconscious life of the spirit of man, *unbewußtes Geistesleben*, one's natural or physical self. One's reason responds to the Word of revelation and the unconscious part receives the creating Word, and each form of the Word functions differently.[2] Through Baptism, the Spirit of God touches man's spiritual life, which is contained within his nature and establishes a relationship between one's nature and God. Thus Baptism is effective on the natural part of man, which contains his spiritual life. The preached Word is directed to a person's conscious self and appeals to one's freedom. While Baptism creates a new relationship, *Verhältniß,* the Word creates a new attitude, *Verhalten*, in the person. Each form of the Word performs a distinct function.[3] What is worked in the unconscious part of the individual Zezschwitz calls faith, which is defined as one's nature instinctively grasping what the Holy Spirit works in Baptism.[4] A conscious appropriation of justification is accidental to his understanding of what faith is.

In Zezschwitz's anthropology, one's unconscious part lies side by side with one's rational and conscious part, but the unconscious part is the superior of the two, since it has a closer relationship to God by its being the vestige of the original creation. The unconscious life has the spiritual or supernatural qualities and is referred to as the spiritual basis of nature, the human spirit and the spirit of life, *geistiger Naturgrund*, *Menschengeist*, and *Geistleben*. The rational or conscious part is called the *bewußtes Ichleben* and acts arbitrarily and independently from the physical, natural life. Zezschwitz uses the term *Geist* in a Neo-Platonic way, since spiritual means that which is closest to God.

---

[1] Carl Adolf Gerhard von Zezschwitz, *System der christlichen kirchlichen Katechetik*, 2 vols. (Leipzig: J. D. Hinrichs, 1863), 1:250.
[2] Zezschwitz, *System,* 251.
[3] Zezschwitz, *System,* 254.
[4] Zezschwitz, *System,* 255.

ERNST HORY

In 1872, Ernst Hory wrote a monograph on infant Baptism entitled *Die Taufe als Kindertaufe auf Grund heiliger Schrift,* with views in line with those who held that Baptism was effective on an infant's natural or physical life. Martensen saw a connection between infant Baptism and the incarnation, a theme that Hory developed in more detail. Basic to this understanding is that the fellowship God has with Christ is reflected in the fellowship Christ has with man. Christ stands between God and man, and His relationship to believers is fashioned after His relationship to the Father. Each is called a natural fellowship or communion in nature. The *Naturgemeinschaft* between Christ and the individual does not involve that person's conscious personality. A conscious fellowship with Christ will develop later out of the natural fellowship.[5] Christ's relationship with the Father sets the standard for the relationship between God and man. The incarnation of Christ is analogous to the union of body and soul in a man. The soul exists before it gives active evidence of its existence. This is similar to the union of the divine and human in Christ. Before Christ was conscious of His union with God, He already possessed it. It is no more foolish to say that a person can have fellowship with God and still not be conscious of it than to say that a person can have a soul and not be conscious of it. Just as it is possible for one to be alive physically and not be aware of it, so one can be a child of God and not be aware of it.[6]

Essential to his view that one can have an unconscious relationship with Christ is Hory's explanation of Christ's unconscious relationship with the Father. The union between Christ's divine and human natures takes place in that part of the personality that has not yet awakened to consciousness or is just beginning to awaken to it. Christ was conscious of His deity only to the extent to which His personality awakened to consciousness, that is, to the degree that it developed out of the natural part of His existence into the ethical one.[7] Christ's developing consciousness of His relationship with the Father corresponds to a child's developing conscious of God. Just as God was in communion with Christ when His personality was

---

[5] Hory, *Die Taufe als Kindertaufe auf Grund heiliger Schrift* (Stuttgart: n.p., 1872), 104.

[6] Hory, *Die Taufe als Kindertau*fe, 110.

[7] Hory, *Die Taufe als Kindertaufe,* 114–15.

unconscious and awakening to consciousness, so God has fellowship with human beings during their development from unconsciousness to consciousness. Baptized infants can receive the Holy Spirit, who then dwells in them without their being aware of it. In infant Baptism a mysterious incarnation of Christ takes place that is based on the historical incarnation. The *kenosis* of the mysterious indwelling of Christ in the heart of the child conforms to the historical *kenosis* of Christ.[8]

The natural relationship the child has with God through Baptism is without faith. A child cannot have the personal relationship with God that is worked by the preached Word, but he does have a relationship to the personal Word, who is Christ, and His kingdom. The absence of faith in the child does not prevent Baptism from working. Where faith is not present, Baptism condescends and works at that level where there is receptivity for it. Baptism is described as a canal through which the kingdom of God flows into the child's natural side, in which the personality remains hidden. God's grace subjects itself to the laws and rules of the organism in which it is working and limits itself to each stage of a child's development. God's condescending grace in children resembles the condescending personal grace of God, Jesus Christ; in the incarnation.[9] Underlying Hory's discussion of what infant Baptism effects in the child is the presupposition that Christ's relation to God is the norm for Christ's relationship with men. This means that the lesser mystery of how God works in Baptism depends upon and is explained by the greater mystery of the incarnation. In systematic theology, a correlation exists between all the topics, including Baptism and the incarnation, but whether the greater mystery of the incarnation provides a definition for the latter mystery of Baptism is another matter. Hory's anthropology plays a key role in his Christology and also in his theology of Baptism. Christ's relationship with the Father is described as a *Naturgemeinschaft* out of which His personal relationship to the Father grows. According to this particular anthropology, nature is the basic part of the human being, from which the conscious "I" emerges.

---

[8] Hory, *Die Taufe als Kindertaufe,* 116–17. *Kenosis* was a theory set forth by the Erlangen theologians that in the incarnation Christ retained those attributes by which he was related to God, the *opera Trinitatis ad interna*, but surrendered those attributes which related to the created world, e.g., omniscience, omnipotence, omnipresence, the *opera Trinitatis ad externa.* See Pieper *Christian Dogmatics*, 3 vols. (St. Louis: Concordia, 1917–1924), 2: 105–108.

[9] Hory, *Die Taufe als Kindertaufe*, 119–20.

Hory's position is open to challenge, not because he sees a correlation between Baptism and the incarnation, but because it is based on an anthropology that may be more of a philosophical construct than a biblical one. Different views of anthropology and the incarnation would render different understanding of the effects of Baptism in infants. Thus a Christology in which Jesus is ascribed all the attributes of God would be the basis for concluding that a baptized child knows and trusts in Christ. Using the historical Jesus model, one could draw no conclusions as to what Baptism works in a child.

RUDOLPH ROCHOLL

Also belonging to those theologians who taught a so-called naturalistic operation of Baptism on the nature of the child was Rudolph Rocholl. His contribution to the discussion was a four-page article in *Neue Kirchliche Zeitschrift* in 1902, entitled "*Vom Kinderglauben*." Though not extensive, it provides the philosophical arguments for the anthropology that divided the human being into unconscious or natural and conscious or rational parts. This concept was basic for understanding that Baptism had a naturalistic effect on the nature of the child and that the preached Word worked on the reason of the more mature person. Rocholl also named the philosophers responsible for this anthropology. He purposes in "*Vom Kinderglauben*" to show that infant faith is tenable if it can be established that there exists within the human being an unconscious part where this faith can exist. He maintains that the inner spiritual man is not located in the powers of reasoning and reflection but rather in the nature of man. In support of this, he mentions the philosophers Descartes, Schelling, and Fichte. Descartes asserted that the child was already conscious in his mother's womb. This Rocholl interprets to mean the unborn child already had a personality but without the powers of reflection. Indeed, it may never awaken to consciousness. An awakened consciousness is only half of the entire personality. Schelling, the philosopher of Romanticism, is also called upon to support the dichotomy of a man into conscious and unconscious parts. Often the holiest part of a man, the unconscious part of human life, was in Schelling's view too often destroyed through the powers of reflection. One's identity is located in one's unconsciousness, that is, the depths of one's personality.[10] A sound psychology requires consideration of both the conscious and the unconscious parts of the individual. Without the unconscious part, the conscious part would disintegrate into a multitude of bodily functions. Acts of the mind would be nothing more than acts of the body.[11] Rocholl says that the concept of an unconscious region existing beneath the conscious one removes any difficulty in holding to infants' faith, defined as the indwelling of Christ in the nature or the unconscious part of the child.[12] Höfling had already defined faith in this way. Rocholl did not advance the argument beyond that of the other Erlangen theologians, but he did identify the philosophers whose ideas were incorporated in it.

FRANZ DELITZSCH

The notable Old Testament scholar Franz Delitzsch followed Höfling, Martensen, and Thomasius in holding that Baptism gave the actual gift of grace to the person receiving this Sacrament and that the preached Word had a declaratory function in presenting a gracious God. While the preached Word was only for those of mature reason, Baptism worked on all those who received it regardless of their mental development. Baptism had objective efficacy in working salvation apart from the attitude of the one who was baptized, whether believer or unbeliever, a view resembling the Catholic doctrine of *ex opere operato*, that the Sacrament was efficacious apart from faith.

---

[10] Rudolph Rocholl, "Vom Kinderglauben," *Neue Kirchliche Zeitschrift* 13 (1902): 672–73. Albrecht Peters mentions other influential philosophers for these ideas. "Diese in sich geschlossene Schau hat kaum noch Luther zum Vater, sie geht über Schelling und Steffens, Oettinger und Bohme auf Parazelsus." Albrecht Peters, *Realpräsenz: Luthers Zeugnis von Christi Gegenwart im Abendmahl* (Berlin: Lutherisches Verlagshaus, 1960), 16.

[11] Rocholl, "Vom Kinderglauben," 673.

[12] Rocholl, "Vom Kinderglauben," 674. After leaving the Evangelical Church of Prussia, the union of Lutherans and Reformed, and then the territorial Lutheran Church of Hannover, Rocholl joined the Evangelisch-Lutherische Kirche Altpreussene. Cf. F. Hübner, Rocholl, Rudolf," *Die Religion in Geschichte und Gegenwart*, ed. Kurt Calling, (Dritte, völlig neu bearbeitete Auflage; Tubingen: J. C. B. Mohr, 1959) 1131. Vilmar, who also held to a naturalistic working of Baptism, also became a member of the same Church. Cf. Heinrich Martin, "*Die Selbtständige Ev. Luth. Kirche,*" *Evang.-Lutherische Freikirche in Deutschland*, ed. Ulrich Kuns (Frankfurt am Main: Lutheraner Verlag, 1953), 23.

Delitzsch does not specifically discuss infant Baptism in his *Vier Bücher von der Kirche*, but what he says about Baptism applies to that of infants. In line with the other Erlangen theologians, Delitzsch compares Baptism to the preached Word and finds three differences. First, when Christ is offered in the Word, He must be received by faith, but when He is offered in Baptism, He is received by all those who are baptized. Second is the way in which salvation is offered. When the preached Word offers salvation, it can be refused, but a person who is baptized receives all the gifts of Baptism whether he believes or not. Gifts of Baptism received in unbelief contribute to the recipient's damnation. The third difference has to do with the effects of each on the individual. Where the preached Word has been refused, there is no change in the individual. Salvation proclaimed in the preached Word remains as distant as if he had never heard it and becomes evidence to accuse him. However, with every baptized person God establishes the relationship of the new covenant in which later by faith the baptized person gives heed to the blood of the covenant. Central to all three differences is that Baptism is efficacious apart from faith, while the efficaciousness of the preached Word depends on faith. An *ex opere operato* concept of Baptism for Delitzsch does not mean Baptism works salvation in each application, but it does mean that it leaves an indelible mark on all who are baptized. Irrespective of faith or the lack of it, they receive Christ, are planted into His death, and are caught up in the net of God's love, a condition God has created and no man can change.[13]

Delitzsch's concept of Baptism is related to his definition of the body of Christ, whose members are those who are baptized and participate in the Lord's Supper. The body of Christ can be known quantitatively, since it is the collective number of those who have been baptized into His body and who drink of the same Spirit. Membership in the body of Christ is determined not by faith but by Baptism. A baptized unbeliever is as much a part of the body of Christ as is a baptized believer. To demonstrate the point, Delitzsch says that both Hengstenberg and Wislicenus are members of the body of Christ. To prove his point, Delitzsch has chosen two very impressive examples. Hengstenberg was a leading conservative biblical theologian in nineteenth-century Germany. Wislicenus was an apostatized and unfrocked pastor.

---

[13] Franz Delitzsch, *Vier Bücher von der Kirche* (Dresden: Justus Naumann, 1847), 30–33.

Delitzsch takes the case further. By virtue of their Baptism, Protestants, Roman Catholics, Socinians, and Unitarians are all members of the body of Christ. Thus the body of Christ expands itself through the administration of Baptism. Everyone who has been baptized has been placed into a new relationship with Christ and becomes a possession of Christ. Unless the baptized person commits the unforgivable sin, he remains until he dies under the power of the Holy Spirit, because through Baptism he is made a member of the body of Christ. Since the Holy Spirit is active in the body of Christ, he actively works on every baptized person. The same Spirit nourishes, purifies, and rejuvenates the life of the body of Christ through the means of grace.[14]

For Delitzsch, Baptism has replaced faith as the most consequential element in salvation. Faith no longer determines membership in the body of Christ. Baptism does. Since it makes its recipients members of the body of Christ regardless of their personal disposition, Delitzsch can claim that baptized Socinians and Unitarians are members of Christ's body. Like others who held to a naturalistic efficacy of Baptism, Delitzsch did not distinguish, as had the older Lutheran theologians, between Baptism's inherent efficacy and reception of its benefits by faith. Baptism is continually efficacious in that it continually offers salvation, but apart from faith it does not produce personal salvation in persons.

CONCLUSION

A summary and a critique of infant Baptism as held by the Erlangen theologians revolves around (1) their anthropology, (2) how they understood the relationship of Baptism to the preached or spoken Word, (3) their understanding of grace, and (4) how they redefined infant faith.

ANTHROPOLOGY

The Erlangen theology's understanding of man was taken over from the philosophy of Romanticism. Man's basic nature consisted of matter, from which his individuality as a person would emerge with maturity. As this physical nature developed, it would be able to reflect upon itself, and the mind or reason of an individual would come into existence. Since the natural part existed before and was the source of

---

[14] Delitzsch, *Vier Bücher,* 41.

the mental part or the reason, the natural part was basic to the essence of a man. The mental or spiritual part was not basic, and a human being could exist without it. This was the case with children who lack consciousness and reason. Even though Naturalism speaks of a person having natural and mental parts, man even in his maturity really only has a natural part, since the mental part, also called the consciousness or the spiritual personality, consists of the accumulated conscious experiences of the awakened nature. The consciousness is a product and function of the natural side of a person.

The Erlangen Lutheran theologians incorporated a Romanticist philosophical view of man into their theology in holding that God had preserved the natural side of man for His own particular saving activities. Even after the fall, man's natural side remained closely contected with God. One's mental life or the mind was distant from God and a hindrance to the working of grace. The superiority of the man's physical nature to his mind is reflected in their understanding of regeneration. Through Baptism God could work regeneration in children in whom the reason or their mental capacities remained undeveloped. Adults are disadvantaged in having to push their reason to the side before God could work regeneration through Baptism directly on their physical natures. It follows that for these theologians every Baptism had to be an infant Baptism, that is, a Baptism working directly on the physical nature. Luther saw children as better candidates than adults for Baptism, but not because their minds had not emerged from their physical natures. He did not identify the soul with reason, the activity of the mind that fought against the truth of God's Word. The anthropology of the Erlangen theologians, influenced as it was by the philosophy of Romanticism, has at best only a superficial resemblance to the biblical view of man. Paul, as does Luther, speaks of the struggle between the old man and the new man in Christ, but this struggle takes place in man's spiritual self or his soul. Also, the soul or the spirit determines the good or evil character of a person and not the physical nature. Conversion involves both soul and body, but the soul, and not the physical side, is where faith arises and the individual is regenerated. Here was a dichotomy unknown to the New Testament. While Neo-Platonism's detachment of the soul from the body is evident in Romanticist influenced Erlangen anthropology, it differed from Neo-Platonism in seeing man's physical nature as primary in time and as the basis for the soul.

THE RELATIONSHIP OF BAPTISM TO THE SPOKEN WORD

A second critique is directed at how the Erlangen theologians viewed the relationship of Baptism to the preached or spoken Word. Luther held that Baptism, the Lord's Supper, and the preached Word each had its own *proprium*, its individual and separate character, making one distinct from the other, but all gave the forgiveness of sins. The Erlangen theologians saw forgiveness as the gift of Baptism and not of the preached Word.[15] The preached Word offered salvation to the individual, but did not actually convey it to his person so that he could claim it as his own. Baptism did this by bringing a person into a direct relationship with God and by giving the baptized person Christ and the Spirit. Preaching had a cognitive effect in giving knowledge of salvation but without actually conveying it. Even though Baptism brought Christ to the individual, it could not give the knowledge that was seen as necessary to faith. Baptism worked regeneration, but it was regeneration without faith. With these definitions, the preached Word was no longer a means of grace, since it pointed to the grace in Baptism but did not convey any grace to the hearer. In this scheme, Baptism had a completeness that the preached Word lacked. In the case of children, Baptism was sufficient at least until they became adults. For adults, the spoken Word by itself was insufficient for salvation. Regeneration came only first with Baptism. In this scheme, the preached Word occupied a position lower than Baptism, since it alone was decisive for membership in Christ's body and for possession of the Spirit. Baptism and not faith determined who possessed grace. Baptized children without faith were included in Christ's body, but unbaptized believing adults were not. Delitzsch carried this to a logical extreme by including baptized Socinians and Unitarians in the body of Christ, an astonishing claim since traditional Christian churches rarely recognize Baptisms administered by these groups.[16]

---

[15]The theologians for whom Baptism's efficacy was different from the Word's also taught that the Lord's Supper had different effects. Just as Baptism brought the person's nature into direct contact with God, so the Lord's Supper effected a direct union with God. This was different from Luther's doctrine that the gift or *proprium* of the Sacrament of the Altar was that of the Word also, "der totus vivus Christus in seiner gottmenschlichen Person." Peters, *Realpräsenz,* 134.

[16] In the matter of the Lord's Supper, Peters shows that here also the Erlangen theolgians did not give faith its proper place. Peters explains the difference between Luther and the Erlangen theologians. "Wohl ficht Luther darum, daß der Geist nur in äusseren Mittel wirken will, wohl streitet er wider allen Spiritualismus für den 'Deus

GRACE

A third critique has to do with how the Erlangen theologians understood grace. It was not considered the proclamation of God's gracious attitude to men because of the death of Jesus Christ. They were definite in holding that the proclamation of the Word was powerless in transmitting grace. Grace came in Baptism and was not so much an attitude in God as it was an objective impersonal quantity or substance. The grace of Baptism was the actual impartation of Christ to the nature of man, but this impartation did not require faith or involve in any way one's spirit or his mental attitude. The New Testament knows of certain graces or gifts being given to certain individuals to carry out particular functions in the Church. These graces served to make public God's gracious attitude in Christ, but cannot be confused with God's saving grace, which was not a thing or substance given to a person. By not requiring faith in children receiving Baptism, the Erlangen theologians compromised the Luther's doctrine of *sola fide* for the sake of an extreme monergistic concept of grace.[17] By doing this, they established one way of obtaining salvation for children, who could be saved by Baptism alone without faith, and another for adults for whom Baptism and faith were required.

---

corporeus,' aber von einer besonderen Betonung unserer Leiblichkeit, wie sie mit den Erlangen Theologen auch in die Abendmahlslehre Eingang gefunden hat, ist er weit entfernt. Für ihn ist der totus Christus mit Fleisch und Blut sowohl im Herzen wie im Leibe gegenwärtig. Die Gegenwart des Herrn zum Leibe, das Proprium des Abendmahles, wird nicht der Anlaß, die Leibseite zu betonen." Peters, *Realpräsenz,* 138–39. This critique could also be made against the Erlangen theologians in regard to Baptism. Just because Baptism is an application of physical water to our physical bodies does not necessarily allow any material operation apart from faith.

[17] Peters shows how in the matter of the Lord's Supper, the Erlangen theologians violated the Lutheran principle that salvation is given through the Word to faith. In this critique Peters does not use the word *Glauben* to describe faith, but rather *Herz.* It is wished that Peters would have been more explicit; however, the meaning is obvious. "Aber nun doch nicht so, wie Vilmar und Rocholl es darstellen, daß der Leib dem Leibe, der Geist dem Geiste begegne, vielmehr ist derselbe eine Christus sowohl dem Herzen in Wort als dem Munde in den Elementen gegenwärtig, beide, Herz und Mund, ziehen ihn in sich hinein. Dabei ist die manducatio oralis der manducatio cordalis zugeordnet, nicht umgekert die cordalis der manducatio oralis. Ein Herauslösen der leiblichen Nießung aus dem Gesamtvollzugist unmöglich. Der Leib Christi wirkt wohl unmittelbar auf unseren Leib, aber nur in Zusammenwirken mit der Nießung des Herzens. So gibt es kein Einwirken des Christusleibes auf die unterbewußten Tiefenschichten unserer Existenz ohne die bewußte erfahrene Begegnung der Herzene mit dem totus Christus." Peters, *Realpräsenz,* 194. So, Peters holds that in regard to Baptism it can be said there is no saving activity on the body apart from faith.

INFANT FAITH

A fourth critique has to do with how, like the Rationalists, the Supranaturalists, and Schleiermacher before them and by whom they were influenced, the Erlangen theologians denied the possibility of faith to infants.[18] Some did speak of infant faith, but it was redefined. They held that faith was a trust in God, but it was possible only in persons with the appropriate level of consciousness or reason to understand the spoken Word. Baptism laid the foundation for faith, but it could not create it. Faith was denied infants because they were incapable of this conscious relationship with God, and Baptism was powerless to create it.

With the Rationalists and Schleiermacher, the Erlangen theologians saw faith as a conscious or rational act of man, and with traditional Catholicism grace was given in Baptism and received apart from any response from the baptized. Here synergism and monergism were placed side by side. The Erlangen theologians wanted to see themselves in the Lutheran tradition, but their views were influenced by Rationalism,[19] Schleiermacher, and philosophical Romanticism.[20]

---

[18] Apparently Brinkel speaks of the Erlangen theologians as holding to infant faith. as did the theologians of Lutheran Orthodoxy but immediately adds that this faith was a mystery of nature. He writes: "Nur die sogenannten 'älteren Erlanger' und noch einige andere hielten an der Lehre vom Kinderglauben bei der Kindertaufe fest und lehrten mit der luth. Orthodoxie, daß dieser Glaube im Kind durch das- Mittel der Taufe gewirkt werde. Allerdings verstanden die 'älteren Erlanger' dabei die Taufe meist als ein 'Naturmysterium,' das auf die 'geistleibliche' Natur des Menschen wirke, . . . " Brinkel includes the following among the Erlangen theologians: Höfling, Th. Kliefoth, Heinrich Schmid, Martensen, Zezschwitz, and Vilmar. Karl Brinkel, *Die Lehre Luthers von der fides infantium bei der Kindertaufe* (Berlin: Evangelische Verlagsanstalt, 1958), 105, n. 2.

[19]Brinkel calls the denial of infant faith a result of Idealism and Humanism. He writes thus. "Fragen wir danach, was sich eigentlich in diesen, sich auf das Bewußtsein des Menschen berufenden Einwünden gegen Luthers Lehre von der fides infantium für ein Denken kundtut, so ergibt sich, daß es letztlich nicht in biblischen und reformatorischen Aussagen, sondern in idealistisch-humanistischen Voraussetzungen gründst." Brinkel, *Die Lehre Luthers von der fides infantium*, 95.

[20] Concerning Luther's position on the sacraments in comparison with naturalistic positon as taught by the Erlangen theologians, Peters says: "Es ist da keine 'höhere geist-leibliche Natur,' kein 'himmlischer' Mensch, der, durch das Sakrament gestärkt, der ewigen Vollendung entgegenharrt, wie Parazelsus und Böhme es sehen, auch kein 'wiedergeborener Leibeskeim,' der durch die Taufe in uns hineingesenkt, durch das Sakrament mit Christi himmlischer Leiblichkeit gespeist, das Angeld des Auferstehungsleibes in unserem Leibe der Sünde und des Todes bildet, wie die durch Schelling von Böhme inspirierten lutherischen Theologen des vorigen Jahrhunderts es darstellen." Peters, *Realpräsenz*, 160.

CHAPTER V

INFANT BAPTISM AT THE END OF THE NINETEENTH CENTURY

INTRODUCTION

At the turn of twentieth century, some Lutheran theologians followed Luther in valuing Baptism as a real means of grace. Their theologies nonetheless incorporated principles that had characterized the approach to infant Baptism of the Rationalists and Schleiermacher. Among these was that the New Testament intended Baptism for adults and bore no evidence of infant Baptism. Faith can be produced by the preached Word only and not by Baptism, and, in any event, children are incapable of believing. Their lack of faith makes their Baptisms incomplete. This incompleteness is corrected when a child comes to faith through the preached Word, which may correspond with his confirmation. On these points, they agreed with the Erlangen theologians, but they did not hold to their naturalistic concept that Baptism had a mysterious effect on the inner, unconscious self. Since infants did not have faith, their Baptism signified future salvation. By saying that Baptism had future significance for children, these theologians attempted to give infant Baptism a role in the process of salvation without agreeing to Luther's doctrine of infant faith. The Erlangen theologians did not attribute faith in any conventional sense to infants in Baptism but did use the word, redefining it as God's activity in the child without the child's cognitive participation. Rationalist theologians at the end of the nineteenth century were explicit in their denial of infant faith especially as Luther had developed it.

Chosen to represent this view are Ernst Bunke (1866–1944), Reinhold Seeberg (1858–1935), and Adolf Schlatter (1852–1935). Bunke emphasizes infant Baptism as the personal call of God to the child and as His promise of regeneration. Seeberg explains infant Baptism as a reversal of the New Testament concept that required that faith be present before Baptism was administered. Salvation made objectively available for infants in Baptism may later be appropriated subjectively in faith. Schlatter sees in infant Baptism an excellent expression of the priority of grace over faith. While these theologians wanted to set forth their doctrine of infant Baptism in a Lutheran context, some of their views, especially in regard to faith and its creation, were already set forth by Calvin.

ERNST BUNKE

At the turn of the twentieth century, Ernst Bunke was a Lutheran pastor in Münsterberg, Schlesien. Though Bunke is not widely known today, he was referenced by others for what he had written about infant Baptism. In his *Zur Systematischen Theologie*, Reinhold Seeberg complimented Bunke for having advanced the understanding of infant Baptism. Particularly pleasing to Seeberg was Bunke's denial that infant Baptism could bring about regeneration in the child. Instead of being the Sacrament of regeneration for the child, it was the Sacrament of personal calling for the child.[1] Bunke had first set forth his views in the *Deutsche Evangelische Kirchenzeitung*, edited by Adolf Stöcker. His first in a series of articles appeared under a pseudonym as "Dr. Lepsius contra Professor D. Cremer."[2] In the third article, Bunke confessed to being Dr. Lepsius. During the same years, 1899 and 1900, Bunke contributed other articles to the same periodical. In some way or another they all had to do with infant

[1] "Es heißt jetzt: 'die Kindertaufe ist nicht die Wiedergeburt,' sondern 'das Sakrament der persönlichen Berufung (Bunke, vgl. Kähler, Kirn). Dieser Gedanke bezeichnet fraglos einen erheblichen Fortschritt zur Erkenntnis des Wesens der Kindertaufe." Reinhold Seeberg, *Zur Systematischen Theologie* (Leipzig: A. Deichert, 1909), 257.

[2] *Deutsche Evangelische Kirchenzeitung* 13 (1899): 265–67, 209–10, and 321–23. Hereafter this periodical is cited as *DEKZ*. Cremer dedicated to Lepsius the second edition of *Taufe, Wiedergeburt und Kindertaufe* with the words "meinem lieben Freund und Gegner Herrn Pastor Dr. Lepsius." Hermann Cremer, *Taufe, Wiedergeburt und Kindertaufe* (Zweite, völlig neubearbeitete Auflage; Gütersloh: C. Bertelsmann, 1901), iii.

Baptism, as their titles indicate: "*Taufe und Glaube*,"[3] "*Was ist die Kindertaufe?*"[4] "*Glaube und Kinderglaube*,"[5] and "*Wort und Sakrament*."[6] In 1900, he summed up his views in a book entitled *Der Lehrstreit über die Kindertaufe*,[7] whose forward was contributed by Adolf Stöcker.[8] For Bunke, infant Baptism does not regenerate[9] but is the sacrament of the personal calling into the kingdom of God.[10] With this, Seeberg was in agreement. For Bunke, regeneration is present only where there is faith, which can only be present in conscious individuals. This excludes children. Hence it is impossible that children can be regenerated in Baptism, but they can be called to regeneration. Bunke's polemical interest in infant Baptism is obvious in the title of his book, *Der Lehrstreit über die Kindertaufe* (*The Doctrinal Controversy over Infant Baptism*). He first defines his position over against that of the Lutheran Confessions and Luther. Then he examines the positions of those Lutherans whose views were prominent in that day. These men included Höfling, Martensen, Cremer, and the older Paul Althaus. The remainder of this section is devoted to defining Bunke's views of Baptism, faith, and regeneration according to the Lutheran Confessions and the Scriptures.

Bunke begins by examining what the Lutheran Confessions and Luther say about Baptism. In his view, they correctly teach that Baptism is the offering of salvation, but they are incorrect in teaching that Baptism works faith in infants. Saving faith must be present for justification. Bunke claims that his position is supported by the Augsburg Confession, the Apology, and the Smalcald Articles, in which he argues that nothing is said about the faith or regeneration of infants. The Augsburg Confession, Bunke claims, contains no clear statement about the effects of Baptism on children. It says only that Baptism is necessary for children and that the essence of this

---

[3] Ernst Bunke, "Taufe und Glaube," *DEKZ* 13 (1899): 282–84.

[4] Ernst Bunke, "Was ist die Kindertaufe?" *DEKZ* 13 (1899): 352–53, 361–62.

[5] Ernst Bunke, "Glaube und Kinderglaube," *DEKZ*, 14 (1900): 281–82.

[6] Ernst Bunke, "Wort und Sakrament," *DEKZ* 14 (1900): 286–87, 295–97.

[7] Ernst Bunke, *Der Lehrstreit über die Kindertaufe Innerhalb der lutherischen Kirche* (Kassel: n.p., 1909).

[8] Adolf Stöcker, in addition to being the editor of the *DEKZ*, was also active in the Christian Socialist Party and took part in programs for the welfare of the working class. Cf. "Stoecker, Adolf," *Lutheran Cyclopedia*, ed. Erwin L. Lueker (St. Louis: Concordia, 1954), 1011. Stöcker approved of Bunke's position.

[9] "Die Kindertaufe ist nicht die Wiedergeburt." Bunke, *Lehrstreit*, 127.

[10] "Die Kindertaufe ist das Sakrament der persönlichen Berufung ins Reich Gottes." Bunke, *Lehrstreit*, 130.

Sacrament is the offer of divine salvation.[11] Similarly, the Apology does not teach that, in itself, Baptism works regeneration or that baptized children have justifying faith. Baptism signifies that through it one is offered salvation and taken into the congregation, where salvation is imparted to those who believe through Word and Sacrament.[12] From the Smalcald Articles, Bunke is given to understand that the salvation offered in Baptism can be received only by that faith that is brought about by the spoken Word of God. Bunke finds it impossible for children to receive the regeneration offered in Baptism because they do not possess that saving faith created by the preached Word. Bunke says that in the Smalcald Articles Luther said nothing about the faith of children or their regeneration, but that for Luther in this confession Baptism was the personal proclamation of salvation's promises.[13]

Bunke holds in less positive regard Luther's two catechisms and the Formula of Concord, in which he finds that infant faith and regeneration are taught. In regard to Baptism, Luther's Small Catechism teaches that forgiveness of sins and regeneration are brought about where faith meets the Word of God in the water. Bunke concedes that with the words, "It is not the water indeed that does them, but the Word of God, which is in and with the water, and faith, which trusts such Word of God in the water," Luther was ascribing a real and conscious faith to children in connection with their Baptism. He bases his conclusion on the fact that Luther was writing his catechism for those who had been baptized as infants.

While Bunke agrees with what the Large Catechism teaches about the essence of Baptism, he disagrees with Luther's argument for infant Baptism: that since at infancy he and others had received the Holy Spirit in Baptism they had saving faith (LC IV, 49–55). Bunke interprets the essence of Baptism as offering divine salvation, forgiveness of sins, justification, and regeneration to those who receive this Sacrament. Even without faith, Baptism continues to offer these blessings to the individual.[14] Children's possession of the Spirit, for Bunke, does not translate into their faith. It is impossible for children to have such a faith.[15] Bunke agrees to Luther's premise that

---

[11] Bunke, *Lehrstreit*, 3.
[12] Bunke, *Lehrstreit*, 6–7.
[13] Bunke, *Lehrstreit*, 10.
[14] Bunke, *Lehrstreit*, 14.
[15] Bunke, *Lehrstreit*, 11.

those who had the Holy Spirit received Him in Baptism and still possessed Him. Through Baptism, infants possess the Spirit in the sense that the promise of grace given them in this Sacrament remains valid, and on the basis of this promise, one can and should receive faith, forgiveness of sins, regeneration, and the gift of the Holy Spirit. Bunke acknowledges that Luther was convinced that his arguments about great men having the Spirit provided the evidence that they had faith as infants.[16] He also points out Luther's belief in infant faith in that he said that the child is carried to Baptism in the hope that God would give him faith (LC IV, 57).

Luther leaves unexplained how inarticulate children can have a faith worked by the Word and accompanied by conversion. According to Bunke, Luther ascribes to a child the faith that normally belongs to an adult but does not develop the idea any further.[17] Bunke accepts what Luther has to say about the nature or essence of Baptism as the offering of forgiveness, but he denies that it can create faith in infants. The Formula of Concord follows the Large Catechism in ascribing to children the New Testament faith of adults with everything that is involved in producing such a faith.[18] Without faith, Baptism has no saving activity in the infant. In the Formula of Concord, regeneration is said to be dependent on justification, which, in turn, is dependent on saving faith. Thus, children are regenerated and saved because of their saving faith.[19]

Bunke is quite critical of Luther's doctrine that children believe through their Baptism. He says that even though Luther and the other reformers rejected Augustine's doctrine of the magical operation of Baptism, they accepted a magical effect of prayer with which the Holy Spirit was involved. Disturbing to Bunke was that even though faith is ascribed in infants to Baptism, the Lutheran Confessions do not explain how this happens. Since faith always involves the mind and the will, faith is impossible for infants. Luther did not properly understand the pericope of the blessing of the children, on which the concept of infant faith was established. Since the Holy Spirit cannot be imparted without the participation of the ethical personality, infant faith is impossible.[20] A year before he published *Der Lehrstreit über*

---

[16] Bunke, *Lehrstreit*, 16.
[17] Bunke, *Lehrstreit*, 16–17.
[18] Bunke, *Lehrstreit*, 17.
[19] Bunke, *Lehrstreit*, 23.
[20] Bunke, *Lehrstreit*, 32–33.

der Kindertaufe, he wrote an article entitled, "Was ist die Kindertaufe?" in which he also opposed the concept of infant faith as taught by the Lutheran Confessions. He wrote:

> It is more or less clear that the Lutheran Confessions maintain that newborn children have faith through Baptism. . . . However, the doctrine of infant faith contradicts the Scriptures and experience. What is necessary for human beings to be regenerated is lacking for children in their Baptism. Infant Baptism is not regeneration.[21]

Concerning what Luther says in the Large Catechism about infant faith, he bluntly says that the Reformer erred.[22]

While Bunke self-admittedly denies what the Lutheran Confessions teach about the operation of infant Baptism, he agrees with their teaching on the essence or nature of Baptism. Here follows his own definition of what the confessions teach on infant Baptism. Into this definition, he incorporates his own opinion of infant faith:

> Infant Baptism is the offering and promise of the salvation brought about by Christ to the individuals. It is the foundation and support for the subsequently arising faith in the baptized. The baptized will receive this faith by virtue of the Holy Spirit through the Word. Infant Baptism is not regeneration. This only happens when the baptized comes to faith.[23]

In order to demonstrate what he believes to be the correct understanding of Baptism, as he has just defined it according to his own explanation of the Lutheran Confessions, he gives the exegesis of certain biblical passages dealing with these three topics: regeneration, Baptism and faith, and Baptism and infant Baptism.

Regeneration in the New Testament is an act of God with the first part consisting in justification of the individual and his being freed from the entanglement of human guilt. In this act, the Holy Spirit is

---

[21] Bunke, "Was ist die Kindertaufe?" *DEKZ* 13 (1899), 352. Translation by writer.

[22] "Am ausführlichsten hat sich bekanntlich Luther im Großen Katechismus über die Taufe ausgesprochen. Daß er die Kinder als gläubige Empfänger der Taufe darin ansieht, hörten wir schon, aber erinnern wir uns daran, daß er in diesem Punkt geirrt hat." Bunke, "Was ist die Kindertaufe?" 353.

[23] Bunke, *Lehrstreit*, 34. Translation by writer. In the *Inhalts-Verzeichnis* Bunke describes infant Baptism as "Der Begriff der Kindertaufe nach den Bekenntnißschriften ohne die Annahme des Glaubens." (*Lehrstreit*, x). Bunke acknowledges that his view is not that of the Lutheran Confessions.

given and inaugurates the new life in power. The other part of regeneration is conversion and faith. Only those who through conversion have come to faith may be considered regenerate, and there can be no faith unless the Word has awakened it. Faith is as much the means of regeneration as are the Word and Baptism. Bunke argues that both the New Testament and the Lutheran Confessions hold that faith necessarily belongs to regeneration and justification.[24]

Numerous passages are cited to show that Baptism is efficacious only for those who have come to faith. Important in Bunke's argument is Matthew 28:19–20, which makes faith a prerequisite for the saving effectiveness of Baptism. The command to make disciples (μαθητεύσατε) involves the preaching of the Word and its being received in faith. Since making disciples is prior to Baptism, preaching of the Word is a prerequisite for receiving Baptism. Baptizing (βαπτίζονται) and teaching (διδάσκονται) do not belong to the process of making disciples but are applied to those who are already disciples. For Bunke, the baptizing is an outward call that makes the person certain of his election. Reception of Baptism is the outward sign that the disciple belongs to Jesus. Without Baptism, the disciples could not have regarded themselves as His disciples. Baptism was the seal of the state of grace for those who had by faith received the salvation proclaimed to them. Without Baptism, it would not be perceptible that the apostles belonged to the exalted Lord and to His congregation. Teaching refers not to the preaching of salvation but to the instruction that the baptized person needs to be worthy of his calling and of his position as a disciple.[25] For Bunke, the preaching of salvation is included in the making of disciples. Baptism

---

[24] Bunke, *Lehrstreit*, 86–88.

[25] Bunke, *Lehrstreit*, 92–93. Bunke's interpretation differs from Martensen's, though both use the words "teaching" and "baptizing" in Mt 28:19–20 in developing their theologies of infant Baptism. For Martensen, the imperative of the making of disciples is carried out by baptizing and teaching, which is the same as preaching. For Bunke making disciples is the self-contained act of preaching, to be followed by baptizing and teaching. Preaching and teaching are different. Bunke puts the imperative of making disciples on the same level as the participles baptizing and teaching. Making disciples means to bring to faith by preaching; baptizing and teaching are subsequent and do not contribute to the making of disciples. A formula can be used to show the difference.

Bunke: making disciples (or faith) + Baptism + instruction = complete discipleship.

Höfling: Baptism + instruction in the Word = making disciples or complete discipleship.

and teaching are acts that are then applied to those who through faith in the Word have already become disciples.[26]

Bunke advances his position on the relationship between faith and Baptism with other passages: Mark 16:16; Acts 2:38; Romans 6:3ff.; 1 Corinthians 12:13; Galatians 3:26ff; Ephesians 5:26; 1:13; Colossians 2:11ff.; Hebrews 10:22; and 1 Peter 3:19–22. From these he concludes that the New Testament teaches that Baptism is applied only to those who already have come to faith. Even if faith is not mentioned specifically in connection with Baptism, it is implied that if Baptism is to have any saving efficacy, faith must be present. Since Baptism is never discussed apart from faith, it is not possible to determine the essence of Baptism apart from faith.[27] For him, Baptism is that Sacrament through which God offers and promises to the individual the grace of salvation, which is communicated through the Holy Spirit, who makes the Baptism efficacious.

Bunke discusses how Baptism is efficacious in three different situations. If Baptism contains the offer of grace and leads an unbeliever to faith, Baptism may be said to work regeneration and impart the Spirit. If faith is already present at the time of the application of Baptism, then it completes regeneration by imparting the Holy Spirit as the principle of the new life. It confirms to the consciousness of the individual that he has been justified. If the entire justification including the impartation of the Spirit has taken place, then Baptism is the sign that the Triune God has been active with His grace in the baptized. At the same time, Baptism is for all who receive it the reception into the congregation of the exalted Lord. This congregation He rules through the activity of the Spirit in Word and Sacrament. Thus, Bunke lists three possible recipients of Baptism: (1) those without faith, (2) those who have faith but have not received the Holy Spirit, and (3) those who have faith and have received the Holy Spirit.

In the first classification, Bunke finds a place for infants. They are baptized without faith and led to regeneration by the Holy Spirit.

---

[26] This position reappeared in the theologies of Karl Barth and Johannes Schneider. Barth writes: "Die Taufe ist im Neuen Testament die unentbehrliche Frage des zum Glauben gekommenen Menschen." *Die kirchliche Taufe* (München: C. Kaiser, 1947), 30. Johannes Schneider writes: "Die Taufe im Neuen Testament setzt die umkehr des Menschen zu Gott, seinen Glauben an Christus und Bekenntnis diesen Glaubens voraus. . . . Die neutestamentliche Taufe ist Taufe der Christus-gläubigen." *Die Taufe im Neuen Testament* (Stuttgart: W. Kohlhammer, 1952), 75.

[27] Bunke, *Lehrstreit*, 107.

In infant Baptism, the child is offered and promised salvation. This offer and promise of salvation is attested by the child's being received into the congregation.[28] Here in the congregation the Triune God is active in saving souls through Word and Sacrament and accomplishes His plan of salvation. For Bunke, infant Baptism is a Baptism of unbelievers and does not fit his interpretation of Matthew 28:19–20 that faith created by the preached Word should precede Baptism.[29] Schleiermacher already proposed that Baptism could be understood as working of regeneration in leading either the child or the unbeliever to faith by placing him in the congregation where God is active with His Word. However, Bunke never goes as far as Schleiermacher in calling infant Baptism an erroneously applied Baptism.[30] Schleiermacher did not call infant Baptism the offering and promise of salvation to the child. Though Bunke gives Baptism a bigger role in the personal salvation of the child than does Schleiermacher, they agree that Baptism does not of itself effect any change in the person of the child.

Essential to Bunke's concept of infant Baptism is his denial of infant faith, for which he finds support in Matthew 18:1–4 and 19:13–15, passages traditionally used to support infant Baptism. He already has made it clear that regeneration requires justification and saving faith.[31] Thus, without faith, children according to his definition are unregenerate, which is the central theme and purpose in writing *Lehrstreit über die Kindertaufe*.

Matthew 18:1–4, for Bunke, does not deal with the relation of children to the kingdom of God but with the believers' relation to God and to their fellow men. This passage concerns strife over rank among the disciples. Jesus' blessing of a child with the word "convert" and the phrase "become as little children" explain each other and refer to self-humiliation. It is not the ethical condition of children that is placed before the disciples as an example, since their condition is not worthy of praise in every instance. Rather, the child standing in this circle of strangers is an example of modesty. So this pericope concerns not how children relate to the kingdom of heaven

[28] Bunke, *Lehrstreit*, 114–15.

[29] Bunke, *Lehrstreit*, 115.

[30] Friedrich Schleiermacher, *Der Christliche Glaube*, 2 vols. (Dritte unveränderte Ausgabe; Berlin: Druck und Verlag von Georg Reimer, 1836), 2:385–86.

[31] Bunke, *Lehrstreit*, 115.

but the attitude God requires of Christians toward Himself and to one another if they are to enter it.[32]

Bunke sees Matthew 19:13–15 in a similar way. Jesus is referring not to the faith of children but to their attitude; hence it cannot be used to demonstrate infant faith. Bunke explicates the pericope in this way. According to custom, children were brought to the leaders of the synagogue for the laying on of their hands with prayers spoken over them. These mothers believed that the blessings of Jesus on their children would be much more effective. The disciples discouraged this because their Lord was heavily burdened and because they did not think very highly of the personalities of children. Inarticulate children could have no relationship to the kingdom of God. Jesus reprimands them for hindering His giving of a blessing to the children, because the kingdom of heaven belongs to those who are like children. The phrase "of such" refers not to the children since the kingdom of the Messiah cannot belong to them. They cannot carry out the requirements for entering the kingdom set forth in the Sermon on the Mount. The words τῶν γὰρ τοιούτων refer not to children but to those who have a childlike attitude. Since children are examples of those who receive blessings, the passage refers to them as objects of grace. Their attitude of simplicity and humility is a goal for those who want to belong to the kingdom. The concept that children can be objects of grace fits Bunke's understanding of infant Baptism, according to which they are objects of the promise and offer of grace.[33]

Bunke argues differently from the parallels in Mark and Luke but comes to the same conclusion: that the kingdom of God does not belong to the children, and thus they do not have faith. He begins by asking whether the kingdom of God was already available when Jesus spoke these words. Was it not rather something to be given in the future? The Greek word ἐστίν in the phrase "of such is the kingdom of God" is of little value in determining whether it was there then or coming in the future, since it is doubtful whether in speaking Aramaic Jesus would have used the word "is." Even if the kingdom of God was present at that time, it was not present in the fullness of its gifts. It was only present in the person of the king, who would distribute its gifts in the future when He had completed the work of redemption. The blessing the Lord gave to the children was a pledge of their future

[32] Bunke, *Lehrstreit*, 122–23.
[33] Bunke, *Lehrstreit*, 123.

participation in His kingdom. In reaching the age of understanding, they would be able to comprehend the redemption by Jesus Christ, and the grace He promised them as children would work on them. This would allow them to return to the simplicity and humble attitude of a child and to enter the kingdom of God. So Bunke finds in these passages support for his view that infant Baptism is the promise of future regeneration.

Pericopes of the blessing of the children support the Baptism of infants but offer no evidence that it creates faith or regenerates them. Jesus' blessing of the children was not the blessing of the Holy Spirit. This is given only to believers through Baptism. When Jesus blessed the children, it was not the Baptism of the Holy Spirit that worked regeneration; this was only possible after Pentecost. So Bunke concludes that the pericopes of the blessing of the children do not prove that Baptism has the same saving effect on children as it has on adults.[34]

Bunke finds that the Lutheran Confessions do not do justice to what the Scriptures say about children's lack of faith and regeneration. Great blessing would occur if it was recognized that the Scriptures and the Lutheran Confessions are not agreed on infant faith. Luther and the reformers erred in equating John's Baptism with the Baptism of the Spirit in spite of the clearest evidence in the New Testament to the contrary. So they also erred in ascribing to the children blessed by the Lord the same regeneration that the believers experienced only after Pentecost. Bunke is conscience-bound to put aside the Lutheran Confessions and to remain by what he considers to be the true understanding of the Scriptures and, therefore, to give up what he calls the fiction and invention of infant faith. Since infant faith is contrary to the Scriptures, it is useless to theorize about a magical operation of the Spirit accomplished in the Word through the Sacrament or on account of the petitions of others. These theories do not require the ethical participation of the personality and hence are worthless.[35] Bunke agrees with the Lutheran Confessions on what

---

[34] Bunke, *Lehrstreit*, 123–24. If, as according to Bunke, children could not have believed when blessed by Jesus, because the kingdom of God had not come in its fullness and the Holy Spirit was still not the Spirit of regeneration, then it follows at that time adults also could not have believed. Bunke has proved too much. It can be agreed that the Spirit's work after the resurrection was greater than before, but this cannot be used to show that children could not believe any more than that adults could not.

[35] Bunke, *Lehrstreit*, 125.

they teach about the creation of faith, but their doctrine that infants believe and are regenerate in conjunction with their Baptism, he argues, cannot be supported by the Scriptures.[36]

Bunke cannot incorporate the doctrine of infant faith, which for him is erroneous, into his argument for baptizing infants. Colossians 2:11–12, where Baptism is compared to circumcision, provides him with a place to initiate his defense of infant Baptism. Baptism is one in the Spirit and ushers the baptized, who is assumed to have faith, into the fellowship of Christ. Nothing here is specifically said about the nature and efficacy of infant Baptism. Without faith, children cannot receive the Baptism of the Spirit. Nonetheless, a basis can be found here for demonstrating how infant Baptism can be shown to be in harmony with Scripture. Circumcision was the sign of the old covenant, which, according to Romans 2:25–29, did not give all the grace that was in the old covenant. A certain share of the spiritual gifts was given in circumcision to the covenant people under the condition that the Jew would conduct himself according to its regulations. Circumcision was not an insignificant ceremony but was the evidence of obedience to God's ordinances and the vow that they wanted to dedicate their children to the fellowship of God's covenant. For His part, God gave the assurance that He would regard the circumcised child as a member of the covenant people, that He desired to accomplish His plan of salvation in the child, and that He would bestow the blessing of religious training on him. With this interpretation of circumcision, infant Baptism was to be practiced and understood. Jesus' blessing the children indicates that the new covenant is not to be any smaller in scope than the old. Since the benefits of the new covenant surpass those of the old, infant Baptism exists on a higher level than circumcision. The powers of grace are greater in the new covenant than they were for the people of Abraham and Moses. Infant Baptism and circumcision are identical in that in both rites the child does not come to the personal and assured possession of salvation. This can happen only when faith arises, which is the necessary prerequisite for the new covenant relationship. Likewise, the Holy Spirit is not effective in the child through infant Baptism, but in Baptism, God promises and guarantees to the child that the Spirit will be effective in him by virtue of the means of grace that are present in the congregation of the new covenant. Through the

[36] Bunke, *Lehrstreit*, 127.

means of grace, faith is awakened, which is the necessary prerequisite for regeneration.[37]

This does not mean that infant Baptism is merely a Baptism with water as opposed to the Baptism of the Spirit. It cannot be a mere Baptism with water, since the promise made to the child is from God through the Holy Spirit and not from man. Thus, for Bunke, infant Baptism is a Baptism of the Spirit, since the Spirit is there with the promise of regeneration from God. Still, infant Baptism may not be called the Baptism of regeneration, since, as has been shown above, it does not effect regeneration. Bunke prefers to call it "disciples' Baptism." In "disciples' Baptism," the command of the Lord to make disciples of all nations is fulfilled. Through Baptism, children are received into the sphere of the discipleship of Jesus. Here in this sphere the grace of Jesus is active. Bunke summarizes his own understanding of infant Baptism as follows:

> Infant Baptism in the new covenant corresponds with circumcision in the old covenant. It transfers its object out of the sphere of the corruption of sin into the sphere where God is active in extending His grace. It also gives the right of future possession and guarantees the claim for the personal possession of salvation. *Infant Baptism is the sacrament of the personal call into the kingdom of God.*

Such a definition of infant Baptism Bunke finds to be in harmony with the Lutheran Confessions as long as what is called the untenable theory of a directly worked infant faith is not maintained.[38]

Since infant Baptism is defined as the personal call into the kingdom of God, it is essential to see what Bunke understands by "personal call." Infant Baptism is the seal that God has called those individuals who have been born within Christendom into His kingdom. The call sealed in Baptism promises to the child that he will inherit the Father's blessings, which have been prepared by the Son and which are distributed to the congregation by the Spirit. The personal possession of the inheritance comes to the child when he believes. What Paul says about the Jewish people in Galatians 4:1 is now made valid for the New Testament congregation: "That the heir, as long as he is a child, differeth nothing from a servant, though he be lord of all; but he is under tutors and governors until the time

[37] Bunke, *Lehrstreit*, 127–29.

[38] Bunke, *Lehrstreit*, 129–31. Italics in original. Translation by writer.

appointed by the father." For the baptized child the appointed time comes when he as the heir comes to faith through the Spirit's work of grace that was guaranteed to him in Baptism. At this time, the baptized child becomes an actual son of God. Through the Spirit's testimony about Baptism the child is brought to regeneration.[39]

CONCLUSION

Bunke's underlying thought throughout his work on infant Baptism has been the defense of the proposition that man is saved alone through faith or that without faith there is no regeneration. This thought is underscored by the closing sentence of his book: "We steadfastly cling to the watchword of the Lutheran Church: *sola fide, alone through faith*."[40] For him it is a scriptural and confessional principle that faith is necessary for regeneration. Children, in his reckoning, are not regenerate because they lack faith.

Though Bunke speaks much about regeneration, he never speaks of salvation in regard to children; it seems only right that he should apply the same *sola fide* principle. This he never does, thus avoiding the conclusion that all children, since they are incapable of faith, are not saved but damned. Bunke's failure to treat of the salvation of baptized children perhaps stems from fear of the logical conclusions of his own *sola fide* principle. Since Bunke nowhere says that baptized children are damned—in fact, he says that they have a claim to future salvation—it can be safely concluded that Bunke believes they are saved and without faith. Here he violates his own *sola fide* principle.

Similarly, when Bunke, while denying infant faith, defines infant Baptism as the Sacrament that gives the guarantee and promise of the forgiveness of sins, he argues that the child actually has the guarantee and promise of the forgiveness of sins and regeneration but not the actual possession of these. Insofar as the child possesses the promise, he possesses a gift of grace but without the benefit of faith. Again, *sola fide* is violated. One has to ask whether it is possible to have a promise from God without having faith. Wherever God gives a promise, it is to be accepted in faith, and there is no promise for the individual unless he has faith. Abraham accepted the promise in faith, and now Christians accept Christ's promise of eternal life in faith.

---

[39] Bunke, *Lehrstreit*, 131.

[40] Bunke, *Lehrstreit*. Translation by writer. Italics in original.

God does make promises to those without faith, but He makes them to individuals so that they will believe them. Thus, the giving of a promise in Baptism without the possibility of faith is a violation of the *sola fide* principle, because only by faith can Christians accept, or possess, promises of God.

Bunke's differentiation between regeneration and the promise of regeneration is also open to question. Could it not be said that he who has the promise from God has what the promise offers? Thus, whoever has the promise of the forgiveness of sins does have the forgiveness as a possession that he can rely on. Therefore, might it not be said that he who has the promise of regeneration has regeneration, at least in some sense? What to Bunke appears as two distinct propositions, that infant Baptism is not regeneration and that infant Baptism is the promise of regeneration, are not really so different as Bunke makes them out to be.

It is also difficult to see precisely in Bunke's position the difference between the baptized and unbaptized children of Christian parents. He says that Baptism is the seal of the common call of God to children born within Christendom. One would have to ask whether an unbaptized child born within Christendom is any less called than a baptized one. After all, birth determines the call of which Baptism is only a seal. If both baptized and unbaptized children of Christians are equally called, there would be no real need of Baptism. This is especially true if one remembers that Bunke says that Baptism is a seal to the consciousness. It is on account of the children's lack of consciousness that Bunke has denied infant faith. If children do not have consciousness, how can Baptism as a seal to the consciousness be of any benefit to them? Thus, it appears that Baptism does not really change the lot of children born within Christendom. The real "means of grace" is being born of Christian parents and not Baptism. Baptism would have no effect on children born of heathen parents, since it is the seal of the call only to children born within Christendom. In the case of children born outside of Christendom, there is no call to seal. Baptism would be a seal without any content.

Bunke's position also involves a downgrading of the Sacrament of Baptism in relation to the preached Word. Even though he may speak about Baptism producing regeneration and completing regeneration, it is the preached Word alone that works it. Baptism can be said to work regeneration in the sense that it puts the baptized into a position within the congregation to hear the preached Word, a concept propounded previously by Schleiermacher. It is really the preached Word that works faith, which is the necessary constituent for regeneration. Bunke makes it quite plain that it is the preached Word and not Baptism that works faith. Thus, the preached Word has a power that Baptism does not have: the power to convert. Without the preached Word, Baptism can effect nothing. The promise made to the child in Baptism is a promise that in reality is not able to effect anything in or for the child. For Bunke it is not the Word of God in and with the water that does such great things, but the preached Word of God accompanying and following Baptism. This is evident when Bunke says that a child can be brought to regeneration in the Word about Baptism. The Word is really apart from the water. Bunke does speak about Baptism giving the Spirit to those who have already come to faith, but in the matter of faith, conversion, and regeneration, Baptism is powerless. It is not only because of the lack of consciousness that infant faith is denied but also because of the impotence of Baptism.

Against Bunke as well as against those who have a similar understanding of infant faith, the charge of synergism can be leveled, insofar as they demand a certain level of consciousness in the person before God can create faith by His grace. Thus, the operation of grace becomes dependent on the level of consciousness attained by the individual. Having faith or not having faith is made to depend on consciousness.

One cannot be satisfied with Bunke's exegesis and the way he applies his own results. This is especially true in two passages: Matthew 28:19 and Colossians 2:11. From Matthew 28:19, he understands that Baptism is to be applied only to those who by faith are now disciples. But then he turns around and uses the same passage to support an idea he calls "disciples' Baptism." Infant Baptism is "disciples' Baptism," since it makes the children members of the outward circle of disciples. Thus, he uses the word disciples in one case to refer to those who have come to faith through the preached Word and in another case to refer to those who participate only in outward membership. The concept of outward discipleship blatantly contradicts his own exegesis of the passage.

About Colossians 2:11 he says that the Baptism referred to here is the Baptism of the Spirit that is applied to adult believers. For him, this passage makes no reference to infant Baptism at all. Still, it is this passage that gives him the clue for the understanding infant Baptism because it refers to circumcision. Whether one agrees with Bunke's exegesis is not the point at hand. The point is that if he says that the passage has no reference to infant Baptism, then he should not use it to establish infant Baptism. Even though Bunke uses Matthew 28:19 and Colossians 2:11 in his understanding of infant Baptism, it must be frankly said that for him infant Baptism is provable neither by biblical command nor by example.

Bunke through biblical exegesis has attempted to prove that infant faith is not taught in the Scriptures. However, it should be stated that this is denied not only on biblical grounds but also on psychological ones. In connection with his discussion on the Smalcald Articles, he says that infant faith is completely excluded according to his psychological conceptions.[41] Bunke denied infant faith because of psychological reasons even before he attempted an exegesis of Matthew 18 and 19. His exegesis only served to prove what he had already accepted as true apart from the Scriptures. His conclusions would be established even before he examined the evidence.

There can be no doubt that Baptism does play a more important role in the personal salvation of the child with Bunke than it does with Schleiermacher. For Bunke, it was the promise of regeneration, while for Schleiermacher it was a matter of indifference whether it should even be continued. However, their basic understandings concerning Baptism was the same. The major difference was that Bunke wanted Baptism to play a role in the salvation of the child in spite of the conclusions of his own research, while Schleiermacher followed the same results to their logical conclusion and expressed his willingness to give up infant Baptism.

---

[41] Bunke, *Lehrstreit*, 10. "Wiederum müssen wir sagen, daß nach unseren psychologischen Vorstellungen hierdurch völlig ausgeschlossen ist, daß die Kinder diesen zum Empfang der Wiedergeburt in der Taufe notwendigen Heilsglauben besitzen." Ernst Bunke, at one time the director of the Johannesstift in Berlin, wrote a biography on the great English Baptist preacher, *Charles Haddon Spurgeon: Prediger von Gottes Gnade, Zeugen des gegenwärtigen Gottes* (3rd ed., 1958) and another one on the German Lutheran Pietist, *August Hermann Francke*: *Der Mann des Glaubens und der Liebe* (1939, 1960). Subtitles for these biographies indicate Bunke's proclivities towards an Evangelical or revivalistic understanding of faith that surfaced in his denial of infant faith. Spurgeon, preacher at the London Metropolitan Tabernacle, opposed baptismal regeneration.

REINHOLD SEEBERG

Reinhold Seeberg gave his most extensive treatment of infant Baptism in a series of lectures at the University of Berlin, which were subsequently published in 1909 under the title *Zur Systematischen Theologie*. His understanding of infant Baptism resembles that of Bunke: both wrestled with the problem of trying to keep infant Baptism as an integral part of the process of personal salvation without accepting the doctrine of infant faith. Seeberg saw Bunke's definition of infant Baptism as the Sacrament of the personal call of God as a considerable advance in the understanding of infant Baptism.[42] Like Bunke, Seeberg defined infant Baptism as the promise of forgiveness and regeneration, placing its saving significance in the future.[43] By so doing, Bunke and Seeberg avoided the Rationalist position that Baptism had no significance for children, Luther's view that it created faith in the child,[44] and the view of the Erlangen theologians that it had an effect on the nature of the child.[45]

Seeberg discussed the continued use of infant Baptism in the light of the common view among scholars that the New Testament knew only of adult Baptism and not infant Baptism.[46] A reason for infant Baptism is found in its connection with the *Volkskirche*.[47] It originated with the *Volkskirche* and has a place as long as this type of church exists. For Seeberg, infant Baptism was the Baptism of the *Volkskirche*.

For Seeberg, Baptism and the preached Word have the same effects. What the Scriptures attribute to the Word in one place they elsewhere attribute to Baptism. Baptism and the Word both can give regeneration, the forgiveness of sins, and the gift of the Holy Spirit. Therefore, Baptism brings not just a portion of the gifts of salvation to the individual, but it brings all of them. In regard to their contents, there is no difference between Baptism and the preached Word. Baptism does not bring any gifts to the individual that the Word does

---

[42] Reinhold Seeberg, *Zur Systematischen Theologie* (Leipzig: A. Deichert, 1909), 257.

[43] Reinhold Seeberg, *Grundriß der Dogmatik* (Leipzig: A. Deichert, 1932), 99. Cf. pp. 133–36.

[44] Seeberg, *Zur Systematischen Theologie*, 255.

[45] Seeberg, *Zur Systematischen Theologie*, 256.

[46] Seeberg, *Zur Systematischen Theologie*, 254. "Ein biblischer Beweis der Kindertaufe läßt sich nicht bringen." Seeberg, *Grundriß der Dogmatik*, 98.

[47] Seeberg, *Zur Systematischen Theologie*, 257.

not also bring. This does not, however, allow for Baptism to be substituted for the preached Word, because Baptism is only effective on a person if the Word has preceded and accompanied Baptism. Without the preached Word, Baptism is nothing or it is just a step in the process of the Word's operation. Within this latter understanding, Seeberg finds a place for infant Baptism: it is a step in the process of the Word's operation. Only after the Word has worked on the soul does a person comprehend the gifts of Baptism. As the person is led to comprehend the gifts of Baptism, he is led by the same degree into a deeper understanding of the Word. It should be noted that this is not Luther's position that Baptism's effect is derived from the Word in the water. Rather, for Seeberg, the New Testament teaching is that the Word precedes and accompanies the water of Baptism.[48]

Seeberg offers this scenario for how people became Christians. A catechumen was first instructed about Christ and Christianity, and through this he was brought to an awareness of God's presence, a consciousness of guilt, a temporary experience of forgiveness, and a perception of the agitating power of the Spirit. All this was accomplished by the preached Word, but it was just preparatory for one particular act through which the catechumen, by virtue of his confession, would become a member of God's people and would receive forever a portion in the new covenant. This all important act was Baptism, which collected and concentrated the feelings of the soul in one moment. Baptism made what was previously just sentiment and inspiration a permanent conscious possession, but it did not work mechanically, as if its working were dependent on the recitation of some sentence before the act. Neither did it work magically as if it effected something *ex opere operato* within the person.

For Seeberg, Baptism was the concluding act of a psychological process through which the soul was inwardly prepared for the experience of the wonderful. When this psychological preparation brings the individual to a realization of salvation, he is made capable of making a confession about salvation. Through Baptism, he becomes conscious that there is grace and forgiveness for his guilt, and he feels himself drawn into the fellowship of Christ's life and death. He is circumcised in the inner man. Single gifts that were previously held before him are brought together as a unit in Baptism through the guarantee of the Spirit. In Baptism, he has reached the

[48] Seeberg, *Zur Systematischen Theologie*, 265–67.

ultimate salvation possible on earth, and now he can regard himself as an heir of the new creation and of the eternal consummation.[49] Briefly, Baptism for Seeberg is the culminating point of the psychological process worked by the Word. Baptism and the Word share the same essence or content, but each has a distinct psychological effect. Baptism brings together in one act what the Word does in many acts.

Seeberg sees Baptism as a particular point of time in the process of salvation. Baptism has a dual role as the goal to which the preached Word strives and the point where the new life begins under the preached Word. For the catechumen, Baptism makes the feelings and thoughts produced by the preached Word a permanent possession of the soul. Where Baptism has already created a permanent consciousness of salvation in the individual, then this permanent consciousness becomes the soul's agency of appropriating additional Christian preaching. Thus Baptism has a place in the middle of the process of salvation by which one is brought to Christ. Here the road leading to salvation begins, where it ends. Baptism makes the contents of the preached Word a permanent possession and leads the Christian into a new life under the Word.[50]

The Word is applied in a series of acts, bringing forgiveness and the Spirit gradually in many phases, but Baptism is a one-time act. These separate acts are directed to that one-time act of Baptism by which the confessing Christian can be assured that the gifts of God's people will abide in him. By the one-time act of Baptism, he also enters into a lasting fellowship with God. Thus, Baptism as a one-time act administered in the congregation is distinct from the Word. What the Word gives, it gives again and again. What Baptism gives, it gives once and for all time. For the mature Christian, Baptism can serve as a source of strength and comfort. A person's consciousness of sin may become weak and the efficacy of the preached Word may stop. Should this happen, Baptism can serve as a support to which the person can go back. In Baptism, the individual can find a source of motivation that makes a person aware that there he has entered into fellowship with God and has been made a member of God's people.

Baptism as a one-time act performed before others is a source of comfort and power because it can present the gifts of Baptism as realities in those times when the individual is not subjectively aware

[49] Seeberg, *Zur Systematischen Theologie*, 268–69.
[50] Seeberg, *Zur Systematischen Theologie*, 271.

of them. The mere fact that Baptism has been performed in the presence of others can give the Christian the inward confidence of the salvation received through the Word. He can have certainty from his Baptism because through it he is participating in the historical benefits of a large fellowship. Through Baptism, salvation becomes for the Christian a historical fact of enduring significance. Baptism by engrafting the personal experience of the believer into the fellowship of the Church makes salvation a historical reality. Because Baptism works this certainty in the believer, it is the beginning point of that life in which the gifts of salvation develop to perfection.[51]

Since Seeberg claims that the preached Word and Baptism both have the same content and give the same gifts, it follows that each works regeneration. Explaining how both the Word and Baptism can work forgiveness is not difficult, but how both can work regeneration is another matter. The question arises of how a person can be regenerated twice, once by the Word and then by Baptism. To address this issue, Seeberg speaks of different aspects of regeneration. The Word regenerates insofar as it gradually works faith and love through a series of successive acts. Baptism works regeneration in making faith and love permanent possessions of the soul. Regeneration through the Word is the development of the new life in the soul, and regeneration through Baptism is the permanent condition of the Christian life. Regeneration through Baptism and the Word are related as *being* (*Sein*) and *becoming* (*Werden*). Both work regeneration with the same inner effect, but the regeneration of Baptism produces a lasting effect (*Sein*) in the individual, while the Word's regeneration is only a momentary action.[52]

For Seeberg, the origins of infant Baptism lie in darkness; no New Testament passage says anything definite about it. 1 Corinthians 7:14 deals with an unbelieving spouse being sanctified through the believing one. To substantiate the holiness of the unbelieving partner, the holiness of their children is mentioned. Seeberg says that if these children had been baptized, offering them as evidence would have been senseless. Passages in Acts where entire households are reported as being baptized can only be valid to prove infant Baptism if it can first be established on other bases. This does not convince Seeberg, since historical evidence for infant Baptism is lacking. Thus, the

[51] Seeberg, *Zur Systematischen Theologie*, 271–73.
[52] Seeberg, *Zur Systematischen Theologie*, 273–74.

baptizing of entire families is not legitimate evidence for infant Baptism. Dogmatical arguments for the practice are ruled out.

Infant Baptism was not known until the last half of the second century and gradually became regular Church practice. By the fifth century, it was in common use. As infant Baptism became the common practice, some raised conscientious scruples against its introduction because it seemed to resemble the magical theories of the mystery religions. Scruples against infant Baptism only disappeared with the rise of the *Volkskirche*, which assured that the baptized child would be brought up in a Christian environment.[53] Dogmas associated with infant Baptism resulted from the Church becoming a *Volkskirche,* at which time infant Baptism replaced adult Baptism. Theories and concepts associated with adult Baptism were carried over to infants in their Baptism. The baptismal rite for adult catechumens was also used for infants. So faith was required of children, the devil was exorcized, and they were brought to the Church during Lent as a sign of penance.[54]

From a dogmatical perspective, Seeberg maintains that infants are not capable of receiving the high spiritual gifts in Baptism of which the adult is capable because they do not possess the ability to undergo the psychological preparation required for responding to the preached Word. This preparation is a prerequisite to receiving any of Baptism's benefits. Neither Scripture nor experience for Seeberg allow for any ability on the part of the child to receive the new life of faith and love.[55] Infant faith is as impossible as it is foolish. It militates against sound reason. Such things as infant faith have no place in religion.[56]

---

[53] Seeberg, *Zur Systematischen Theologie*, 274–76.

[54] Seeberg, *Zur Systematischen Theologie*, 276.

[55] A similar position on infant faith was held by Albrecht Ritschl. "Der Glaube an Christus kann nur im reifern Lebensalter erwartet werden. . . . Was als für die Folgezeit sich als das umfassende Motive des christlichen Lebens bewährt, kann im Kindesalter nicht direkt weder zum Verständniß gebracht noch erlebt werden. Weil im System der Glaube an Christus als Hauptmotiv alles Guthandelns dargestellt wird, versucht man es, den unmündigen Kindern die Liebe zum Heiland beizubringen und durch diese Argument die sittliche Erziehung methodisch zu leiten. Man kann ja zugeben daß im Kindesalter die Liebe zum Heiland dem Glauben an Christus analogus ist. Indessen die letzere Leistung ist etwas sehr Ernsthaftes, das Erste aber ist Spiel. Denn sonst würde es dem Kinde nicht zugänglich sein." *Die christliche Lehre von der Rechtfertigung und Versöhnung*, 3 vols. (Zweite verbesserte Auflage; Bonn: Adolf Marcus, 1883), 3:556.

[56] Seeberg, *Zur Systematischen Theologie*, 277.

Comparing the differences between infant and adult Baptism provides Seeberg an opportunity to define them. In the Baptism of adults, which is the Baptism of the New Testament, the psychological preparation under the preached Word is followed by the certainty given in Baptism. With children, this process is reversed. They receive the objective element of salvation in Baptism and then follows the subjective action of the Word upon the soul. For adults, Baptism includes an immediate inner experience. Since it involves the consciousness, it is subjective in character. On the other hand, for children, Baptism has a purely objective character. Only when the preached Word is applied to them do they have an inner and subjective experience. For adults, the so-called becoming (*Werden*), achieved through the Word, precedes the permanent condition of salvation (*Sein*), given in Baptism. With children, it is reversed. They receive the permanent assurance of salvation, its objective part (*Sein*), first. This *Sein,* which they have from Baptism, is the starting point for the future development under the Word (*Werden*). If infants are baptized without the anticipation that the Word will be applied in the future, their Baptism becomes magic, an external ceremony with no effect. Only under the condition that the Word will follow does infant Baptism offer anything. Only in the Word will the Spirit be effective in the child's life.[57]

A child born within Christendom has the advantage over an adult proselyte who must of his own free will and decision enter into that fellowship where the Word is effective. Through birth, the child has already entered into this fellowship. The only thing left for the parents and the congregation to do is to bring the child up as a conscious member of the fellowship. For the adult catechumen, faith first takes on a historical dimension when he enters this fellowship through Baptism. From its inception, the faith of a child is presupposed to be historical, since through birth the child and the congregation are destined for one another. His birth is the historical connection between his life and that of the congregation. What the catechumen has through a gradual process in the preaching of the Word, the child already possesses through birth. By birth within the Christian fellowship, the child is already positioned to hear the Word and to come under its influence.

Seeberg recognizes three conditions for administering infant Baptism. First, parents, sponsors, and the congregation are required to

[57] Seeberg, *Zur Systematischen Theologie*, 273–74.

have faith in the efficacy of God's Word. Second, the child must be born into the Christian congregation as evidence that God has elected him to be his own. Third, parents and congregation must desire to place the child under the influence of the preached Word. When these conditions are met, an infant can be baptized with the assurance that he will be brought under the influence of the Word, through which he will receive the gifts of the new covenant. With the assurance that the Word will be applied, it is not presumptuous to make a promise and guarantee to the child that he will have a part in the Christian congregation and in the benefits of salvation that are connected with it. Since the child by Baptism is put into a position of requiring further development in the Word, the parents, sponsors, and congregation are obligated to give the child a Christian education. Thus, the function of the sponsors is not to confess the Christian faith in the child's stead but to obligate the child to the faith that comes from the Word.[58]

Seeberg recognizes that some children may never come to faith and others may come to faith later in life instead of earlier. A baptized child who has not come to faith is similar to the proselyte who, after he comes to faith, is baptized. Such a person has the choice of remaining in the faith into which he was baptized. A child has the choice of whether or not he will live up to the faith his Baptism requires. It might appear that the adult who has come to Baptism of his own free will has a better opportunity for living up to what his Baptism requires than does a child. The adult has willingly elected to be baptized, while the child has not. In response, Seeberg sees certain conditions in the child's life that provide good opportunities to remain faithful to what Baptism requires. Influential in bringing a child to faith are the parents' will and example and the child's environment, which includes religious education and Christian customs. Upon reaching consciousness, the unconscious mind upon which Christian elements have already worked has a permanent possession of salvation that is in no way inferior to what the adult has. The Holy Spirit's work in the child is in direct proportion to the degree in which he has come under the influence of the congregation where the Spirit works.[59] Seeberg does not see infant Baptism as a practice of the New Testament but finds a place for it under New Testament definitions. He uses the metaphor of adoption to explain how children possess

---

[58] Seeberg, *Zur Systematischen Theologie*, 280–81.

[59] Seeberg, *Zur Systematischen Theologie*, 281–82.

salvation. An adopted child is born humbly and without dignity but through adoption possesses many things, including the highly developed, refined culture and privileges of his adopted parents. He begins to possess all these things gradually as he becomes subjectively capable.

Similar is the situation of the child who through Baptism is placed under the working of the Holy Spirit in the congregation. The baptized child can make the benefits which he has received as a permanent possession through Baptism meaningful for his soul as he becomes subjectively capable. Spiritual gifts can be possessed in two ways. They can be possessed in the sense that they are available and insofar as they are made personal possessions. Objective possession of salvation is possible without the subjective possession of it, but Seeberg does not reverse this so that spiritual gifts can be possessed without objectively possessing them. Children are capable of objectively possessing these gifts in the sense that the possibility of inheriting them is open to them. The child only becomes capable of the subjective possession of salvation when he becomes capable of the spiritual acts of love and faith.[60]

By maintaining that the child is not subjectively capable of the salvation offered in Baptism, Seeberg does not believe that he is taking anything away from Baptism or detracting from the omnipotence of God, who can deal with individuals as He wants. Seeberg is quick to add claims that God's miracles are never done against the laws of nature He Himself has established. God's miracles that are defined as His working towards a definite purpose in a particular form of these established laws. Miracles are manipulations of the laws of nature and not transgressions of them. Faith for infants is as impossible as their conceiving children, discovering planets, and preaching sermons. If God had wanted infants to believe, He would have given them other abilities than what He has. For Seeberg, it is a miracle when God gives spiritual feelings, thoughts, and will to those who are capable. It is nonsensical and not miraculous when a soul that is incapable of will and thought should receive those things that are

[60] Seeberg, *Zur Systematischen Theologie*, 282–83. Karl Girgensohn (1875–1925) endorses Seeberg's position that infant Baptism is not regeneration, but only the objective and effective promise of regeneration. *Grundriß der Dogmatik* (Erlangen und Leipzig: A. Deichertische Verlagsbuchhandlung, 1924), 173.

only possible for willing and thinking persons. One who accepts infant faith arbitrarily twists God's ordinances.[61]

In Baptism, the child does not subjectively receive regeneration, but he receives it as an objective possibility that may later develop into a subjective reality. A baptized child can only be considered regenerate when he becomes a pious child. This occurs when the child has begun a life of love and faith and has entered into a reciprocal fellowship with God. Such a life of faith and love results from the preaching of the Word in the home, school, or Church.[62] Even for a baptized child, the cause of regeneration is the preached Word as it is for adults. Infant Baptism leads to the goal of regeneration. "We will say accordingly that the child's Baptism is not regeneration, but *it is the objective and effective promise of regeneration; nevertheless it points to the goal of regeneration.*"[63]

Seeberg summarizes his concept of infant Baptism in three points: (1) Baptism is the acceptance of the child into the fellowship of the Christian Church. (2) Through Baptism the child is adopted by God through the Spirit who acts within the Church. (3) For a child, Baptism is the objective and effective promise of regeneration.[64]

Though Baptism does not regenerate the infant, it has an important function in providing the basis of the child's Christian life, which begins with receiving Baptism and then develops so that the child understands it. Baptism inaugurates the efficacy of the Word, which propels the child to experience subjectively what has been objectively promised in Baptism. A time comes in the religious development of the baptized child under the influence of the Word when the objective possession of Baptism becomes the personal possession of his life. By Church custom, confirmation has been established as the time when this should occur. After a period of religious instruction, the child in confirmation makes a public confession of his faith before the congregation. Confirmation is not only an outward Church ordinance, but it fulfills an inner need. Even without confirmation a child can come to the point when he can feel himself to be a child of God, a member of the Church, and a possessor of its gifts. Confirmation does not confer new gifts on the

---

[61] Seeberg, *Zur Systematischen Theologie*, 283–84.
[62] Seeberg, *Zur Systematischen Theologie*, 284.
[63] Seeberg, *Zur Systematischen Theologie*, 285. Italics in original. Translation by author.
[64] Seeberg, *Zur Systematischen Theologie*, 285.

child that Baptism has not already given, but it is only the recognition that the gifts given in Baptism have become a personal possession. For Seeberg, a child who has not made his confession remains in the state of receptivity. His connection to the Church is through his parents. When the child himself makes a personal confession, this connection is activated as his own.[65]

Seeberg allows for infant Baptism only under the condition that the child will be brought into a Christian environment. Problematic is the case of a child born into a household estranged from religion where positive religious sentiments are completely lacking. Where Christianity belongs to the culture, as is the case where the state and Church are brought together in the *Volkskirche*, infant Baptism can be practiced. Since children can receive some Christian education in the school, it is important that the *Volkskirche* be continued. Continuing the Baptism of infants depends on the life of the *Volkskirche*. Should the people revert to heathenism, the Church would lose its character as a *Volkskirche*. If the state should break its connection with the Church, it would no longer be a *Volkskirche*, and it would assume its original character as a missionary Church. With this, the Baptism of infants would give way to the Baptism of adults. As long as there is a *Volkskirche*, children should receive Baptism as the customary way for them to come to God. Along this way, the Spirit will lead them to salvation.[66] For Seeberg, infant Baptism and the *Volkskirche* are so intimately connected that he holds that the struggle to keep the *Volkskirche* is the struggle over infant Baptism.[67]

CONCLUSION

Seeberg takes over concepts offered by Schleiermacher: (1) Infant Baptism is not the Baptism of the New Testament. (2) The Baptism of the New Testament is adult Baptism. (3) Faith can come only through the preached Word and not through Baptism. (4) Children cannot receive faith because they are not sufficiently conscious to receive the preached Word. (5) Infants' lack of faith makes their Baptisms incomplete. (6) This incompleteness is corrected by the application of the preached Word that can take place in confirmation. (7) Both Baptism and the preached Word can be said to work regeneration, but

---

[65] Seeberg, *Zur Systematischen Theologie*, 285–87.
[66] Seeberg, *Zur Systematischen Theologie*, 289–91.
[67] Seeberg, *Zur Systematischen Theologie*, 292.

this requires that regeneration be understood in two different ways. (8) Baptism is a particular point of time in the process of the application of the preached Word.

While Schleiermacher would prefer dropping infant Baptism altogether, a position Karl Barth put forth in the mid-twentieth century, Seeberg provides a definition for Baptism that allows for it to be continued within Christian families and, where this is lacking, within the framework of the *Volkskirche*. Since infant Baptism originated within the *Volkskirche*, it can remain the ordinary custom as long as the *Volkskirche* remains in place. Should the *Volkskirche* cease to exist, infant Baptism would have to give way to adult Baptism.

Seeberg cannot find any biblical basis for infant Baptism. In order to maintain infant Baptism in place as the customary practice, he defines Baptism as the act that concentrates in one moment that which is offered in the preached Word over a longer period of time. In the New Testament, it is given only to those who already believe to make their possession of salvation more permanent. Baptism assures the believer of his salvation. For children, Seeberg takes the biblical definition and reverses the order. They receive Baptism first and then later, when they come to maturity, they come to faith through the preached Word. In Baptism, they receive the objective element of their salvation and in preaching they receive faith, the subjective element.

Seeberg's position on infant Baptism is open to critique in several places, of which the most prominent might be that he does not provide a rationale for why the *Volkskirche* should be seen as an acceptable replacement for the New Testament concept of the Church. He never addresses this question. Thus he bases his arguments for infant Baptism on a historical development but at the same time concedes that the Scriptures know only of the practice of adult Baptism. Schleiermacher and Barth came to this conclusion and admitted that infant Baptism was not ideal but within their circumstances allowed for it with the greatest reluctance. Seeberg found a reason for infant Baptism within the institution of the *Volkskirche* but not in apostolic teaching and practice. Also open to critique is Seeberg's concept that Baptism gives salvation objectively and preaching creates faith as the subjective part of salvation. This has a faint resemblance to Luther's concept that Baptism stays in place, offering its gifts even where faith is not present. Seeberg approaches Luther's view, but in the case of children, they possess Baptism's gifts even without faith. He provides a positive insight in distinguishing between the functions of Baptism and the Word, but his division is too sharp in holding that Baptism gives salvation and the Word creates the faith that accepts these gifts. Baptism does regenerate in the sense that the preached Word alone does not, but the Word that is present in Baptism and makes it a Sacrament creates faith.

Seeberg recognizes that New Testament Baptism was applied only to those who first had come to faith. Without offering any reason, he then reverses this order so that Baptism with its objective gifts precedes their subjective appropriation by faith. This allows for baptizing infants. In the New Testament, believers had the subjective element of salvation that was then made certain by Baptism. If, by faith, adult believers have the certainty of salvation, it has to be asked how Baptism can improve their situation. Children possess salvation by Baptism but only have the certainty of it later by faith. For children and adults, the roles of Baptism and faith are switched. Children possess salvation objectively by Baptism and are given the personal certainty of it by faith in the preached Word. Adults possess salvation subjectively by faith in the preached Word and are made certain of it by Baptism. Though Seeberg speaks of a child possessing Baptism objectively, such a Baptism is without any significance for the child until the preached Word is applied to faith. Seeberg seems to have offended his own principle that Baptism and not faith gives the certainty of salvation.

Seeberg claims that he simply reversed the New Testament process by applying the objective part of salvation first by Baptism to the child and then following with the subjective part by the application of the preached Word to faith. However, he has done more than simply reverse the order. He has changed the meaning of the objective part of salvation. In the case of adults, Baptism makes such a psychological impression that salvation becomes a permanent possession of the soul. In the case of children, it simply puts salvation at their disposal. Children are not personally involved as are adults. Baptism for adults makes them certain of salvation. In the case of baptized children the certainty is given by confirmation. Confirmation approximates in its effects Seeberg's New Testament definition of Baptism.

Seeberg is a good example, perhaps the best one, of those nineteenth-century Lutheran theologians who understood that New Testament Baptism was given to adults who had faith but at the same time did not have the heart to do away with infant Baptism. Luther's doctrine of infant faith was an unacceptable solution to their dilemma. Seeberg wanted to avoid the Charybdis of infant faith, which was found to be psychologically impossible, and the Scylla of giving up infant Baptism, which would spell the end of the *Volkskirche*, an institution embedded in German culture. He found a solution by bifurcating salvation so that its essence—the *Sein*, the objective part of salvation—was given in Baptism and faith—the subjective part, the *Werden*—was given in the preached Word. This scheme allows for infant Baptism but not within the New Testament dimensions. Children possess salvation objectively but not subjectively, that is, by faith. Seeberg has come no further than Calvin in attributing salvation to children but without faith.

ADOLF SCHLATTER

Adolf Schlatter, professor at Berlin and later Tübingen, discusses infant Baptism in his *Das Christliche Dogma*. Like Bunke and Seeberg, Schlatter wrestles with the same problem of attempting to keep infant Baptism an integral part of salvation without coming to an acceptance of infant faith. Bunke resolved the problem by defining infant Baptism as God's personal call of regeneration to the child. Seeberg emphasized infant Baptism as God's promise of regeneration or forgiveness to the child. Schlatter attempts to resolve the problem of keeping infant Baptism an integral part of salvation without accepting infant faith by putting a strong emphasis on the grace given in Baptism. The child is said to be caught up in grace through Baptism before he comes to faith. Between the giving of grace in Baptism and the arising of faith, there is a considerable lapse of time. Such a separation between the giving of grace in Baptism and the arising of faith in the child is said by Schlatter only to be an accurate reflection of the fact that grace precedes faith. Like other theologians of the nineteenth and early-twentieth centuries, Schlatter offers a strong polemic against Luther's doctrine of infant faith.

For Schlatter, Baptism belongs to those acts through which Jesus makes visible His will and gifts and unites individuals to His congregation. It indicates that Christ has given His Gospel not only in Word but in deed. In Baptism, Christ gives all of His gifts, including participation in His death and life, deliverance from sin and the flesh, and justification. In other words, the entire Gospel is connected with Baptism, with the understanding that it does not offer a special gift not found in the Word.

God confronts the individual with the entire power of His Gospel in Baptism. The baptized is expected to respond to God's action in Baptism with repentance and faith. This relationship established in Baptism is the relationship the believer has with God throughout his entire life. Within the relationship of Baptism, God takes away sin and guilt, but in it He also unites us in fellowship with Christ. Schlatter places the blessings of Baptism into negative and positive categories. First, Baptism removes sin, guilt, and anything that is detrimental to one's salvation, and, second, it effects a new relationship with Christ.[68] Repentance worked in Baptism condemns a person and places him before God as unjust. This repentance also demands that, rather than concerning ourselves with our own unrighteousness, we should concentrate on God giving us grace, with which we can believe and have certainty of our salvation.

Schlatter initiates his discussion on infant Baptism by examining Luther's concept of infant faith. He notes that Luther's study of the New Testament drew him to see an indissoluble connection between faith and Baptism. Thus, Luther reasoned that a child having the grace of Baptism would require that he have faith to accept this grace. Faith was created in the child by the congregation imploring God to give him saving faith. Luther did not maintain that the congregation believed vicariously for the child, but that it assisted the child to come to faith through its prayers. Schlatter claims that by attributing faith to the child, Luther was not compelled to delay the child's Baptism to maturity. Luther taught that this faith was worked by Christ in the act of Baptism through the Holy Spirit.[69] Schlatter does not disagree with Luther that the Spirit works in the child. In his opinion Luther went too far in delineating what could be known of the Spirit's work. Luther's concept of infant faith is only a conjecture based upon a syllogism[70] in order to provide a basis for a concept that lacked much

[68] Adolf Schlatter, *Das Christliche Dogma* (Calw & Stuttgart: Verlag der Vereinsbuchhandlung, 1911), 456–60.

[69] Schlatter, *Das Christliche Dogma*, 461–63.

[70] It is difficult to say exactly to which of Luther's syllogisms Schlatter refers. Baptism and faith are inseparable in the New Testament. Children are to be baptized. Therefore children have faith. Another possibility attributed to Luther is found in a theological opinion prepared by the Theologische Facultät der Martin-Luther-

support. Schlatter urges men called by the Church not to accept Luther's conjecture about infant faith. They should perform their pastoral tasks with a good conscience, which cannot be based on inferences. Infant faith is a dangerous conjecture, because what the Church believes about faith is at stake. For Schlatter, faith is an act of the mind that involves hearing and understanding the preached message. It also involves an act of the will that undergirds the Word. Whatever happens in children through Baptism can have no resemblance to the faith of an adult person. Faith is stripped of its meaning when it is defined as an unconscious process. By denying infant faith, Schlatter believes he has protected the concept of faith that is the cornerstone of the Church's preaching.[71]

Schlatter also condemns the concept that children should be baptized to prevent them from going to hell. Fear of hell more than their having faith was the dominant motive in baptizing children. The Augsburg Confession is cited as an example of the false teaching that infants should be baptized to save them from going to hell. Schlatter, who presents himself as a Lutheran theologian, sides with the Anabaptists and against the Augsburg Confession, which condemns them for holding that children are saved without Baptism. In his view, baptismal practice cannot be based on fear and so the fear of hell is not a valid reason for baptizing children. Such a motivation is without faith and sinful. There should be no fear concerning the fate of children who die without Baptism. Faith should be in Christ and not in the water. Even though the water of Baptism is lacking, Christ is not lacking. The grace of God is not dead, if the child should die before he receives Baptism.[72]

Schlatter also objects to Baptism's sole purpose as a remedy for original sin. This would make Baptism an indispensable Sacrament for newborn children, a view he cannot accept. This view surrenders the Reformation heritage and contradicts the New Testament. Rather, Baptism embraces everything sinful in man. If Baptism were directed only against original sin, it would become one means of salvation among other means. Baptism's efficacy would have to be complemented by the application of other means of grace, and it

---

Universität Halle-Wittenberg in response to a request from the Consistory of Saxony. Children are not excluded from salvation. Salvation can only be appropriated in faith. Therefore children can believe. "Votum zur Kindertaufe," *Theologische Literaturzeitung*, 87/11 (November 1962): 872.

[71] Schlatter, *Das Christliche Dogma*, 463.

[72] Schlatter, *Das Christliche Dogma*, 463.

would become impossible for the individual to reach a permanent state of grace.[73] This is in line with Schlatter's understanding that all of God's grace is located in Baptism.

Schlatter sees no value in arguing for infant Baptism based on its role in preserving the *Volkskirche*, an arrangement in which the population of a particular political jurisdiction belonged to one Church. This was the argument the Reformed theologians in Zürich had used in maintaining the custom, and seeing a correlation between the Old Testament rite of circumcision and Baptism. They wanted to bind the Church and the people to one another and so make the people Christian through the Church. The ideal was that the Church and people were one unit as it was in the Old Testament. Since circumcision was used in the Old Testament for doing this, infant Baptism was chosen as the means through which Church and people would become united to each another.

Schlatter holds that the Anabaptist controversy arose as a protest against such a union of Church and people. The Anabaptists wanted to establish the Church on a voluntary basis. With them, Schlatter agrees that infant Baptism should not be used as a means of binding Church and people to one another. Even though many problems might arise by separating the Church from the people, infant Baptism is a separate issue that should be settled on its own merits. It cannot be maintained simply as a means of continuing the *Volkskirche*. Baptism must be used for the purpose for which it was instituted. If infant Baptism does not fulfill the purposes of Baptism, it should not then be maintained for the sake of other benefits such as the *Volkskirche*.[74]

After this discussion of what he considers to be invalid motives for baptizing children, Schlatter presents what for him are valid motives. He holds that faith is necessary for participation in God's forgiveness and redemption and for fellowship with Christ. A Baptism not confirmed by faith is received in vain. However, the relationship between divine grace and human faith is only properly understood where the priority is given to grace. Grace is first, and faith is second. Grace gives, and faith takes what grace gives. Grace and faith stand in a cause and effect relationship with each other. Faith is also a limitation on grace, insofar as that without faith, grace remains without effect.[75]

---

[73] Schlatter, *Das Christliche Dogma*, 463–64.
[74] Schlatter, *Das Christliche Dogma*, 464–65.
[75] Schlatter, *Das Christliche Dogma*, 465.

Schlatter condemns the concept that a man must first believe before God is gracious to him. If this were the case, then the individual would create through his own attitude the ability to receive divine grace. Faith would then be endangered since it would be misled to rely on itself. Faith would not rely on God, who is the strength of faith. Therefore, the Baptist question that asks whether the faith of the candidate for Baptism is sufficient can never be answered, since it separates faith from grace. Faith does not consist in measuring one's faithfulness, through which a person then creates the grace of God. In infant Baptism, Schlatter finds an excellent means through which the proper relationship between grace and faith can be expressed. The proper order is that grace precedes and calls forth faith.[76] This is exactly what happens in infant Baptism. Here God's grace precedes and calls forth faith from the child.[77]

The call of God to faith in Baptism does not limit itself to the time of Baptism, but it extends over one's entire lifetime. Schlatter calls Luther's concept of infant faith unnecessary and dangerous since, he says, it compresses the grace of Baptism into one moment.[78] Rather than having only momentary significance, Baptism places one under the will of God and is valid throughout one's entire life. On this account Baptism does not have to be repeated, if a person is restored after having fallen into a period of serious and long unbelief. Baptism

---

[76] Schlatter has emphasized here the importance of divine grace in connection with Baptism in order to avoid the necessity of accepting the doctrine of infant faith. A French Protestant theologian, Paul Lobstein (1850–1922), emphasized love in order to accomplish the same thing. He writes: "Er hat uns zuerst geliebt, er ist größer als unser Herz—er kann sich selbst nicht verleugnen—das ist die dreifache Wahrheit, an die uns die Kindertaufe erinnert, diese selige Unterpfand der göttliche Liebe, die sich darin kundgibt und offenbart in ihrem unverdienten Zuvorkommen, ihrer königlichen Unabhängigkeit und ihrer unwandenbaren Treue." By emphasizing the love of God, Lobstein wanted to avoid Luther's doctrine of infant faith, which he called a psychologically and morally untenable fiction. *Zur Rechtfertigung der Kindertaufe*, translated into German by Pfr. Kupsch (Freiburg i. B. and Leipzig: J. C. B. Mohr, 1895), 295. Theodor Kaftan (1848–1926) avoided the doctrine of infant faith by emphasizing God's election. He writes: "Das ist ein Verständnis der Taufe der Fülle des Evangeliums heraus. 'Nicht ihr habt mich erwählt, sondern ich habe euch erwählt.' In der Kindertaufe gewinnte die Taufe ihre normale Gestalt." *Auslegung des lutherischen Katechismus* (Schleswig: Druck und Verlag von Julius Bergas, 1892), 344.

[77] Schlatter, *Das Christliche Dogma*, 456–66.

[78] Luther does not teach this. Cf. Harry G. Coiner, "The Inclusive Nature of Holy Baptism in Luther's Writings," *Concordia Theological Monthly* 33 (November 1962), 645–57.

is given for all time and through it we know that God does not want to repel us from Himself, but that He wants to receive us in faith. However, as long as a person is without faith, grace cannot become his personal possession. Still, in spite of the lack of faith, the grace of God is not unreal. Even though a person resists the grace of God, it does not leave. It stays and attains its purpose when a person comes to faith. In faith, the grace of Baptism is imparted to us. As already shown, Schlatter dismisses the concept of infant faith as false. Still, infant Baptism is not an erroneous Baptism because faith is lacking. Infant Baptism could only be described as erroneous if it could be shown that children lack the grace of God and that they were excluded by Christ from His congregation. But Schlatter claims that just the opposite is the case. According to the words of Jesus and the universal character of His work and lordship, children are promised divine grace. Christ Himself is the forgiveness of sins for the entire world and has reconciled it to God. Insofar as children belong to the world, they belong to those for whom Christ was sent; there is no need to have any anguish over the fate of unbaptized children. In fact, the reason for baptizing children is not that they stand outside of God's grace, but because they already stand in it. Infant Baptism is to be administered in connection with the future application of the preached Word. Where the possibility of dispensing the Word to the child in the future is not present, infant Baptism should not be applied. On this account, infant Baptism should not be carried out in heathen areas. For Schlatter, Baptism by itself is not a sufficient means of grace. Without the preached Word, Baptism cannot be the means of grace. On this account, the Church is obligated to give the child the Word as he grows.[79]

Since the dispensing of infant Baptism is to be carried out in connection with the future preaching of the Word, Schlatter suggests that infant Baptism be discontinued where Christian education is no longer possible. If the society has become hostile to Christianity, there is little reason to continue the union of the people and the Church in the *Volkskirche*. At such a time, the unity between the Church and the people would only be a fiction. Therefore, the Church should never continue with the practice of baptizing infants as if it were indispensable for its existence. If the *Volkskirche* would ever cease to exist, the situation would be like the Christian Church during

[79] Schlatter, *Das Christliche Dogma*, 466–67.

the time of the Roman Empire when both children and adults were baptized.[80]

SEEBERG AND SCHLATTER ON THE *VOLKSKIRCHE*

Both Seeberg and Schlatter attach the continuance of infant Baptism to the existence of the *Volkskirche*. If the *Volkskirche* should cease, infant Baptism would also have to be discontinued. But apart from the question of continuing infant Baptism, Seeberg and Schlatter disagree on what the relationship between infant Baptism and the *Volkskirche* should be. Seeberg justifies the entire practice of infant Baptism within the framework of the *Volkskirche*. On the other hand, Schlatter believes that they should remain separate issues. For Schlatter, the worth of the *Volkskirche* is that it provides Christian education, which must necessarily follow infant Baptism. But apart from this, infant Baptism and the *Volkskirche* are to remain separate matters. Seeberg regards both issues as being intimately connected with each other. It might be said that Seeberg regards infant Baptism as the Baptism of the *Volkskirche*. Schlatter, on the other hand, regards infant Baptism as a Baptism that can be defended in its own right quite apart from the issue of the *Volkskirche*.

EVALUATION OF SCHLATTER'S THEOLOGY

As previously mentioned, Schlatter's strong emphasis on grace was probably the most distinctive element in his discussion of infant Baptism. But it is precisely on this point that Schlatter is most vulnerable to criticism. First of all, he has maintained that every grace is the grace of Baptism. Still, he does not carry through with this principle, since he claims that faith is an effect of the preached Word and not of Baptism. If Baptism gives every grace, it should also give the grace to believe. This is, of course, denied by Schlatter. Second, infant Baptism is called a good expression of the priority of grace over faith.[81] No one would deny that grace is prior to faith and that

---

[80] Schlatter, *Das Christliche Dogma*, 467–68.

[81] None of the three men discussed in this chapter comment on the baptismal rite. Such comments are frequently helpful in understanding a theological position. In order to overcome this lack here, a few remarks about an article by Johannes Bauer, (1860–1933), professor of practical theology at the University of Heidelberg, will be included. Like Schlatter and Bunke, Bauer no longer accepted Luther's doctrine of infant faith. Since the child is not to be baptized on the basis of his own faith, Bauer suggests that either the Apostles' Creed no longer be used in the rite of infant Baptism or that infant Baptism be given up. Here follows the pertinent portion. "Der

this would hold true for infant Baptism too. However, from the priority of grace over faith, Schlatter justifies his conclusion that there can be a lapse of time between the giving of grace in Baptism and the arising of faith in the child. But in the matter of the personal application of grace, the priority and precedence of grace before faith is a logical sequence and not a temporal one. Second, in the matter of the objective justification of the world, grace precedes faith temporally by such an extent that it cannot be measured in units of human time. This means that the salvation established before the foundation of the world precedes temporally the faith of a man. However, in the matter of personal salvation or subjective justification, grace as a personal possession does not temporally precede faith. The possession of salvation presupposes faith. Thus, when Schlatter says that infant Baptism is an expression of the priority of grace over faith, this might be true insofar as the objective justification of the world is concerned, but it is not true so far as personal salvation is concerned. In maintaining that infant Baptism can be justified by the concept that grace precedes faith, Schlatter is confusing objective and subjective justification. In objective justification, grace precedes faith temporally, but in subjective justification, grace only precedes faith logically. There is no lapse of time between the personal possession of grace and faith.

A third objection against Schlatter's concept of infant Baptism regards his claim that children are baptized because they already stand in grace and because they belong to those for whom Christ and the Spirit were sent. Schleiermacher rightly protests against such

---

Einwände, die man heute gegen den Kinderglauben und gegen die damit zusammenhängende Stellung des Glaubensbekenntnis erhebt, sind unwiderlegbar, und auch lutherische Theologen der Gegenwart haben die Position Luthers aufgegeben; sie widerspricht der evangelischen Auffassung des Glaubens als eigener persönlicher Entscheidung und als einer inneren Bestimmtheit und Erfahrung des seelischen Lebens. Und je höher man die Wirkung der Taufe stellt, je mehr man geneigt ist, die objektive Kraft des Sakraments und seine Unabhängigkeit vom menschlichen Glauben zu betonen, um so schwieriger ist die Annahme eines irgendwie vor der Taufe vorhandenen oder hervorgerufenen Kinderglaubens oder eines stellvertretenden Glaubens durch die Paten.—Dabei ist es völlig einerlei, ob man das Glaubensbekenntnis einschränkt, ob man nur das Bekenntnis zu Vater, Sohn, und Geist, vorausschickt: die Formel 'auf das Bekenntnis taufen,' d. h. 'auf Grund eines dem Kind irgendwie zugeschriebenen Glaubenstaufen,' läßt sich bei der evangelischen Kindertaufe nicht aufrecht erhalten—oder man muß die Kindertaufe selbst aufschaffen." Johannes Bauer, "Bekenntnis und Kindertaufe," *Christliche Welt* 27 (1913): 209. Like Schlatter, Bauer has so emphasized grace that there is no need for faith in the child.

reasoning. He says that if children already stand in grace, there is no necessity to baptize them. In addition, he says that if we baptize them because they belong to those for whom Christ died, we should also on the same account baptize all men upon whom we can lay our hands.[82] Here again Schlatter has confused objective and subjective justification. Just because children belong to those for whom Christ and the Spirit were sent does not mean that they are personally saved. Actually, the Scriptures attribute personal salvation only to those who have faith, not to all who are included in Christ's work of redemption. The entire world has been included in His redemption, but this does not mean that everyone is personally saved. The mere fact that children are included in Christ's work of redemption does not mean that they automatically should be baptized. Schlatter's strong emphasis on grace is further seen in that he says that we should have no fear concerning children who die without Baptism because they already stand in God's grace. If such a thought were carried out to its logical consequences, Baptism would really become superfluous for children insofar as personal salvation is concerned.

Schlatter separates original sin from the total sinfulness of man and objects to the idea that Baptism is the means of grace directed only against original sin. Such a concept, Schlatter says, would make Baptism indispensable for newborn children. He is correct when he says that Baptism is directed to the entire sinful nature of man and not just original sin. But on this account Baptism would also be directed against original sin. If children do have original sin, then it is absolutely necessary that Baptism or some other means of grace be given them so that they can be saved. One can use the same data as Schlatter does and come to the opposite conclusion. If Baptism is directed to the total sinfulness of man, it would also be directed to every part of this sinfulness. Therefore, it would also be directed against original sin. On this account, children should be baptized.

A similar objection can be raised when Schlatter says that Luther's concept of faith is both unnecessary and damaging, since it compresses the effects of Baptism into the actual moment of the act. Schlatter says that Baptism is to be valid for the entire life and not just for one moment of it. If Schlatter is right when he says that Baptism is valid for our entire life, then one can come to a conclusion exactly opposite from Schlatter's. If Baptism is valid for the entire life, it is then also valid for the time of infancy. Should Baptism really

[82] Schleiermacher, *Der Christliche Glaube*, 2:384.

be valid for infancy, Luther's concept of infant faith would be quite necessary and edifying. It would be necessary, since as Schlatter himself admits, the benefits of Baptism can only really be enjoyed in faith.

Schlatter is a good example of those theologians who wanted to keep infant Baptism in God's plan of salvation for the individual without accepting the doctrine of infant faith. It is true that he has emphasized grace, but, unfortunately, he did so by eliminating faith from any role in the salvation of children.

CONCLUSION

In their understanding of infant Baptism, Bunke, Seeberg, and Schlatter embodied concepts previously found at the beginning of the nineteenth century in the writings of Wegscheider, Reinhard, and Schleiermacher, but they added a new dimension. Even though Baptism does not effect any change in the child, it has personal significance for the child's salvation in the future. With this, they attempted to reconcile two of their basic premises: (1) that Baptism has significance for salvation in connection with faith, and (2) that infants do not believe.[83] That Baptism was to have future significance for the child's salvation was expressed variously. Bunke called infant Baptism the personal call of God, which the child was able to answer only at a more mature age. Seeberg said that infant Baptism was the promise of future regeneration and forgiveness. Schlatter said that

[83] One of the more interesting attempts to solve the problem caused by the infant's lack of faith at the time of Baptism was provided by a theologian simply known by his last name, Kalchreuter. In order to bridge the tension caused by "1) ohne Glauben keine Taufe (kein Sakrament); 2) kein Glauben bei Säugling," he says that the faith of the infant's father can be substituted for the infant's faith. He writes: "Ist nun aber nach dem Obigen ein Glaube der Kinder unmöglich und doch die Beschneidung der Kinder eine göttliche sanctionirte Ordnung, so werden wir schon hier auf den einzig möglichen Ausweg hingewiesen, der uns auch bei dem Institut der Kindertaufe allein übrig bleibt, nämlich die Statuirung der *fides aliena* und zwar des Hausvaters, der einstweilen für das Kind eintrat." ("Der stellvertretende Glaube und die Kindertaufe," *Jahrbücher für deutsche Theologie* 11 [Drittes Heft, 1866]: 533). Kalchreuter claims that his concept is built on the unity and solidarity of the family, the congregation, the people, and the Church on one side, and the lack of faith in the infant on the other side (536). Just as the life of the child is potentially in the mother, so the faith of the child is potentially in the parents (542). It must be asked whether faith can be potentially present in parents who are hypocrites. Kalchreuter's position resembles that of the Roman Catholic doctrine which teaches that children are baptized on the faith of the Church or *fides aliena*.

infant Baptism was an excellent expression that grace precedes faith. Grace is present for the child long before he comes to faith.[84] There was a lapse of time between the giving of grace in Baptism and the arising of faith through the preached Word.

What these theologians did not address is how children incapable of faith possess the grace offered in Baptism. In the case of children, Luther held that it was by their own faith. For him a category between faith and unbelief, even for children, did not exist, but for these theologians, it did. Children are offered grace in Baptism, but incapable of faith they cannot appropriate it to themselves. Thus, a category between faith and unbelief has been set up for children who are offered grace through Baptism but who still do not have the maturity to accept it. Should they die before they come to faith, they are saved. Schlatter goes one step further in saying that there should be no concern about children who die without Baptism. If children are saved without Baptism, they are also saved with Baptism. This is implicit in the theologies of Bunke and Seeberg, neither of whom speaks of the damnation of baptized children. Baptized children are saved even without faith. Here lies the problem, since they hold that faith plays an important role in regeneration. A child only experiences regeneration first when he comes to faith, but a baptized child can be considered in a state of grace and saved without faith. Baptized children are saved as they wait for faith. In maintaining that children are saved without faith, these theologians establish a state between belief and unbelief.

This raises the question of whether Baptism effects salvation for the child in any sense at all, since it can be omitted without serious effect on the child's salvation. Thus, Schlatter holds that children are baptized because they already stand in grace, a position closely resembling that of Calvin. Similarly, Bunke calls Baptism the seal of the call the child already possesses through his birth. Seeberg holds that the birth of a child into a Christian environment gives him the permanent possession of Christianity (*Sein*). Since the birth of such a child gives him these blessings, Baptism does not effect anything new

---

[84] Theodor Kaftan tried to mediate between the ideas that only in faith can salvation be received and that children have no faith by saying that children were led on the road to faith. "Das geschieht, indem unter uns nur solche Kinder getauft werden, von denen wir wissen, daß sie in ihrem Heranwachsen den Weg zum Glauben werden geführt d.h. christlich erzogen werden." *Auslegung des lutherischen Katechismus*, 344. Of course, this does not solve the tension. A person on the road to faith is still without faith.

for the child. Baptism only confirms what the child already has through birth. It points to a child's future faith and regeneration, but at the time of his Baptism, the child is not given anything that he does not already possess. Baptism is considered the call to regeneration, but at the time of the Baptism, the call is without effect on the child. When the child is regenerated, the preached Word, and not the call in Baptism, affects him. Hence infants can be baptized only with a guarantee that the preached Word will follow. The preached Word is absent in Baptism for the infant and hence cannot create faith in the child. This can only be done when the Word is preached.[85]

[85] The second and third editions of *RGG* do not address the views of these theologians. Ferdinand Kattenbusch in *Realencyklopädie für protestantische Theologie und Kirche* does discuss the views of Kähler, Gottschick, and Scheel. R. Seeberg identified his views with those of Bunke and Kähler. See footnote 1 above. Of Kähler, Gottschick, and Scheel, Kattenbusch says, "Dem Kinde wird es, darauf rechnet die Gemeinde, zu seiner Zeit zum Bewußtsein kommen, was es heiße, im Leben unter einem gnädigen Gott zu stehen, von Beginn des Lebens an in diesen Gott 'getauft' zu sein. Wer die Bibel und was Christus gesagt und 'Verordnet' hat, nicht als Gesetz, sondern als Evangelium versteht, weiß, daß die Taufe nicht als 'bedingter Grund' der Gnadenszuwendung Gottes gedeutet werden darf. Er versteht es aber, daß sie als ein spezifischer Moment in dieser gewertet werden darf. Denn es ist nur ein Ausdruck dafür, daß wir Gott lebendig als Person empfinden, wenn wir ihn und seine Gnade im konkreten Momente zu sehen vermögen, ja darin suchen." F[erdinand] Kattenbusch, "Taufe. II. Kirchenlehre," *Realencyklopädie für protestantische Theologie und Kirche*, ed. Albert Hauck (Dritte verbesserte und vermehrte Auflage; Leipzig: J. C. Hinrichsche Buchhandlung, 1907), 19:424.

Chapter VI

Paul Althaus and Hermann Cremer

Introduction

Contemporary with Bunke, Seeberg, and Schlatter, who saw Baptism as a call and promise to the child, Paul Althaus Sr. and Hermann Cremer were writing monographs asserting that Baptism worked complete regeneration in a child but without attributing faith to him. Althaus termed this concept *Taufwiedergeburt*, baptismal regeneration, but in the case of children, it was a regeneration without faith. This he presented as the correct New Testament concept of Baptism. *Taufwiedergeburt* was solely an act of God and did not involve any change in the person. The individual received something from Baptism but did not experience an internal change. In baptismal regeneration, *Taufwiedergeburt*, God gave all the blessings of salvation, including justification and faith, to the baptized. Faith resulted from baptismal regeneration but was not part of it. Since faith was not necessary to receive baptismal regeneration, children who could not believe still were able to participate in it. When faith arose in the child, it did not bring any new blessings to the child. All blessings came from and through Baptism and not through faith. Faith would arise in the child at a time when his consciousness would be able to deal with the preached Word. Here Schleiermacher's influence is still seen. Faith created by the preached Word was the response to regeneration that the child already possessed through Baptism. Since faith played no part in receiving Baptism's benefits, it had for Althaus and Cremer a strongly objective character, a view that set them off from their contemporaries. Baptism was not only objective according to its nature, as Luther held, but also in its effects. Its effects were not dependent on any change in those who were baptized.[1] Hermann Cremer (1834–1903) was the mentor of Paul Althaus Sr. (1861–1925), but since Althaus was the first to engage the topic of Baptism, his views shall be discussed first.

PAUL ALTHAUS SR.

Paul Althaus Sr. would be overshadowed by his more famous son, Paul Althaus Jr. who, together with Werner Elert and Hermann Sasse, would be recognized as one of the leading confessional Lutheran theologians of the first half of the twentieth century. From 1897–1912, the older Althaus was professor of systematic and practical theology at the University of Göttingen. He finished his academic career as professor of systematic theology and New Testament in Leipzig. His first book on Baptism was given as a lecture for the Whitsunday conference in Hannover in 1892 under the title "*Die historischen and dogmatischen Grundlagen der hannoverischen Taufliturgie*" ("The Historical and Dogmatic Bases for the Baptismal Liturgy for [the Lutheran Church] in Hannover"). It was edited for publication in 1893 under the title *Die historischen und dogmatischen Grundlagen der Lutherischen Tauftliturgie*.[2] Under the direction of Hermann Cremer, Althaus was awarded the licentiate degree in theology on February 8, 1896, at the university in Greifswald for another work on Baptism. It appeared in 1897 under the title *Die Heilsbedeutung der Taufe im Neuen Testamente*.[3] Althaus and Cremer were of the same mind on Baptism and would remain friends until the latter's death in the fall of 1903. Althaus turned down an opportunity

[1] This assessment is supported by Kattenbusch: "Eine sittliche Erneuerung, eine 'subjektive Veränderung unserer Beschaffenheit' ist die Taufe nicht. Ebendeshalb ist sie als Kindertaufe genau das gleiche wie als Erwachsenentaufe. In dem Maß als dem Menschen (Kinde) zum Bewußtsein kommt, was Gott an ihm gethan, erwacht der (Heils-) Glaube und mit ihm die sittliche Kraft und Lust." F[erdinand] Kattenbusch, "Taufe. II. Kirchenlehre," *Realencyklopädie für protestantische Theologie und Kirche*, ed. Albert Hauck (Dritte verbesserte und vermehrte Auflage; Leipzig: J. C. Hinrichs'sche Buchhandlung, 1907), 19:423. Kattenbusch, in his survey of the nineteenth century, places Cremer and Althaus side by side and calls them the *Konstruktionen*. Of them he says, "die Taufe bedeutet eine acktuale Wiedergeburt."

[2] Paul Althaus, *Die historischen und dogmatischen Grundlagen der Lutherischen Taufliturgie* (Hannover: Verlag von Heinr. Feesche, 1893).

[3] Paul Althaus, *Die Heilsbedeutung der Taufe im Neuen Testamente* (Gütersloh: C. Bertelsmann), 1897.

arranged by Cremer to join him on the theological faculty of Greifswald and, in 1897, joined the theological faculty at Göttingen, where he became a full professor in 1899. A few days before coming to Göttingen, Ernst Schurer, soon to be his colleague, was not pleased with Althaus's doctrine of Baptism and vowed to oppose it. In 1912 he joined the faculty in Leipzig where he remained until his death on February 24, 1925. Even though *Die Heilsbedeutung der Taufe im Neuen Testamente* does not address infant Baptism specifically, his discussion of regeneration is applicable to it. Althaus views regeneration as an act of God without involving faith or any change in the recipient of Baptism. Since he does not discuss one Baptism for adults and another for children, what he says about Baptism is applicable to both.[4]

An effect of Baptism is dying and rising with Christ. The dying and rising with Christ effected by Baptism is not to be considered an ethical dying to sin or resurrection. Rather, the dying and rising with Christ are to be considered acts of God's grace through which the baptized actually and personally participates in the death and resurrection of Jesus. Through these acts, Jesus as the Messiah achieved redemption. Like the dying and rising with Christ, man's regeneration is not to be understood as an ethical renewing. Rather, regeneration is to be understood as an act of God's saving activity through which He gives salvation to those who have been baptized. Through this regeneration, the baptized are rescued from their former condition of imprisonment under death and made participants in the life created by Christ.[5] According to its essence, Baptism takes away the guilt of the individual on the basis of the redemptive work of Christ and hence is the bath of regeneration. This bath has been prepared by the grace of God. By virtue of the redemptive work in Baptism, we are placed into the fellowship of salvation. Althaus denounces those concepts of regeneration that hold that in Baptism regeneration is incomplete, that it is made possible, or that it is only signified and symbolized. According to Althaus, these unacceptable views are based on a false understanding of the Greek word for regeneration (*paliggenesia*) as an ethical restoration of the individual. This erroneous interpretation must first be discarded before coming to terms with the Pauline concept that regeneration takes place through

[4] Althaus, *Die Heilsbedeutung der Taufe,* ix. "Das Neue Testament rechnet mit den unterschiedlichen Arten der Erwachsenentaufe und der Kindertaufe nicht."
[5] Althaus, *Die Heilsbedeutung der Taufe*, 256.

Baptism, *Taufwiedergeburt*. Baptismal regeneration means that Baptism is the sacramental means ordained by God through which He makes salvation the possession of the individual. Through Baptism, the individual is placed into a personal relationship with the God of salvation. By virtue of this relationship created through Baptism, God's will to save the world becomes for the baptized person God's particular will to save him. Through Baptism, the objective redemption that is available for the entire world becomes the personal possession of the individual.[6] Through Baptism, God works regeneration. To be regenerated means to be saved from the condemnation of death and to participate in Christ's life. Althaus's concept of baptismal regeneration, *Taufwiedergeburt*, sets the stage for how he views infant Baptism and faith.[7]

Althaus calls the bestowal of faith in Baptism and the ethical conversion magic, resulting from the erroneous opinions of the dogmaticians.[8] He objects to the views of both Luther and Quenstedt that children believe through their Baptism. Althaus realizes that for Quenstedt infant faith was unlike the full and conscious faith of adults, the *fides reflexa*. In response Althaus says that the way in which infant faith was described could not really be distinguished from the self-conscious, active faith of an adult. Such a faith was incongruous with a child's nature. Luther is held responsible for what Althaus called the hypothesis of infant faith. At first, Luther believed that faith was given before the act of Baptism. Later he changed his mind and held that faith was given right in the act of Baptism.[9] Luther's and Quenstedt's doctrine of infant faith cannot be supported by the New Testament.[10]

Althaus's denial of infant faith follows naturally from how he understands faith as a conscious act. The idea of infant faith contradicts what God requires of an individual before He can give a new will, a new nature, and a new disposition. An individual must actively and consciously participate with God before He can create faith. Without a person's participation, God would be ignoring the individual's personal freedom and his ethical personality.[11] Since Althaus regards a personally conscious and active participation as a

---

[6] Althaus, *Die Heilsbedeutung der Taufe,* 257.
[7] Althaus, *Die Heilsbedeutung der Taufe*, 257–58.
[8] Althaus, *Die Heilsbedeutung der Taufe*, 308.
[9] Althaus, *Die Heilsbedeutung der Taufe*, 295.
[10] Althaus, *Die Heilsbedeutung der Taufe*, 296.
[11] Althaus, *Die Heilsbedeutung der Taufe*, 309.

requirement for God's creation of faith, it can be seen why he says that Luther's and Quenstedt's views on infant faith are unknown to the New Testament.

A fuller understanding of Althaus's concept of Baptism can be seen in how he relates Baptism to adult faith. Before Baptism, the faith of an adult is a gift of God, but it is not saving faith. Faith does not bestow the gifts that Baptism does.[12] When Baptism is given, the faith which existed before Baptism becomes a faith that receives and holds salvation. What faith desired before Baptism it receives in Baptism.[13] Faith cannot bring or add anything to Baptism. It can only receive and make use of that which is once and for all time given in Baptism. Baptism demands that faith follows, but faith is not required in order that Baptism may become effective. Faith is the *organum leptikon* by which Baptism can subjectively come into force.[14]

Even though Althaus does not specify what infant Baptism does and does not do in infants and children, this can be concluded from his understanding of the nature and effect of Baptism that one Baptism is valid for both adults and children. Baptism does work regeneration in young children but without working faith. Since children possess salvation through Baptism, its role has been confused with the one traditionally given to faith. According to Luther's understanding, God gives salvation through Baptism, but Baptism is God's means of giving salvation and is not the means by which the baptized accepts it. Faith is the only means by which one applies salvation to oneself. It is hard to see that according to Althaus a baptized unbeliever would not thereby be personally and subjectively justified. Objective justification becomes indistinguishable from subjective justification. By maintaining that regeneration does not have to do with any ethical change in man, Althaus makes regeneration a thing with an objective and autonomous existence apart from the disposition of the one who possesses it. Unless regeneration involves the ethical condition of the baptized, an unbeliever can possess it. This is the case of children who cannot believe but possess baptismal regeneration.

For Althaus, the order of salvation is grace, Baptism, personal salvation, and, last of all, faith. Faith is not the channel through which Baptism works, but it is a product of regeneration given in Baptism.

---

[12] Althaus, *Die Heilsbedeutung der Taufe*, 298.
[13] Althaus, *Die Heilsbedeutung der Taufe*, 303.
[14] Althaus, *Die Heilsbedeutung der Taufe*, 308–10.

Saving faith is not the prerequisite for regeneration, but regeneration is the prerequisite for saving faith. The blessings that God gives do not come through faith but through baptismal regeneration. Althaus does say that Baptism comes into force subjectively through faith; however, Baptism has a personal saving effect before and apart from faith. By saying that Baptism is brought into subjective force through faith, Althaus means that through faith the person becomes conscious of what Baptism has done to him and then he lives accordingly. However, even apart from Baptism coming subjectively into force through faith, Baptism works regeneration. Baptism is merely given a different but a higher place in the economy of salvation than the preached Word. By itself, the preached Word can produce faith in its hearer, but only Baptism changes an ordinary faith into a saving faith.

For Luther, Baptism possessed an objective character, since it was God's work, but reception of its benefits depended on faith. For Althaus, the benefits are given without faith. God works regeneration in the individual apart from his ethical condition. The subjective personality is not involved. However, when it comes to the creation of faith, Althaus completely reverses himself. If God were to create faith in the individual without his active and conscious participation, it would be a violation of that person's freedom and ethical personality. On the one hand, God gives salvation to the individual apart from his ethical disposition and, on the other hand, God does not create faith without the person's active participation. A synergistic view of faith lies side by side with a monergistic view of the bestowal of salvation. This dichotomy is dependent on Althaus's seperation of the giving of the benefits of salvation from faith. His concept of baptismal regeneration (*Taufwiedergeburt*) was soon to appear in the writings of his mentor, Hermann Cremer, who applied this concept specifically to children.

HERMANN CREMER

Cremer had been Althaus's mentor and the elder of the two, but his books on Baptism were published after Althaus's and shortly before his own death in 1903. The influence that each had on the other probably began when Althaus was preparing his dissertations under Cremer's tutelage. Cremer's first book on Baptism appeared in 1899 under the title *Wesen und Wirkung der Taufe.*[15] The second one was published in 1900 with the title *Taufe, Wiedergeburt und Kindertaufe* and was a response to Johannes Lepsius, who had criticized his 1899 work.[16] An enlarged edition of *Taufe, Wiedergeburt und Kindertaufe* appeared in 1901.[17] This edition was virtually a different book from the 1900 edition in size and content. In the first edition, it appears that Cremer denies infant faith, and in the second he accepts it. This conundrum may account for the different evaluations of Cremer. His contemporaries, Ernst Bunke[18] and Reinhold Seeberg,[19] held that Cremer did not teach infant faith. Writing half a century later, Karl Brinkel claims he did.[20] When Bunke criticized Cremer, he had the works of 1899 and 1900 at his disposal. Seeberg had these in addition

---

[15] Hermann Cremer, *Wesen und Wirkung der Taufe* (Gütersloh: C. Bertelsmann, 1899).

[16] Hermann Cremer, *Taufe, Wiedergeburt und Kindertaufe in Kraft des Heiligen Geistes* (Gütersloh: C. Bertelsmann, 1900), 3–5.

[17] The first edition of 1901 had 76 pages and the second was more than twice the length with 165 pages. (Hermann Cremer, *Taufe, Wiedergeburt und Kindertaufe in Kraft des Heiligen Geistes* [Zweite, völlig neubearbeitete Auflage; Gütersloh, 1901]). A reprint for the second edition was published posthumously by son Ernst Cremer in 1917. Citations to the second edition are taken from the third edition. Cremer, *Taufe, Wiedergeburt und Kinderstaufe in Kraft des Heiligen Geistes*, ed. Ernst Cremer (Dritte unveränderte Auflage; Gütersloh: C. Bertelsmann, 1917).

[18] Bunke writes: "Aber daß die Kindertaufe die Wiedergeburt sei, muß anders bewiesen werden. Übrings müssen wir festfallen, daß nach Cremer zur Erlangung der Tauf-Wiedergeburt-Rechtfertigung ein minderwärtiger Glaube ausreichend ist, den man dem Glauben nach der Taufe (das ist doch dann der seligmachende Glaube) nicht gleichsetzen darf. Ob die Kinder wenigstens diesen minderwärtigen Glauben haben, ist hier nicht ausdrücklich behauptet." *Lehrstreit über die Kindertaufe* (Kassel: n.p., 1900), 59. He further says, "Luther hatte sich die Wiedergeburt in der Kindertaufe gesichert, daß er den Heilsglauben der Kinder behauptete. . . . Cremer hat diese Aufnahme aufgegeben" (62).

[19] Seeberg writes: "Andere wieder verdünnten den Begriff der Wiedergeburt so, daß er identisch wurde mit dem Begriff der Rechtfertigung (so Ritschl und Cremer). Dann handelte es sich nicht mehr darum bei der Taufe, daß dem Kinde ein neues Leben geschenkt werde (Cremer). Den 'Kinderglauben' konnte man bei dieser Anschauung beiseite schieben, aber man kam doch zu keiner deutlichen Aussage darüber, was denn die Taufe eigentliche gebe. Man sagte, die Rechtfertigung, aber diese ist doch nur dort wirksam, wo sie im Glauben erfaßt, und Glaube war eben nicht da." *Zur Systematischen Theologie* (Leipzig: A. Deichert, 1909), 257.

[20] Brinkel writes: "Der Biblizist Wilhelm Cremer kam auch zur Annahme eines Kinderglaubens bei der Kindertaufe. Dieser Glaube werde bei der Taufe im Kind durch göttliche Begnadigung gewirkt, und sei 'so lange in der Begnadigung eingeschlossen, bis er sich zeigt, wenn das Erkennen, das Bewußtsein' sich zeige." *Die Lehre Luthers von der fides infantium bei der Kindertaufe* (Berlin: Evangelische Verlagsanstalt, 1958), 105.

to the one of 1901. Brinkel refers only to the 1901 edition. Since Cremer seems to have changed his position on infant faith between the appearing of the 1900 and 1901 editions, attention has to be given to each edition of *Taufe, Wiedergeburt und Kindertaufe*.

The 1900 edition of *Taufe, Wiedergeburt und Kindertaufe* contains the same basic thoughts of the more modest *Wesen und Wirkung der Taufgnade* of 1899. Unique in the 1900 work is that children are said to be completely regenerated in Baptism, even though they are not able to come to faith, a view put forth by Althaus. How Cremer understands regeneration is reflected in his view of infant Baptism, which must be either a real Baptism—which of necessity involves the washing away of sins, regeneration, and a renewal of the Holy Spirit—or not a Baptism. A third possibility does not exist.[21] Regeneration given by Baptism consists of the pardoning grace of God (*Begnadigung*) and the forgiveness of sins. To be regenerated in Baptism means that, through the forgiveness of sins, life is given anew and the individual is released from sin and judgment. Through grace and forgiveness, the baptized comes to possess eternal life.[22] Regeneration does not involve faith.[23] This definition allows Cremer to attribute regeneration to children who for him are incapable of faith.

Grace in Baptism has a primacy over faith in Cremer's doctrine of regeneration. This is evident in that before children accept and believe in salvation, it is available for them as their own possession. Faith is not a condition for receiving grace, but faith is created by grace. That faith is worked by grace is substantiated by a reference to the conversion of three thousand on Pentecost. Baptism, not the preaching of Peter, created saving faith in their hearts. Only after the hearers of Peter's sermon had been baptized could they say that they had experienced the grace of God. Such an experience could not be produced by the preached Word alone. This proves for Cremer that in Baptism grace becomes the personal possession of the individual. Cremer says that lack of faith in children does not prevent their being baptized. He reasons that there is no one time that is perfectly suited for the reception of Baptism. At no time is anyone capable of making

---

[21] Cremer, *Taufe, Wiedergeburt und Kindertaufe* (1900), 15.

[22] Cremer, *Taufe, Wiedergeburt und Kindertaufe* (1900), 32.

[23] In the 1901 edition of *Taufe, Wiedergeburt und Kindertaufe* Cremer included a chapter entitled "Die Notwendigkeit des Glaubens" (93–112). The addition of a chapter on the necessity of faith might indicate that Cremer was sensitive to his critics that his prior definition of regeneration excluded faith.

the decision to believe. The time for being baptized cannot be the time of repentance, since repentance is a lifetime task. Baptism should not be administered only at the time of death, since this would support the false concept that Baptism is directed only at those sins that have been committed before the reception of Baptism.[24] Since no one time is perfectly suited for receiving Baptism, it may be received during infancy as well as any other time.

Cremer speaks of children having faith (*Glauben der Kinder*), but whether this refers to infant faith is another matter.[25] He criticizes Ritschl for claiming that faith is possible only at maturity. Cremer maintains that it is possible for children to have justifying faith. The faith of children is described as a faith that grasps the Savior and prays the Lord's Prayer. Cremer calls it an evil thing to speak about the impossibility of children having faith (*die Unmöglichkeit des Glaubens der Kinder).* But here Cremer is speaking in defense of children's faith and not infant faith. This is evident in that he goes on to say that children are still not able to believe (*die Kinder noch nicht glauben können*). Since children are not capable of believing, faith cannot be directly produced in them by any means. Infants are not able to know anything about God and the world. Cremer does not want to have anything to do with infant faith and has no use for the older views, obviously a reference to Luther's and the Lutheran Orthodox doctrine of infant faith. Problematic for Cremer is whether children who cannot believe can be baptized.[26] Through the preached Word, children can believe, *Kinderglauben*, but baptized infants do not have *Kinderglauben.* Both baptized infants without faith and baptized children with faith have regeneration and justification from their Baptism.

Children's sinfulness alone is not reason enough to baptize them. If this were the case, then the children of Jews and heathens should be baptized along with those of Christians. However, Christians have the right and duty to baptize children who are born within Christendom, so that through Christian service and the power of the Holy Spirit

---

[24] Cremer, *Taufe, Wiedergeburt und Kindertaufe* (1900), 61–62.

[25] Ordinarily *Kindertaufe* refers to infant Baptism, but etymologically it can mean the Baptism of children who may not be infants, an ambiguity Cremer used to his theological advantage. Kurt Aland, who saw no biblical evidence for infant Baptism, used the same tactic in his *Taufe und Kindertaufe* (Gutersloh: Gerhard Mohn, 1971).

[26] Cremer, *Taufe, Wiedergeburt und Kindertaufe* (1900), 63–64. In the previous year, 1899, Cremer called infant faith a fiction. "Sollen wir denn wirklich mit der Fiktion des 'Glaubens der Kinder' rechnen müssen?" *Wesen und Wirkung*, 15.

they may receive what is necessary for their salvation. Birth from Christian parents gives these children a close relationship to God's salvation and with it the right to be baptized, a right the children of heathen do not have. They are in a position to come more easily and quickly to faith than the children of the heathen. From the very beginning, the children of Christians have a place in the Christian congregation and thus they come under the influence of God's Word.[27] The children's right to receive Baptism is based less on their need to be forgiven and more on the circumstances of their birth.

Factored into Cremer's understanding of Baptism is his definition of the Church, where God is present and dwells in the Spirit. Here are available the supernatural blessings of God, who is effective through the Spirit, who wants to gain the world to participate in redemption. Since children are born within the Church, they are born within that sphere where the Spirit is effective, and so from the beginning children stand under grace. Grace is not merely intended for them, but actually belongs to them. Through their birth, the children of Christians are called and chosen. Over these children hovers the grace of forgiveness and not merely the patience of God that hovers over the Jews and heathen. Even before they come to faith, God's grace is imparted to them. Before believing, they are upheld by grace and grow up into faith. There is never a time of decision for them. As their conscious life unfolds, it is already the conscious life of faith. Baptizing children presupposes that their life will become a life of faith. That Baptism and faith belong together follows necessarily from the connection between the Word and Baptism. A child's faith consciousness will depend for its content on the faith of the parents and the congregation into which the child was born.

Consciousness of faith comes to the child from his parents and consists in awareness of his own election and adoption by God. It does not involve a mental reflection of everything belonging to this adoption. As soon as the child has faith, his faith grasps this consciousness and joins it to Baptism. Unknown is the time and the way this takes place.[28] Cremer addresses the issue of whether the child's will is abused in being baptized. Rather than an act of force against a child's will, Baptism, as a child's birth into Christendom, gives him an advantage in coming to faith. Only when a baptized

[27] Cremer, *Taufe, Wiedergeburt und Kindertaufe* (1900), 65–67.
[28] Cremer, *Taufe, Wiedergeburt und Kindertaufe* (1900), 68–70.

child renounces or gives up the faith does such a child come under the condemnation of God.[29]

Cremer defines infant Baptism as the bath of regeneration and as the renewing in the Holy Spirit in which the child is given his new life which is saved from death, judgment, and destruction. A child's lack of knowledge of his salvation does not mean that he does not possess it. If baptized children do not come to faith, they lose what their Baptism gave them. Since children are called, justified, and reborn in Baptism, their not coming to faith is a falling away, an experiencing of the second death. New Testament warnings about falling away apply to those baptized as children because they have been baptized.[30] It should be noted here that Cremer is speaking of falling away from the grace of Baptism and not from faith. Even if a child who has been baptized never comes to faith, his refusal to come to faith is called a falling away. Since the Church in baptizing children is acting in accordance with the ordinances of the Lord in appropriating salvation, it acts in the power of the Holy Sprit. Thus, in Baptism, the Spirit appropriates to the child the eternal grace of the Triune God, the eternal redemption, and the eternal forgiveness of sins. In Baptism, the child is justified and sanctified. When the child later comes to faith, he has the assurance that he already has the grace given in Baptism.[31]

Since at the time of Baptism the child does not have the knowledge requisite for faith, it is very important that everything be done to insure that such a baptized child receive this knowledge. As mentioned, the children of the heathen should not be baptized, because they cannot understand the influence of the Word that is present within Christendom. Baptism should be refused to those children who are born of parents who oppose Christianity or where a Christian education cannot be guaranteed. Such a child is not an object of the divine election, but may become one later. Refusing Baptism to children for whom a guarantee of Christian education cannot be given can be a blessing and will not hinder them from coming to faith later. In order to determine which parents are fit to have their children baptized, Cremer suggests smaller congregations, so that the commitment of the members of the congregation will be

[29] Cremer, *Taufe, Wiedergeburt und Kindertaufe* (1900), 72.
[30] Cremer, *Taufe, Wiedergeburt und Kindertaufe* (1900), 72–73.
[31] Cremer, *Taufe, Wiedergeburt und Kindertaufe* (1900), 73–74.

more easily known. Unless this is done, it will be impossible to have a sincere and blessed dispensation of the Sacrament of Baptism.[32]

Cremer's concept of Baptism in 1900 in *Taufe, Wiedergeburt und Kindertaufe* is more extensive and clearly set forth than in the year before in *Wesen und Wirkung der Taufsgnade*, but his views remained the same. Three of his views were set forth by Schleiermacher and those influenced by him (see Chapters Two and Three). (1) Faith comes only through the preached Word, not Baptism. (2) Infants do not have faith. (3) As long as children do not come to faith through the preached Word, their Baptism is incomplete. Since in some places it might appear that Cremer contends for the exact opposite position, each point needs clarification.

Cremer calls faith an effect (*Wirkung*) of Baptism but nuances this by calling it a saving faith, a faith that is distinct from faith as knowledge. Baptism gives faith its saving quality. As mentioned, those who heard Peter's sermon on Pentecost experienced the mercy of God only after Baptism. Peter's sermon and not Baptism conveyed the knowledge of Him whom faith should believe. Only the preached Word and not Baptism provides knowledge. Thus, baptized inarticulate children do not possess faith as knowledge. They derive the consciousness of faith from their parents and the congregation. The Word and Baptism necessarily belong together. The Word provides the content or object of faith, and Baptism gives eternal life and other blessings. This necessary connection between faith and Baptism requires that infant Baptism be administered only when the Word can be preached later. Where there is no certainty of this, Baptism should be omitted.

Cremer agrees with Schleiermacher that infants cannot and do not have faith, even though he speaks of *Kinderglauben*. German allows an ambiguity that English does not. He can say that it is evil to speak of the impossibility of the faith of children ("*die Unmöglichkeit des Glaubens der Kinder*") but then goes on to say that Baptism is desirable for children who still cannot believe ("*Denn wir begehren sie Taufe für Kinder, **die noch nicht glauben können***").[33] The use of the word in German (*Kinder* expresses two words in English—infants and children) accounts for this discrepancy. A more precise translation for the English word infant is *Säugling*, but *Kindertaufe*

[32] Cremer, *Taufe, Wiedergeburt und Kindertaufe* (1900), 75.

[33] Cremer, *Taufe, Wiedergeburt und Kindertaufe* (1900), 63–64. Bold italics reflect emphatic spacing in original.

not *Säuglingtaufe* is the ordinary word for infant Baptism. The same holds true for infant faith, which appears in German as *Kinderglauben*. When Karl Brinkel studied Luther's concept of infant faith, he entitled his book *Die Lehre Luthers von der fides infantium bei der Kindertaufe*, but he consistently used *Kinderglauben* as the reference to infant faith and not simply children's faith. No ambiguity exists in the Latin *fides infantium*, since *infans* means "not able to speak." Newborn children lack the ability to articulate words, at least so that they can be understood. Cremer uses the double meaning in German to affirm that children can believe but infants cannot.

Like Schleiermacher, Cremer holds that the Baptism of infants is incomplete and needs to be supplemented by a conscious act of faith created by the preached Word. Without explanation, Cremer avoids saying that New Testament Baptism was not for infants or intended only for adult believers. With Althaus, he argues for an objective efficacy of Baptism, so that apart from the faith of the infant, it is justified and regenerated. Bunke, Seeberg, and Schlatter did not go this far and held that Baptism gave the child the promise of the forgiveness of sins and regeneration. Martensen and the Erlangen theologians held that Baptism effected a change within the physical or natural part of a child's existence. Following Luther, Friedrich Adolph Philippi (1809–1882) and Francis Pieper also taught that Baptism effected regeneration in infants, but regeneration was accomplished in the child by faith and not by Baptism alone without faith. On the other hand, Cremer taught an immediate regeneration and justification of the infant through Baptism without any change occurring in the child. In Baptism, God declared the child justified and regenerated without faith. On this point he is emphatic: Baptism is the actual washing away of sin, the washing of regeneration and the renewal of the Holy Spirit, or it is nothing. To this, there is absolutely no response from the infant. Faith does not play a role in the child's justification and regeneration. The spoken Word has only a cognitive function in informing the hearer that salvation is found in Baptism, but without the Word, the baptized person is ignorant of what Baptism has given him.

Cremer makes a clear distinction between the regenerate and the unregenerate.[34] The baptized are regenerate and the unbaptized are not regenerate. Though faith does not effect regeneration, loss of faith

---

[34] This differs from views offered by Bunke, Seeberg, and Schlatter, who allowed for an intermediate category.

deprives a baptized person of justification and regeneration. Faith is not a condition for receiving regeneration, but it is a condition for retaining it. In the expanded second edition of 1901, Cremer assigns a more prominent role to faith. Whether this was a real or just as apparent change must be determined.

HERMANN CREMER'S POSITION IN THE 1901 EDITION OF *TAUFE, WIEDERGEBURT UND KINDERTAUFE*

In 1901, Cremer published the second edition of his *Taufe, Wiedergeburt und Kindertaufe,* just one year after Ernst Bunke had written his *Lehrstreit über die Kindertaufe,* in which he criticized Cremer for teaching the regeneration of children without faith.[35] Bunke also had at his disposal Cremer's *Wesen und Wirkung der Taufgnade*, written in 1899. The 1901 edition of Cremer's work would be his final and most developed discussion on infant Baptism.[36]

Cremer's discussion begins with John's Baptism. Jesus' Baptism was superior to John's, since it actually took away sins. When John baptized, the forgiveness of sins was still not available, but it gave a guarantee of and promised forgiveness to those who confessed their sins. Actual forgiveness was not present in the preached Word but would come with the Messiah.[37] Similarly, the Baptism administered by the disciples in Jesus' name like John's Baptism did not work forgiveness of sins but only guaranteed forgiveness, because at that time the Lord had not completed His work of salvation. Forgiveness was present in the person of Jesus, but only when He completed His work would its content and value be revealed.[38] With the completion of the work of redemption, Baptism was instituted by God as the actual washing away of sins in the name of the Triune God. Since the apostolic Baptism is the actual washing away of sins in the name of

[35] Bunke, *Lehrstreit über die Kindertaufe*, 55–57. Bunke had a chapter entitled "Cremer-Althaus."

[36] *Taufe, Wiedergeburt und Kindertaufe*, (1901), 32–33. In this edition Cremer mentions specifically Bunke's critique of his *Wesen und Wirkung* and *Taufe, Wiedergeburt und Kindertaufe* (1900). Against Bunke, Cremer maintains that he never taught that Baptism was useful without faith. Striking is the inclusion in the 1901 edition, absent in the 1900 edition, of the chapter entitled "Die Notwendigkeit des Glaubens." Cremer may have taken Bunke's critique more seriously than he was ready to admit.

[37] Cremer, *Taufe, Wiedergeburt und Kindertaufe* (1901), 19.

[38] Cremer, *Taufe, Wiedergeburt und Kindertaufe* (1901), 21.

Jesus, it therefore follows that those who have been baptized are united with Christ, who died for them, was buried, and then rose again. By Baptism, one grows with Him like branches of the vine.[39]

Baptism in the New Testament is closely connected with the preaching of salvation, in which God is present in the Holy Spirit, who awakens a need and desire for salvation. This desire for salvation dare not be equated with that faith that possesses in Christ the redemption from sins or that experiences the mercy of God. A faith created by the preached Word before the person is baptized realizes that salvation is for the entire world and desires it for itself, but without Baptism the person does not possess it. It is incomplete and is only beginning. Thus, Cremer distinguishes one kind of faith created by preaching before Baptism and another kind of faith after Baptism. Faith is necessary to receive what Baptism offers; nevertheless Baptism is dependent not on this faith but on the Word and the will of God. Through faith, Baptism reveals its content, power, and meaning, but these do not come from faith but from the Word and the will of God. Possession of grace and eternal life is connected with Baptism, through which one becomes a Christian and a member of the congregation as the fellowship of salvation. This does not happen through hearing the spoken Word, which can condemn the person who loses what Baptism gives. Baptism gives all the grace of God, makes a sinner a child and heir of God and a fellow heir with Christ, and transplants the person out of death into life. If the Church practice of infant Baptism is to be the Baptism of Christ, it must be the bath of regeneration, the washing away of sins, and the burial and resurrection with Christ. Without these, infant Baptism is no Baptism.[40] For Cremer, Baptism gives to infants the same blessing as the Baptism of the New Testament.

At the heart of Cremer's concept of New Testament Baptism as the washing away of sins are his concepts of regeneration and faith. Baptism is the bath of regeneration that makes one a Christian, brings him into the state of grace, and cleanses him of the guilt of sin. No one has ever become a Christian without Baptism.[41] Baptism itself is regeneration. Over against the regeneration in Baptism stands faith. Regeneration is the reality that faith then encounters. To explain the differences between what faith and Baptism do, Cremer speaks of

[39] Cremer, *Taufe, Wiedergeburt und Kindertaufe* (1901), 23–24.
[40] Cremer, *Taufe, Wiedergeburt und Kindertaufe* (1901), 27–29.
[41] Cremer, *Taufe, Wiedergeburt und Kindertaufe* (1901), 35.

faith as the subjective order of salvation, *Subjektive Heilsordnung*, and regeneration as the objective order of salvation, *Objektive Heilsordnung*, which takes place through Baptism and forgiveness of sins. To come into the kingdom of the Messiah one must undergo Baptism. It is here that one receives regeneration and forgiveness of sins, but this does not involve a change in the person who receives Baptism. If baptismal regeneration involved a change in the individual, God's grace would be dependent on the change which it has brought about.[42] Regeneration is an act of God and first happens apart from the person. New Testament regeneration is the pardon and forgiveness of sins by which a new life is given and frees the baptized from death and judgment. Eternal life becomes a possession through regeneration. Faith personalizes regeneration because only by faith is a person made alive through grace. One believes in one's regeneration and rejoices over it in faith.[43] Faith and not regeneration concerns the inner change in man, not because faith justifies but because it grasps and lays hold of God.[44]

Only by faith can one have what Baptism offers and hence Baptism and faith belong together. If a person loses faith, he no longer possesses what Baptism offers.[45] Faith and Baptism belong together because faith receives what Baptism gives. What Baptism symbolizes, it also gives. In Baptism, the symbol and the reality are bound together.[46] First, Baptism gives regeneration and grace, to which faith then is added. Faith is the operation of grace in Baptism. One's faith is the work of God's grace even though it is the person who says that he wants to believe. Whoever has faith should desire Baptism, because only in Baptism is sin symbolically and actually taken away. There one meets God's mercy. Without Baptism, faith cannot have what Baptism offers.[47]

Cremer carefully distinguishes between Baptism, which alone regenerates, forgives sins, puts one in the state of salvation, and gives eternal life, and faith as man's response to his regeneration. Faith created by the preached Word responds to the high gifts of God in Baptism. There is a faith that is built solely on the preached Word, but it is not saving faith, because it does not yet possess those blessings

---

[42] Cremer, *Taufe, Wiedergeburt und Kindertaufe* (1901), 46–50.
[43] Cremer, *Taufe, Wiedergeburt und Kindertaufe* (1901), 54–56.
[44] Cremer, *Taufe, Wiedergeburt und Kindertaufe* (1901), 96–99.
[45] Cremer, *Taufe, Wiedergeburt und Kindertaufe* (1901), 93.
[46] Cremer, *Taufe, Wiedergeburt und Kindertaufe* (1901), 96–99.
[47] Cremer, *Taufe, Wiedergeburt und Kindertaufe* (1901), 106–10.

that only Baptism can offer. Baptism gives salvation and the preached Word creates a faith that acknowledges this. Only when Baptism is added to the faith created by the preached Word does it become a saving faith and receive the blessings of salvation that Baptism offers. Regeneration and other blessings of Baptism remain outside of man and by faith one lays hold of them. What is objective becomes subjective by faith. The chapter on infant Baptism is devoted chiefly to a discussion of infant faith, and so it seems that in the 1901 edition of *Taufe, Widergeburt und Kindertaufe,* Cremer has reversed his position set forth in the 1900 edition, where he explicitly denied infant faith.

Perhaps the best explanation for this change in accepting infant faith is that Cremer now realizes the indispensable role played by faith in the plan of salvation. The life of a regenerate child of God is the life of faith. Only by faith does one possess the eternal blessings, pardon from sin, and regeneration. All the blessings of Baptism are connected with faith. Without faith there are no blessings derived from Baptism. Faith and Baptism belong to each other from beginning to end. This connection does not mean that Baptism first becomes effective in faith, but without faith, the baptized person is in a dangerous position. Faith is an effect of Baptism and as such it dare not be separated from Baptism. In order for infant Baptism to be a real Baptism, it must be the washing away of sins, the bath of regeneration, and the renewal of the Holy Spirit. Baptism, and not faith, produces the state of grace for the child, and yet faith is necessary if the grace is to be possessed and enjoyed. Through faith, the person can hold on to this grace when he is in doubt.[48] Since according to his own definition baptismal grace can only be possessed and enjoyed by faith, Cremer comes around to attributing some type of faith to infants and children.

Grace is first given to the child through Baptism and not through faith.[49] Thus, the first bestowal of grace is without faith. In Baptism, children are given faith in pardoning grace (*Begnadigung*), which produces faith, but pardoning grace is present before faith. Faith is produced when God announces (*verkündigt*) in the preaching of the Gospel that one has been pardoned by grace (*Begnadigung*). One is not first pardoned when one believes, but one is already pardoned

[48] Cremer, *Taufe, Wiedergeburt und Kindertaufe* (1901), 106–10.
[49] Cremer, *Taufe, Wiedergeburt und Kindertaufe* (1901), 119.

when the preached Word comes.[50] Cremer is consistent in holding that faith comes from the preached Word and not Baptism. The baptized person possesses pardoning grace (*Begnadigung*) before he believes, but faith is included in pardoning grace (*Begnadigung*) and remains there until it reveals itself when the child exhibits recognition and consciousness.[51] Cremer does not designate the age when this happens. God effects faith in the child through Baptism, but faith is not a condition to receive grace.[52]

To prove his case that faith is given in the gift of grace (*Begnadigung*) Cremer discusses a child's mental development. The mind is there but does not notice that it is there. One awakes, but does not know when one awakes. One loves mother and father but does not begin doing this on a particular day. A person can be self-willed, but this attitude of the mind does not begin on a certain date. Just as the onset of these phenomena cannot be pinpointed to a certain day, so the moment when faith begins is indefinite. The faith God creates in one's soul appears gradually just as does human knowledge, will, love, and emotions and may have many crude features. Those with an awakening faith have memories (*Andenken*) of the heavenly Father and the certainty that they are loved. Even though such a faith is not tested, it is nevertheless true and conscious. It is as conscious as the child is conscious of himself and of his parents. Faith that is included in the pardoning grace of Baptism sometimes is not seen and used. In others, it does not awaken.

With adults, Cremer distinguished between the faith before Baptism and the faith after Baptism. Only the faith after Baptism can be designated as saving faith. With children, there is a distinction between faith before the preached Word and faith after the preached Word. Both types of faith play a role in salvation, but only after the child believes the preached Word, does he trust in the object he knows. The preached Word supplies the cognitive aspect of faith. In the 1901 edition, Cremer speaks of *Kinderglauben* given in Baptism, but until the child is mature, he is incapable of faith. In Baptism, God gives the child divine benefits, and in preaching, he creates faith to accept its benefits and so Baptism is effective without faith. Since Cremer gives a double meaning to *Kinderglauben,* he may seem to be saying just the opposite. Faith created through the Word is an act of

[50] Cremer, *Taufe, Wiedergeburt und Kindertaufe* (1901), 126–27.
[51] Cremer, *Taufe, Wiedergeburt und Kindertaufe* (1901), 133–34.
[52] Cremer, *Taufe, Wiedergeburt und Kindertaufe* (1901), 128.

grace, but such faith does not receive the *Begnadigung*, the grace, which can only be given in Baptism.

In the 1900 edition of *Taufe, Wiedergeburt und Kindertaufe*, Cremer used the term *Kinder* both of infants and older children. This allowed him to support *Kinderglauben* in one place and deny it in another. In the 1901 edition, he attributed *Kinderglauben* to infants, but such faith did not involve trust in God or an awareness of Him. The confusion now lies in the word *Kinderglauben*. Infants can possess faith in Baptism as a gift of God's grace, but only through preaching does faith then become a trust in God. Faith ascribed to infants is a quantity or thing given in Baptism, but as ascribed to older children and adults, faith is a trust in God created by the Word.[53]

It is no wonder that on the basis of the 1901 edition of Cremer's work, Reinhold Seeberg and Karl Brinkel could come to opposing opinions on whether or not Cremer accepted infant faith. Seeberg was close enough to the situation to understand that in spite of the terms *Kindertaufe* and *Kinderglauben*, Cremer had not deviated from his position in denying faith to baptized infants. Differences between the 1900 and 1901 editions of *Taufe, Wiedergeburt und Kindertaufe* were more apparent than real. Bunke had criticized Cremer's 1900 edition because faith was not a factor in the regeneration of children. Cremer's mentioning Bunke in the 1901 edition indicates that he was aware of Bunke's criticism and explains the additional amount of space given to discussing faith. To allow for faith in his definition of baptismal regeneration, Cremer defined faith as if it were a thing or object given in Baptism and not as trust in God. Cremer's basic position on the objective efficacy of Baptism had not changed but became more prominent in asserting that baptized children possessed regeneration and justification without the child being personally involved with his own faith.

CONCLUSION

Althaus set forth the principle of the objective efficacy of Baptism in his exegetical study of Baptism in the New Testament. This principle was applied by Cremer specifically to infants and children. Althaus's and Cremer's understanding of baptismal regeneration was an

---

[53] Martin Chemnitz references the Wittenberg Concord (1536) in showing that faith is ascribed to infants just as it is to adults. *Examination of the Council of Trent*, trans. Fred Kramer, 4 vols. (St. Louis: Concordia, 1974–1981), 2:173–75.

obvious denial of the *sola fide* principle of the Lutheran Church. If their principle would be carried to its logical consequences, Baptism alone would be sufficient in all persons for regeneration and participation in communion with God and Christ. The basic error in Althaus's and Cremer's thought was failure to distinguish between the essence of Baptism and its efficacy. According to Luther's doctrine, the essence of Baptism as an act of God does not depend on faith. It may properly be spoken of as having an objective character. The personal blessing or efficacy (*Wirkung*) of Baptism always depends on faith. Only to faith does Baptism give its blessings. Unless the baptized child or adult responds in faith to Baptism, he does not receive salvation. Without faith, God's saving activity in Baptism can have no effect. Thus, the effect of Baptism is subjective in character in that Baptism works faith and then works through faith. Baptism does not work apart from faith. Althaus and Cremer have ignored the Lutheran distinction between the objective character of the essence of Baptism and the subjective character of its efficacy. For them, both the essence of Baptism and its efficacy are objective in character.

CHAPTER VII

CONCLUSION

Putting aside the views of such nineteenth century confessional Lutherans as Philippi and Walther, who adhered to Luther's views on infant Baptism and faith, the majority of the nineteenth-century German Lutheran theologians agreed on four points: (1) Baptism cannot create saving faith. (2) Saving faith can only be produced by the spoken Word in persons who have reached a certain level of reason or consciousness. (3) Since infants or young children have not reached this level of consciousness, they cannot have faith. (4) Since children are without faith at their Baptism, it is incomplete and needs to be supplemented at maturity by a confession of faith often associated with confirmation. These theologians differed on Baptism's positive effects on the child at the time of Baptism being administered. Since justification by faith alone, *sola fide*, characterizes Lutheran theology, including its doctrine of Baptism, the question remains whether, in spite of their attempts to give faith a role in Baptism, they remained in this point within Luther's heritage.

THE INABILITY OF BAPTISM TO CREATE FAITH

Beginning with Rationalism at the end of the eighteen century and throughout the nineteenth century, the Lutheran theologians denied to Baptism its innate power to create faith. After Schleiermacher, they attributed a soteriological efficacy to Baptism that did not require faith on the part of the baptized. The Erlangen theologians held that Baptism worked on the nature or the physical life of the child and not on the mind or the reason. Bunke, Seeberg, and Schlatter said that Baptism was a promise of salvation to the child, a view similar to

Calvin's. Paul Althaus Sr. and Cremer claimed that salvation was attributed in its entirety to the child through Baptism. Cremer even spoke of a child's faith, but he redefined it. Baptism was a factor in creating faith, because it brought the child into association with the Church, where the preached Word was active. These theologians followed the Rationalists in denying faith to infants and so on this point they departed from Luther.[1] The Erlangen theologians, who had a commitment to classical Lutheranism, attributed a mysterious power to Baptism, but only the preached Word and not Baptism created faith.

THE INABILITY OF CHILDREN TO RECEIVE FAITH

Schleiermacher's ideas of consciousness, self-consciousness, and faith as God-consciousness had a wide influence among nineteenth-century Lutheran theologians who came to agree with him that infants did not have the capacity for faith. The ground for this had already been laid by the Rationalist theologians who saw faith in terms of reason, which in infants was undeveloped. Karl Brinkel, who wrote on Luther's doctrine of infant faith, notes that Rationalists' denial of infant faith is a result of the philosophy of Idealism.[2] Faith partially consists of knowledge and can only be created by its transmission through the senses to the conscious mind. This view did not allow for Luther's doctrine that Baptism created faith in infants. The Erlangen theologians held to the Rationalists' and Schleiermacher's understanding of faith as knowledge communicated through the senses to a conscious mind. They also believed, under the influence of Romanticism, that Baptism had naturalistic effects on the body and not on the mind. This concept that children lacked the mental capacity to have faith was arguably the chief reason for redefining Baptism.[3]

---

[1] Karl Brinkel, *Die Lehre Luthers von der fides infantium bei der Kindertaufe* (Berlin: Evangelische Verlagsanstalt, 1958), 95.

[2] Brinkel, *Die Lehre Luthers von der fides infantium*, 95.

[3] The view persists among Lutheran theologians that God works with infants differently than he does with adults. Infants are capable only of the Word in Baptism but not the spoken or written Word, of which only adults are psychologically capable. "Adults are dependent on the oral and written form of the Word when they come to faith, for they already have the functional psychological components to respond with trust when God addresses them. So far as we know, infants do not. In both cases it is God who is establishing the relations. In the case of infants, he does so with the promise of life won for them by Christ. In a manner beyond explanation, he expresses this promise to the infant through the Word in sacramental form, the Word of

They had to offer explanations of how children without faith could share in Baptism's benefits. This led to an adjustment in interpreting the New Testament passages from which the doctrine of Baptism was drawn. They had to reconcile the fact that New Testament Baptism was administered in faith with their conviction that children could not believe.

THE INCOMPLETENESS OF INFANT BAPTISM

Since infants received Baptism without faith, Lutheran theologians acknowledged that it was incomplete according to New Testament standards. The Rationalists and Supranaturalists addressed the issue holding that a child would come to faith in association with the Church. Schleiermacher favored the position of the Anabaptists in not baptizing infants because of their lack of faith, but he tolerated the custom with the understanding that the elements of faith would be added in their confirmation. The Erlangen theologians taught a naturalistic effect of Baptism on infants but also were aware that the lack of faith made it an incomplete Baptism, and so it was administered to them in regard to their future faith. Bunke, Seeberg, Schlatter, and Cremer did not hold to a naturalistic view of Baptism, but they also believed that infants could receive Baptism on the basis of their future faith. This meant that only children born of Christian parents should be baptized. Cremer favored smaller congregations in which pastors could question the parents to determine which parents had sufficient faith to merit having their children baptized. Baptism was denied to the children of unchurched parents. This mixes together Calvin's view that only children in the covenant by birth from Christian parents were entitled to Baptism along with the views of Catholics in the rites of Christian initiation that assured the proper level of Christian knowledge through catechesis. Traditionally,

---

Baptism." Robert Kolb, "Lutheran View: God's Baptism Act as Regenerative," in *Understanding Four Views on Baptism*, series ed. Paul E. Engle, gen. ed. John H. Armstrong (Grand Rapids: Zondervan, 2007), 104. In response, Thomas J. Nettles observes that "Kolb has two theologies of Baptism—one for infants and one for adults." "A Baptist Response" in *Understanding Four Views on Baptism*, 114. Nettles concludes that without trust children should not be baptized. Of course this is the view to which some Rationalist Lutherans first came.

Catholics and Lutherans only refused Baptism to children when the parental request was intended to make a mockery of Christianity.[4]

Baptizing children in regard to or in anticipation of future faith makes an emergency Baptism problematic when a child's death is immanent, an issue these theologians did not discuss. Calvin followed a more logical route in not allowing for emergency Baptism, especially one administered by a lay person. If the practice of baptizing infants depends on their coming to faith at maturity, then good reason exists not to baptize children who are in immediate danger of dying. Unless these children outlive the crisis, they will not come to faith through the spoken Word. Silence about emergency infant Baptism suggests that its discussion would have uncovered weaknesses in their theological arguments. These Lutheran theologians did hold that through Baptism the child possessed its gifts, but it was a possession without faith. With general agreement that the lack of faith made the Baptism of infants incomplete, these theologians had addressed how it could be completed. Following the Rationalists and Schleiermacher, some saw confirmation as corrective to the faith missing in infant Baptism, an answer that Catholicism had already offered. This was also inherent in Lutheran Pietism that held that after Baptism faith reached a higher goal in self-reflection. Though the Rationalist Lutheran theologians of the nineteenth century were not of one mind concerning Baptism, it was for each of them incomplete.

THE SOTERIOLOGICAL EFFECTS OF INFANT BAPTISM

The Rationalists and Schleiermacher saw Baptism's benefits as the child's incorporation into the Christian community, but these benefits were available even without Baptism. In the strictest sense, Baptism did benefit the child directly. Later, Lutheran theologians believed that according to the New Testament, Baptism offered benefits, but they had to figure out how these could be given to children apart from faith. The Erlangen theologians taught that Baptism had a saving effect on the child's physical or natural self. Bunke, Seeberg, and

[4] The traditional Lutheran position of baptizing infants quite apart from the religion or faith of the parents was preserved by Carl Ferdinand Wilhelm Walther, who led the confessional Lutheran movement in the United States but belonged to the theological world of the land of his birth. *Americanisch-Lutherische Pastoraltheologie* (St. Louis: Druckerei der Synode von Missouri, Ohio u. a. Staaten, 1872), 125–27.

Schlatter spoke about the saving efficacy of Baptism in terms of promise. Cremer and Althaus taught that Baptism gave a completed salvation for the child, even though he did not believe. They were agreed that faith involved the mind or the intellect and only came through the spoken Word. They also believed that this happened within the Christian home or congregation, the view that characterized the positions of the Rationalists and Schleiermacher. Though Schleiermacher saw his theology as a response to Rationalism, both saw the benefits of Baptism as the perfection of the moral or Christian life that came with advantages which were attached to belonging to a Christian community within the congregation.

The mysterious *Naturwirkung* of the Erlangen theologians is far removed from anything taught by the Rationalists; this physical effect of Baptism on the child through Baptism is completed only when that child comes to faith within the congregation of the baptized. Bunke, Seeberg, Schlatter, Althaus, and Cremer also held that Baptism ushers the child into the outward association of believers, where faith can arise. So, in the sense that faith arises within the Christian community, they did not, in this aspect at least, advance much beyond Rationalism and Schleiermacher. The community with the spoken Word and not Baptism effects faith, and so Baptism in creating faith is made subsidiary to the influence of the Christian community. At least in regard to faith, the community and not Baptism is the real means of grace. The connecting of salvation with the outward association of church members is, as Werner Elert points out, a thought originating with Schleiermacher and not Luther.[5]

THE TWO ALTERNATIVES

Luther and the classical Lutheran theologians answered how children could receive Baptism and its benefits by ascribing faith to them, the *fides infantium*. Beginning with the Rationalists, later Lutheran theologians could no longer do this, and they had to show how baptized children could still receive these benefits without faith. An overarching question was whether infant Baptism was the New Testament practice that they agreed had been administered in faith. In the background was the older Lutheran position that Baptism was

[5] Werner Elert, *Abendmahl und Kirchengemeinschaft in der alten Kirche hauptsächlich des Ostens* (Berlin: Lutherisches Verlagshaus, 1954), 5–7.

efficacious for children in whom faith was created by Baptism or even before Baptism by the Word.

For Luther infant Baptism was not only in harmony with Scripture but demanded by it. Not only were children capable of faith, but their sinful condition required the remedy Baptism offered. After the eighteenth-century Enlightenment, Rationlist Lutheran theologians moved away from Luther and their Reformation heritage but without fully disowning it. In their discussions of infant Baptism, this tension was manifested but was not really resolved, or at least it was resolved in ways about which they disagreed with one another. Each of their attempts at resolution compromised the *sola fide* doctrine that distingished Lutheran theology from that of others. By denying the *fides infantium*, they were suspending the applicability of the doctrine for children, a large segment of those who found themselves in the Christian community. By not baptizing infants, Reformation-era Anabaptists and modern Baptists also made the *sola fide* principle inapplicable to children. Francis Pieper, a German born theologian who made his mark in America, takes the bold step of affirming infant faith apart from his discussion of Baptism.[6] Of course, the doctrine of infant faith is contrary to psychological and philosophical presuppositions arising out of Humanism and Rationalism.[7]

Sola fide is so central for the Lutheran doctrine of justification that exceptions cannot be made. The Lutheran Confessions and the classical theologians insist that salvation takes place only by believing the Word, which is also present in Baptism. Children are born of flesh and blood and do not constitute a special class between sinful human beings and perfected angels. A critique can be made of the German Lutheran theologians at several levels, but their denial of the *fides infantium* contravened the Reformation principle of justification through faith: "*Igitur sola fide iustificamur*."[8]

---

[6] Francis Pieper, *Christliche Dogmatik*, 3 vols. (St. Louis: Concordia, 1917–1924), 2:537–36; *Christian Dogmatics*, 3 vols. (St. Loius: Concordia, 1951–1953), 2:448–49.

[7] Brinkel, *Die Lehre Luthers von der fides infantium*, 95.

[8] Apology of the Augsburg Confession IV, 178.

BIBLIOGRAPHY

PRIMARY SOURCES

Achelis, Ernst Christian. *Lehrbuch der Praktischen Theologie*. Vol. 3. Dritte teilweise neubearbeitete Auflage. Leipzig: J. C. Hinrichs'sche Buchhandlung, 1911.

Aland, Kurt. *Die Säuglingstaufe im Neuen Testament und in der alten Kirche: eine Antwort an Joachim Jeremias*. München: C. Kaiser, 1961.

Althaus, Paul, Sr. *Die Dogmatische Begründung der Neutest amentlichen Aussagen über die Taufe*. Gütersloh: C. Bertelsmann, 1896.

________. *Die Heilsbedeutung der Taufe im Neuen Testament.* Gütersloh: C. Bertelsmann, 1897.

________. *Die historischen und dogmatischen Grundlagen der Lutherischen Taufliturgie.* Hannover: Verlag von Heinr.[ich] Fresche, 1892.

Axelsen, J. C. "Die Kindertaufe dargestellt nach ihrem Verhältniss zur Schrift und zum Glauben," *Zeitschrift für die gesammte lutherische Theologie und Kirche*, 8/3 (1847): 1–49.

Bahr, C. *Die heilige Taufe nach den Einsetzungsworten.* Halle: Julius Fricke, 1871.

Barth, Karl. *Church Dogmatics*. Translated by G. W. Bromiley. 5 vols. Edinburgh: T. & T. Clark, 1969.

________. *Die kirchliche Taufe*. München: C. Kaiser, 1947.

________. *The Teaching of the Church Regarding Baptism*. Translated by Ernest A. Payne. London: SCM Press, 1948.

Barth, Markus. *Die Taufe-ein Sakrament?: Ein exegetischer Beitrag zum Gespräch über die kirchliche Taufe*. Zürich: Evangelischer Verlag, 1951.

Bauer, Johannes. "Bekenntnis und Kindertaufe," *Die Christliche Welt*, 27 (1913): 206–209, 225–228, 247–250.

Bretschneider, Karl Gottlob. *Handbuch der Dogmatik der evangelischen-lutherischen Kirche*. 2 vols. Zweite verbesserte und sehr vermehrte Auflage. Leipzig: Barth, 1822.

Brettner. "Die Gnadenmittel, Wort und Sakrament, in ihrem Verhältnisse zu einander betrachtet," *Mecklenburgisches Kirchen-und Zeitblatt*, 13 (1887): 113–125, 129–139.

Brief Statement of the Doctrinal Position of the Missouri Synod. St. Louis: Concordia, n.d.

Bunke, Ernst. "Dr. Lepsius contra Professor D. Cremer," *Deutsche Evangelische Kirchenzeitung*, 13 (1899): 265–267, 298–299.

________. "Glaube und Kinderglaube," *Deutsche Evangelische Kirchenzeitung*, 14 (1900): 281–282.

________. *Lehrstreit über die Kindertaufe*. Kassel: n.p., 1900.

________. "Taufe und Glaube," *Deutsche Evangelische Kirchenzeitung*, 13 (1899): 282–284.

________. "Was ist die Kindertaufe," *Deutsche Evangelische Kirchenzeitung*, 13(1899): 352–53, 361–362.

________. "Wort und Sakrament," *Deutsche Evangelische Kirchenzeitung*, 14 (1900): 286–87, 295–297.

Calvin, John. *Institutes of the Christian Religion.* 1536 edition. Translated by Ford Lewis Battles. Grand Rapids: Wm. B. Eerdmans, 1959.

Corblet, Jules. *Histoire Dogmatique, Liturgique et Archeologique du Sacrament de Bapteme*. 2 vols. Paris: Victor Palm, 1881–1882.

Cremer, Ernst. Vom Kinderglauben: *Eine Studie über das Wesen des christlichen Glaubens.* Gütersloh: C. Bertelsmann, 1902.

Cremer, Hermann. *Taufe, Wiedergeburt und Kindertaufe in Kraft des heiligen Geistes*. Gütersloh: C. Bertelsmann, 1900.

________.*Taufe, Wiedergeburt und Kindertaufe in Kraft des heiligen Geistes*. Zweite, völlig neubearbeitete Auflage. Gütersloh: C. Bertelsmann, 1901.

________. *Taufe, Wiedergeburt und Kindertaufe in Kraft des heiligen Geistes*. Edited by Ernst Cremer. Dritte unveränderte Auflage. Gütersloh: C. Bertelsmann, 1917.

________. *Wesen und Wirkung der Taufgnade*. Gütersloh: C. Bertelsmann, 1899.

Dächsel, K. August. *Vollständige Formulare zur Verrichtung der heiligen Handlung der Taufe.* Berlin: Verlag von Wilhelm Hertz, 1853.

Delitzsch, Franz. *Vier Bücher von der Kirche*. Dresden: Justus Naumann, 1847.

Dienemann. *Die heilige Taufe im Licht des göttlichen Worts und der Gegenwart*. Leipzig: Deichert, 1894.

Döderlein, Johannes Christoph. *Institutio Theologi Christiani*. Edito Quinta. Norimberg und Altorf: n.p., 1791.

Dorner, Isaak August. *System der Christlichen Glaubenslehre*. 2 vols. Zweite Auflage. Berlin: Verlag von Wilhelm Hertz, 1880.

Eckermann, Jakob Christoph Rudolph. *Handbuch für das systematische Studium der christlichen Glaubenslehre*. Vol. IV. Altona: Johann Friedrich Hammerich, 1803.

Eckhardt, D. *Homiletisches Reallexikon nebst Rerum.* St. Louis: Success Printing Co., 1914.

Eisenlohr, M. Christ. Frid. *Historische Bemerkungen über die Taufe*. Tübingen: Jacob Friedrich Herbrandt, 1804.

Frank, Franz Hermann Reinhold. "Initiale und Randzeichnungen zum Sakrament der Taufe," *Allgemeine Evangelisch-Lutherische Kirchenzeitung*, 35 (March 28–May 9, 1902): 293–298, 314–319, 338–343, 362–368, 410–414, 434–436.

________. *System der christlichen Wahrheit*. Dritte verbesserte Auflage. Erlangen und Leipzig: Deichert, 1894.

________. *Über die Lebensmacht der Gnadenmittel im Sinne lutherischer Lehre.* Erlangen und Leipzig: Deichert, 1891.

Freybe, Albert. *Die heilige Taufe und der Taufschatz in deutschem Glauben und Recht, deutscher Sage, Sitte und Dichtung.* Gütersloh: C. Bertelsmann, 1900.

Gemmel, Severin. *Die Herrlichkeit der heiligen Taufe*. Gütersloh: C. Bertelsmann, 1907.

Gennrich, P. *Die Lehre von der Wiedergeburt, die christliche Zentrallehre in dogmengeschichtlicher und religionsgeschichtlicher Bedeutung.* Gütersloh: C. Bertelsmann, 1907.

Gerhard, Johann. *Loci Theologici.* Vol. 4. Edited by Eduard Preuss. Berolini: Gust. Schlawitz, 1866.

Girgensohn, Karl. *Grundriß der Dogmatik.* Leipzig und Erlangen: A. Deichert'sche Verlagsbuchhandlung, 1924.

Gottschick, Johannes. *Die Lehre der Reformation von der Taufe.* Tübingen: J. C. B. Mohr, 1906.

Hahn, August. *Lehrbuch des Christlichen Glaubens.* Zweite durchaus verbesserte Auflage. Leipzig: Friedrich Wilhelm Vogel, 1858.

Haller, A. H. "Der Begriff der Wiedergeburt nach der Schrift," *Neue Kirchliche Zeitschrift*, 11 (1900): 592–620.

Hardeland, Theodor. *Das Bad der Wiedergeburt.* Berlin und Hannover: n.p., 1902.

________. "Die Gemeinschafts Wesen im Sinne der lutherischen Kirche," *Theologisches Jahrbuch auf das Jahr 1899*, 27. Edited by J. Schneider. Gütersloh: C. Bertelsmann, 1899: 1–17.

Harless, A. von, and Thedor Harnack. *Die kirchliche-religiöse Bedeutung der reinen Lehre von den Gnadenmittel.* Erlangen: Andreas Deichert, 1869.

Harnack, Adolf von. *Lehrbuch der Dogmengeschichte.* Vol. 1. Dritte verbesserte und vermehrte Auflage. Freiburg i. B. und Leipzig: J. C. B. Mohr, 1894.

________. *Die Mission und Ausbreitung des Christentums in den ersten drei Jahrhunderten.* Vol. 1. Vierte verbesserte und vermehrte Auflage. Leipzig: J. C. Hinrichs'sche Buchhandlung, 1924.

Haupt, Erich. "Zur Tauffrage und noch einmal zur Tauffrage," *Deutsche-evangelische Blätter*, 32 (1907): 647–656.

Heppe, Heinrich. *Dogmatik des deutschen Protestantismus im sechzehnten Jahrhundert.* Vol. 3. Gotha: Andreas Perthes, 1857.

Hermann, Wilhelm. *Der Verkehr des Christen mit Gott.* Stuttgart: Verlag der J. G. Cotta'schen Buchhandlung Nachfolger, 1896.

Hoenecke, Adolf. *Evangelisch-Lutherische Dogmatik.* 4 vols. 1909–1912. Edited by Walter and Otto Hoenecke. Milwaukee, Wis.: Northwestern Publishing House, 1909.

Hoffmann, Johann Wilhelm Friedrich. *Das Sakrament der Taufe.* 2 vols. Erlangen: Palm, 1846–1848.

________. *Taufe und Wiedertaufe*. Stuttgart: S. G. Liesching, 1840.

Höfling, Johann Christian Konrad, von. "Die christliche Taufe und die Baptistische Frage von Dr. H. Martensen," *Mecklenburgisches Kirchenblatt*, 1 (1845): 187–216.

________. *Der Schriftbeweis*. Vol. 2/2. Nördlingen Druck und Verlag von C. H. Beck'shen Buchhandlung, 1860.

Hory, Ernst. *Die Taufe als Kindertaufe auf Grund Heiliger Schrift*. Stuttgart: n.p., 1872.

Jeremias, Joachim. *Infant Baptism in the First Four Centuries*. Translated by David Cairns. Philadelphia: Westminster Press, 1960.

________. *The Origins of Infant Baptism: A Further Study in Reply to Kurt Aland.* Translated by Dorothea M. Barton, 1963. London SCM Press; Naperville: Allensons, 1963.

Kaftan, Julius. *Dogmatik.* Fünfte und sechste verbesserte Auflage. Tübingen: Verlag von J. C. B. Mohr, 1909.

Kaftan, Theodor. *Auslegung des lutherischen Katechismus*. Schleswig: Druck und Verlag von Julius Bergas, 1892.

Kähler, Martin. *Dogmatische Zeitfragen*. 3 vols. 1907–1913. Leipzig: A. Deichert, 1908.

Kahnis, Karl Friedrich August. *System der Lutherischen Dogmatik*. Vol. 3. Leipzig: Dörffling und Franke, 1868.

Kalchreuter. "Der stellvertretende Glaube und die Kindertaufe," *Jahrbücher für Deutsche Theologie*, 11 (Drittes Heft, 1866): 523–543.

Kapp, Georg Friedrich Wilhelm. *Grundsätze zur Bearbeitung evangelischer Agenden mit geschichtlicher Berücksichtigung der früheren Agenden*. Erlangen: Joh. Jac. Palm und Ernst Enke, 1831.

Kemmler, Gottlob. *Die Kindertaufe Recht und Kraft*. Stuttgart: Verlag der Evangelischen Gesellschaft, 1890.

Kerferstein, Friedrich. *Die Kindertaufe und die Kirchenzucht*. Gütersloh: C. Bertelsmann, 1867.

Kliefoth, Theodor. *Acht Bücher von der Kirche*. Schwerin und Rostock: Stiller, 1854.

________. *Theorie des Cultus der evangelischen Kirche*. Parchim und Ludwigslust: n.p., 1844.

Klöpper, Friedrich Wilhelm. *Liturgik oder Theorie der stehenden Kultusformen in der evangelischen Kirche*. Leipzig: Otto Wigand, 1841.

Kücklich, Ernst Reinhold. *Die biblische Berechtigung der Kindertaufe*. Stuttgart: Christliches Verlagshaus, 1903.

Kuhlemann, W. "Zur Tauffrage," *Protestantenblatt*, 28 (1905): 328–29.

Kühn, Bernhard. *Seufzet nicht wider einander: Ein Wort zum Frieden in der Tauffrage*. Gotha: P. Ott, 1906.

Laetsch, Willis E. "The Doctrine of Baptism," The Lutheran Church—Missouri Synod. *Proceedings of the Forty-Fifth Regular Convention, Cleveland, Ohio, June 20–29, 1962*. St. Louis: Concordia, 1962.

Lehmus, Adam Theodor Albert. *Über die Taufe*. Heidelberg: Mohr und Zimmer, 1807.

Lindemann, Christoph Friedrich Heinrich. "Über die Taufe," *Museum für Religionswissenschaft in ihrem ganzen Umfange* 1/ 8 (1804): 168–178.

Lobstein, Paul. *Zur Rechtfertigung der Kindertaufe*. Translated from the French by Pfr. Kupsch. Freiburg in B. und Leipzig: J. C. B. Mohr, 1895.

Löhe, Wilhelm. *Die Kirche in der Anbetung: Agende für christliche Gemeinde des lutherischen Bekenntnisses*. Vol. 7/1 of Gesammelte Werke. Edited by Klaus Ganzert. Neuendettelsau: Freimund-Verlag, 1953.

________. *Luthers Worte von der heiligen Taufe*. Nördlingen: n.p., 1856.

Lückert, Friedrich. *Grundriss der Evangelischen Dogmatik*. Göttingen: Dieterichsche Buchhandlung, 1845.

Lütgert, Wilhelm. *Gottes Sohn und Gottes Geist*. Leipzig: Deichert Verlag, 1905.

Luthardt, Christian Ernst. *Kompendium der Dogmatik*. Achte verbesserte Auflage. Leipzig: Dörffling und Franke, 1889.

________. *Lutheran Agenda*. St. Louis: Concordia, 1941.

________. *Lutheran Book of Worship*. Minneapolis: Augsburg Publishing House, 1978.

________. *Lutheran Service Book*. St. Louis: Concordia, 2006.

________. *Lutheran Worship*. St. Louis: Concordia, 1982.

Martensen, Hans Lassen. *Die christliche Dogmatik*. Berlin: Verlag von Gustav Schlawitz, 1856.

________. *Die christliche Taufe und die baptistische Frage*. Gotha und Hamburg: Andreas Perthes, 1843.

________. *Die christliche Taufe und die baptistische Frage*. Zweite Auflage. Gotha: Andreas Perthes, 1860.

Mau, G. *Ist das Taufsakrament noch haltbar?: Ein Wort zur Lösung der Tauffrage*. Wismar in Mecklenberg: Hans Bartholdi, 1908.

Michahelles, Karl Friedrich. *Über den christlichen Ritus der Taufe und besonders der Kindertaufe*. Nürnberg: Riegel und Wießner, 1816.

Modersohn, Ernst. *Soll ich mich noch einmal taufen lassen?* Neumünster: n.p., 1913.

Mueller, Adam Lebrecht. *The Faith of Unborn Children*. Translated by Otto F. Stahlke; edited by David R.Liefeldt. Nevada, IA: Lutherans for Life, 1998, 2005.

Mumm, Reinhard. "Trennung von Einsegnung und Annahme: Ein Beitrag zur Reform der Konfirmationspraxis," *Blätter aus der Arbeit der freien kirchlich-sozialen Konferenz*, II (1899): 82–83.

Nitzsch, Carl Immanuel. *System der Christlichen Lehre*. Vierte verbesserte und vermehrte Auflage. Bonn: Adolph Marcus, 1839.

Nitzsch, Friedrich August Berthold. *Lehrbuch der Evangelischen Dogmatik*. Dritte Auflage. Revised by Horst Stephan. Tübingen: Verlag von J. C. B. Mohr, 1912.

Oettingen, Alexander von. *Lutherische Dogmatik*. 3 vols. 1897–1902. München: Beck'sche Verlagsbuchhandlung, 1902.

P. "Über die Kindertaufe," *Allgemeines Magazin für Prediger nach Bedürfnissen unserer Zeit*, 12 (1795): 64–77.

Philippi, Friedrich Adolph. *Kirchliche Glaubenslehre*. 5 vols. Gütersloh: C. Bertelsmann, 1864–1875.

Pieper, Franz. *Christliche Dogmatik*. Vols.1–3. St. Louis: Concordia, 1917–1920.

Pieper, Francis, *Christian Dogmatics*. Vols. 1–3. St. Louis: Concordia, 1950–1953.

Quenstedt, Johann Andreas. *Theologia Didactico-Polemica sive Systema Theologicum*. Lipsiae: Thomas Fritsch, 1715.

Quitman, Henry. *Evangelical Catechism*. Hudson: William E. Norman, 1814.

Rabus. "Wiedergeburt und Wissenschaft," *Neue Kirchliche Zeitschrift*, 10 (1899): 139–168, 219–256.

Reiche, Karl Christoph. *Die Taufe der Christen, ein ehrwürdiger Gebrauch, und kein Gesetz Christi*. Berlin und Leipzig: Georg Jakob Decker, 1774.

________. *Über das Wunderbars und Verwunderung: Ein psychologischer Versuch*. Wittenberg und Zerbst: Zimmermann, 1782.

Reinhard, Franz Volkmar. *Vorlesungen über die Dogmatik*. Edited by Johann Gottfried Immanuel Berger. Zweyte verbesserte Auflage. Nürnberg und Salzbach: J. E. Seidel'schen Kunst- und Buchhandlung, 1806.

Richter. "Kindertaufe, ihr Wesen und Recht," *Theologische Studien und Kritiken* 34 (Zweites Heft, 1861): 219–264.

Ritschl, Albrecht. *Die christliche Lehre von der Rechtfertigung und Versöhnung*. 3 vols. Zweite verbesserte Auflage. Bonn: Adolph Marcus, 1883.

Rocholl, Rudolph. "Vom Kinderglauben," *Neue Kirchliche Zeitschrift* 13 (1902): 672–676.

Romberg, Gotthardt. "Kindertaufe und Wiedergeburt," *Mecklenburgisches Kirchen- und Zeitblatt* 31 (1903): 401–406.

________. "Über Kindertaufe und Kinderglauben," *Mecklenburgisches Kirchen-und Zeitblatt*, 31 (1903), 145–152.

Rutz, Paul. "Taufe und Wiedergeburt mit besonderer Berücksichtigung der Kindertaufe," *Neue Kirchliche Zeitschrift* 12 (1901): 585–620.

Sartorius, Ernst. Wilhelm Chirstian. *Gespräch von der Kindertaufe*. Königsberg: Schultz'schen Druckerei, 1841.

________. *Die Lehre von der heiligen Liebe*. Zweite Auflage. Stuttgart: Liesching, 1855.

Schäder, Erich. *Das Geistproblem der Theologie*. Leipzig und Erlangen: A. Deicherts'sche Verlagsbuchhandlung, 1924.

________. *Theozentrische Theologie*. Vol. 2. Leipzig: A. Deichert, 1928.

Scheel, Otto. *Die dogmatische Behandlung der Tauflehre in der modernen positiven Theologie*. Tübingen: Verlag von J. C. B. Mohr, 1906.

Scheiner, Martin. "Die Taufe-heidnische Magie oder christliches Gnadenmittel?" *Neue Kirchliche Zeitschrift* 24 (1913): 149–189.

Schlatter, Adolf. *Das Christliche Dogma*. Calw und Stuttgart: Verlag der Vereinsbuchhandlung, 1911.

Schleiermacher, Friedrich Daniel Ernst. *Am Grabe des geliebten Kindes*. Mainz: Matthias Grünewald, 1947.

________. *Der Christliche Glaube nach den Grundsäzen der evangelischen Kirche*. 2 vols. Dritte unveränderte Ausgabe. Berlin: Druck und Verlag von G. Riemer, 1836.

________. *The Christian Faith.* 2 Vols. Edited by H. R. Macintosh and J. S. Stewart. New York and Evanston: Harper & Row Publishers, 1963.

Schmid, Heinrich. *Die Dogmatik der evangelisch-lutherischen Kirche*. Erlangen: Carl Heyden, 1843.

Schneider, Johannes. *Die Taufe im Neuen Testament*. Stuttgart: W. Kohlhammer, 1952.

Schott, Theodor. "Das Wesen der Taufe nach den Einsetzungsworten," *Zeitschrift für die gesammte lutherische Theologie und Kirche* 32 (1872): 1–48.

Schultz, Hermann. *Grundriß der Evangelischen Dogmatik*. Göttingen: Vandenhoeck und Ruprecht, 1890.

Schulze, Ludwig. *Die Lehre von der Taufe in der lutherischen Kirche nach ihrer biblischen Grundlage*. Gütersloh: C. Bertelsmann, 1911.

Schwartz, Carl von. "Die Bedingung der Taufe auf dem Missionsfelde," *Neue Kirchliche Zeitschrift*, 11 (1900): 68–88.

Seeberg, Reinhold. *Christliche Dogmatik.* 2 vols. Erlangen und Leipzig: A. Deichert, 1924–1925.

________. *Grundriß der Dogmatik.* Leipzig: A. Deichert, 1932.

________. *Zur Systematischen Theologie.* Leipzig: A. Deichert, 1909.

Sperl, Gustav. "Welches ist das res 'sacramenti' in der Taufe?" *Zeitschrift für kirchliche Wissenschaft und kirchliches Leben* 9 (1888): 615–622.

Stange, Karl. "Die Lehre von den Sakramenten," *Studien des Apologetischen Seminars in Wernigerode.* Gütersloh: C. Bertelsmann, 1920: 37–51.

Steinbeck, Johann. "Die Bedeutung der christlichen Taufe im Hinblick auf neuere Forschungen," *Allgemeine Evangelisch-Lutherische Kirchenzeitung* 24 (June 25–July 2, 1909): 602–607, 624–631.

Steinmetz, Rudolph. "Zusammenhang von Taufe und Wiedergeburt," *Neue Kirchliche Zeitschrift* 13 (1902): 65–80, 144–162, 220–232.

Stier, Rudolph. *Die letzten Reden des Herrn Jesu, des Leidenden, Sterbenden und Auferstanden nach den vier Evangelisten.* Dritte Auflage. Leipzig: W. Langewiesche, 1874.

Storr, Gottlob Christian. *Lehrbuch der Christlichen Dogmatik.* Translated from Latin into German by Carl Christian Flatt. Stuttgart: Johann Benedict Metzler, 1803.

Stosch, Johann Ernst Georg. *Zeitgedanken über die heilige Taufe.* Gütersloh: C. Bertelsmann, 1902.

Strauss, David Friedrich. *Die christliche Glaubenslehre in ihrer geschichtlichen Entwickelung und im Kampfe mit der modernen Wissenschaft.* Tübingen: C. I. Osiander and Stuttgart: F. H. Köhler, 1841.

Thomasius, Gottfried. *Christi Person und Werk.* 3 vols. Zweite Auflage. Erlangen: Blasings, 1852–1861.

Traub, G. "Was halten wir von der Taufe," *Praktische Fragen des modernes Christentums.* Edited by Heinrich Geffeken. Leipzig: Verlag von Quelle und Meyer, 1907: 1–21.

Trenck, H. Frhr. von der. "Wiedergeburt und Bekehrung in ihrem Verhältnis zu einander und zur Taufe, speciell zur Kindertaufe," *Pastoralblätter* 56 (1904):739–759.

Vetter, Karl Wilhelm. *Die Lehre vom christlichen Kultus nach den Grundsätzen der evangelischen Kirche im Wissenschaftlichen Zusammenhange*. Berlin: Verlag der Sander'schen Buchhandlung, 1839.

Vilmar, August Friedrich Christian. *Dogmatik.* Edited by K. W. Piderit. Gütersloh: C. Bertelsmann, 1874.

________. "Einige Bemerkungen über das Taufritual," *Kirche und Welt*, II. Gütersloh: Druck und Verlag von C. Bertelsmann, 1873: 176–187.

Theologische Facultät der Martin-Luther-Universität Halle-Wittenberg. "Votum zur Kindertaufe," *Theologische Literaturzeitung* 87 (November 1962): 867–876.

Wacker, Emil. *Wiedergeburt und Bekehrung in ihrem gegenseitigen Verhältnis*. Gütersloh: C. Bertelsmann, 1893.

Walther, Carl Ferdindand Wilhelm. *Americanisch-Lutherische Pastoraltheologie*. St. Louis: Druckerei der Synode von Missouri, Ohio u. a. Staaten, 1872.

Warns, Johannes. *Die Taufe, Gedanken über die urchristliche Taufe.* Hamburg: Wiegand, 1913.

Wegscheider, Julius August Ludwig. *Institutiones Theologiae Christianae Dogmaticae*. Editio Tertia Emendata et Aucta. Halae: Io. Iac. Gebauer et Filii, 1819.

de Wette, Wilhelm Martin. *Dogmatik der evangelisch-lutherischen Kirche nach den symbolischen Büchern und den älteren Dogmatikern*. Zweyter verbesserte Auflage. Berlin: Verlag von G. Riemer, 1821.

Wetzel, Ed. *Die Kindertaufe in ihrer Notwendigkeit und Schriftgemäßigkeit*. Berlin: W. Schultze, 1865.

Wigand, Paul. *Wiedergeburt und Bekehrung*. Zweite Auflage. Leipzig: A. Deichert, 1896.

Wilbrandt, Adolf. "Die Kindertaufe in ihrer fundamentalen Bedeutung für das Christenleben," *Mecklenburgisches Kirchen- und Zeitblatt*, 31 (1903):41–49, 65–71, 81–90.

________. "Die Kindertaufe und Kinderglauben," *Mecklenburgische Kirchen- und Zeitblatt* 31 (1903): 297–307, 321–325.

Zezschwitz, Carl Adolf Gerhard von. *System der christlich kirchlichen Katechetik.* 2 vols. Leipzig: J. C. Hinrichs, 1863–1872.

SECONDARY SOURCES

Aland, Kurt. *Did the Early Church Baptize Infants?* Translated by with an introduction by George R. Beasley-Murray. Philadelphia: Westminster Press, 1963.

________. *Die Säuglingstaufe im Neuen Testament und in der alten Kirche; eine Antwort an Joachim Jeremias*. München: C. Kaiser, 1961.

________. *Taufe und Kindertaufe*. Gutersloh: Gerhard Mohn, 1971.

Beyreuther, E. "Theodor Lehmus," *Die Religion in Geschichte und Gegenwart*, Vol. 4. Edited by Kurt Galling. Dritte, völlig neu bearbeitete Auflage; Tübingen: J. C. B. Mohr, 1960. Col. 266.

Brinkel, Karl. *Lehre Luthers von der fides infantum bei der Kindertaufe*. Berlin: Evangelische Verlagsanstalt, 1958.

Bridge, Donald and David Phypers. *The Water That Divides*. Downers Grove: InterVarsity Press, 1977.

Coiner, Harry. "The Inclusive Nature of Holy Baptism in Luther's Writings," *Concordia Theological Monthly*, 33 (November 1962): 645–657.

Elert, Werner. A*bendmahl und Kirchengemeinschaft in der alten Kirche hauptsächlich des Ostens*. Berlin: Lutherisches Verlagshaus, 1954.

________. *Der Christliche Glaube: Grundlinien der lutherischen Dogmatik*. Edited by Ernst Kinder. Fünfte und erneute durchgesehene und ergänzte Auflage. Hamburg. Furche Verlage, 1960

Ferm, Vergilius. *Crisis in American Lutheran Theology*. New York and London: The Century Company, 1927.

Freericks, Hermann. *Die Taufe im heutigen Protestantismus*. Münster i. W.: Druck der Aschendorffschen Buchdruckerei, 1924.

Green, Lowell C. *The Erlangen School of Theology: Its History, Teaching and Practice*. Fort Wayne: Lutheran Legacy, 2010.

Grass, H. "Erlanger Schule," *Die Religion in Geschichte und Gegenwart,* Vol. 2. Edited by Kurt Galling. Dritte, völlig neu bearbeitete Auflage; Tübingen: J. C. B. Mohr, 1958: cols. 566–568.

Grudem, Wayne. *Systematic Theology*. Grand Rapids: Zondervan Publishing House, 1997.

Heyder, Karl Ludwig Wilhelm "Schelling, Friedrich Wilhelm Joseph von," *A Religious Encyclopaedia*, Vol. 3. Edited by Philip Schaff. New York: Funk & Wagnalls, Publishers, 1883: 2118–2120.

Hohlwein, Hans. "Rationalismus II. Rationalismus und Supranaturalismus, kirchengeschichtlich," *Die Religion in Geschichte und Gegenwart*, Vol. 6. Edited by Kurt Galling. Dritte, völlig neu bearbeitete Auflage; Tübingen: J. C. B. Mohr, 1961:cols. 791–800.

Hübner, Heinrich. "Rocholl, Rudolf," *Die Religion in Geschichte und Gegenwart*, Vol. 5. Edited by Kurt Galling. Dritte, völlig neu bearbeitete Auflage; Tübingen: J. C. B. Mohr, 1961: col. 1131.

Kantzenbach, Fredrich Wilhelm. *Die Erlanger Theologie: Grunlinien ihere Entwicklung im Rahmen der Geschichte der Theologischen Fakultät 1743–1877*. München: Evangelischer Presserverband für Bayern, 1960.

Kattenbusch, Ferdinand. "Taufe. II. Kirchenlehre," *Realencyklopädie für protestantische Theologie und Kirche*, 19. Edited by Albert Hauck. Dritte verbesserte und vermehrte Auflage; Leipzig: J. C. Hinrichs'sche Buchhandlung, 1907: 403–424.

Kolb, Robert. "Lutheran View: God's Baptismal Act as Regenerative," in *Understanding Four Views on Baptism*. Edited by Paul E. Engle and John H. Armstrong. Grand Rapids: Zondervan, 2007, 91–109.

Martin, Heinrich. "Die Selbständige Ev. Luth. Kirche," *Evang.-Lutherische Freikirche in Deutschland*. Edited by Ulrich Kunz. Frankfurt am Main: Lutheraner Verlag, 1953: 21–27.

Marty, Martin E. *Baptism*. Philadelphia: Muhlenberg Press, 1962.

Mücke, Albert. *Die Dogmatik des neunzehnten Jahrhunderts*. Gotha: Friedrich Andreas Perthes, 1867.

Nettles, Thomas J. "A Baptist Response," in *Understanding Four Views on Baptism*. Edited by Paul E. Engle and John H. Armstrong. Grand Rapids: Zondervan, 2007, 110–114.

Peters, Albrecht. *Realpräsenz: Luthers Zeugnis von Christi Gegenwart im Abendmahl*. Berlin: Evangelisches Verlagshaus, 1960.

Repp, Arthur C. "Reconstructing Confirmation for Our Day," The Lutheran Church—Missouri Synod, *Seventy-Sixth Convention Proceedings of the Western District, June 12–16, 1961*. St. Louis: Concordia, 1961: 29–69.

Riggs, John W. *Baptism in the Reformed Tradition*. Louisville: Westminster John Knox Press, 2002.

Rohls, Jan. *Reformed Confessions: Theology from Zurich to Barmen*. Translated by John F. Hoffmeyer. Introduction by Jack L. Stotts. Columbia Series in Theology Louisville: Westminster John Knox Press, 1997.

Scaer, David P. *Baptism.* Confessional Lutheran Dogmatics. St. Louis: Luther Academy, 1999.

________. *Law and Gospel and the Means of Grace*. Confessional Lutheran Dogmatics. St. Louis, 2008.

________. "Confirmation as Sacramental Rite." *Logia* 15:1 (Epiphany 2006): 49–58.

Schluter, Richard. *Karl Barths Tauflehre*. Paderborn: Verlag Bonifacius, 1973.

Schlink, Edmund. *The Doctrine of Baptism.* Translated by Herbert J.A. Bouman. St. Louis: Concordia, 1972.

________. *The Theology of the Lutheran Confessions*. Translated by Paul F. Koenecke and Herbert J. A. Bouman. Philadelphia: Muhlenberg Press, 1961.

Schneider, Johannes. *Die Taufe im Neuen Testament*. Stuttgart: W. Kohlhammer, 1952.

Schrey, Heinz-Horst. "Walther, Christian: Typen des Reich-Gottes Verständnisses. Studien zur Eschatologie und Ethik im 19. Jahrhundert," *Theologische Literaturzeitung* 87/10 (October 1962): cols. 774–775.

Spitz, Lewis W. "Lutheran Theology after 1580," *Lutheran Cyclopedia*. Edited by Erwin L. Lueker. St. Louis: Concordia, 1958, 638–641.

Spierling, Karen E. *Infant Baptism in Reformation Geneva*. Louisville: Westminster John Knox Press, 2009.

Stasiak, Kurt. *Return to Grace: A Theology for Infant Baptism*. Collegeville: The Liturgical Press, 1996.

Stephan, Horst. *Geschichte der Deutschen Evangelischen Theologie Seit dem Deutschen Idealismus*. Edited by Martin Schmidt. Zweite Neubearbeitete Auflage. Berlin: Alfred Töpelmann, 1960.

Stöcker, Adolf. *The Teaching of the Church Regarding Baptism*. Translated by Ernest A. Payne. London: SCM Press 1949.

________. "Stöcker, Adolf," *Lutheran Cyclopedia*. Edited by Erwin L. Lueker. St. Louis: Concordia, 1958: col. 1011.

Tranvik, Mark David. "The other sacrament: the doctrine of baptism in the late Lutheran reformation." Th. D. Dissertation, Luther Northwestern Theological Seminary, 1992.

Trigg, Jonathan. *Baptism in the Theology of Martin Luther*. Leiden: E.J. Brill, 1994.

Witczak, Michael G. *The Sacrament of Baptism*. Collegeville: The Liturgical Press, 2011.

Subject Index

Persons Index